S0-AII-429

VOICES OF SAVANNAH

*Selections from the Oral History Collection
of the Savannah Jewish Archives*

Compiled by
Valerie Frey, Kaye Kole, and Luciana M. Spracher

Savannah Jewish
ARCHIVES

Savannah, Georgia
2004

COVER:

Torpian Society, 25 December 1926

The theme of this annual costume ball was the "Torpian Ranch," complete with Indians and Cowboys!

JVM 003 Savannah Jewish Archives General Photograph Collection, Item 0748

Copyright 2004
Savannah Jewish Archives, Savannah, Georgia

Cover design by Jere Connan.

All rights reserved. No part of this publication may be reproduced in any form or by any means without prior written permission of the Savannah Jewish Archives, 501 Whitaker Street, Savannah GA 31401.

Savannah Jewish Archives; Valerie Frey, Kaye Kole, Luciana M. Spracher
Voices of Savannah

ISBN 0-615-12633-2

Library of Congress Control Number 2004096517

1. Memoirs, lives of Jews in Savannah. 2. Jewish traditions and culture. 3. Oral histories.
4. Photographic archives.

To purchase copies of *Voices of Savannah*, contact
Savannah Jewish Archives
501 Whitaker Street
Savannah GA 31401
912 - 651-2125

THE SAVANNAH JEWISH ARCHIVES

The Savannah Jewish Archives (SJA) was established in 1994 to preserve and make known the history of Savannah Jewry through the acquisition, preservation, and public access of records of the Savannah Jewish community. SJA serves areas outside of the immediate city and county as well, since the only other Jewish archives in the state is in Atlanta.

In addition to more than 2,300 identified photographs, the collection consists of more than 285 cubic feet of synagogue and organization records, oral histories, copies of the *Savannah Jewish News*, family papers, business records, and a limited number of artifacts. Congregations Mickve Israel and B'nai B'rith Jacob have both deposited much of their archival material in the Savannah Jewish Archives, and gift donations have been made by Congregation Agudath Achim.

Housed in the Georgia Historical Society in Savannah, the Savannah Jewish Archives' collections can be accessed through their library, open to the public Tuesday through Saturday, 10 a.m. until 5 p.m.

For more information regarding SJA membership (available at several levels), volunteer opportunities, or donations of archival materials, please contact the archivist:

Savannah Jewish Archives
c/o Georgia Historical Society
501 Whitaker Street
Savannah, Georgia 31401
(912) 651-2125

TABLE OF CONTENTS

ACKNOWLEDGMENTS

Thank you to all who have donated materials, time, and funds
to the Savannah Jewish Archives,
preserving the community's past for the sake of its future.

Jane Kahn's careful editing of the text was an invaluable service.
Evelyn Scharf transcribed three oral history interviews
for researcher use.

We would like to show our appreciation to all the volunteers
who conducted oral history interviews (in alphabetical order):
Carole Cohen
Valerie Frey
Eleanor Galin
Joan Gefen (OBM)
Suzanne Kantziper
Eric Meyerhoff
Elaine Radetsky
Lisa Robinson
Ross Stemer

The following volunteers each interviewed more than five subjects,
significantly contributing to this growing collection:
Robert Friedman
Gail Robinson
David Rosenzweig

And finally a very special thank you to
Harriet Meyerhoff
who went above
and beyond the call of duty,
conducting fifty-two interviews.

DEDICATION

We dedicate this work to the Savannah Jewish community —
special, strong, and unique.

PROJECT NOTES FROM THE EDITORS

". . . oral accounts provide a wealth of detailed information that puts flesh on the bare bones of records and brings the events to life."

— *From Memory to History: Using Oral Sources in Local Historical Research*
Barbara Allen and William Lynwood Montell
Nashville, TN: The American Association for State and Local History, 1981. Pg. 56

In this age of rapidly expanding information, print sources are abundant. But how well do newspaper articles, identification documents, or formal histories create a vivid understanding about people's daily lives? An oral history, our story in our own words, is a rich supplement to print materials, filling in gaps of knowledge and complementing existing sources. These narratives provide intriguing insights into customs and attitudes, afford an intimate window into the personal domain, and cultivate a sense of community. After working extensively with the Savannah Jewish Archives' oral history collection, we feel strongly that these materials will indeed strike a chord not only with the Jewish community, but with all Savannah residents as well as anyone who had a special childhood game, a favorite grandfather, a first love, a family business, or who simply enjoys wandering down "Memory Lane."

This book was a labor of love and a joy, yet it was also a challenge. How do you combine interviews with one hundred and six individuals (transcribed into an estimated 2,000 pages) and over 2,300 photographs into one small book? The answer is that we had to offer our readers a mere taste of what the Savannah Jewish Archives has to offer, choosing to publicize the collection to a wide variety of researchers, and share highlights that bring the warmth of this particular community into sharper focus, rather than offer a comprehensive or exhaustive view.

We wish very much that we could have included materials from each of our more than 200 donors and could have represented all the Jewish families in Savannah. This book, however, had to fit together like pieces of a puzzle, forming a cohesive sampler of Savannah's Jewish community in the 20th century, while remaining within certain guidelines to facilitate its publication. We read and considered all of the oral history narratives. Each and every one was interesting and useful. Nevertheless, we found that some of the stories either were not compatible with the chapter subjects, or the conversational style between interviewer and interviewee was not conducive to this particular format.

We also considered every photograph in our collection but had to make choices based on print quality, size, and other factors as well as simply by subject matter. All materials donated to the Archives, however, are carefully preserved for use in future projects and by other researchers. Regardless of whether we were able to include your donated materials in this project, we appreciate your consideration and generosity to the Archives and the community.

The material included in this volume represents the experiences of Savannah's Jewish community in their own words, relating their own memories and perceptions. Occasionally, memories may become flawed or skewed over time. We have made no attempt to change the content of the narratives. Since we were dealing with recorded interviews, we took some liberty with grammar and punctuation to help the narratives flow smoothly as a whole. The original taped interviews and full transcripts, which can provide meaningful context for each oral history, are available to the public through the Savannah Jewish Archives.

We hope you enjoy this volume as much as we have enjoyed bringing it to life!

As you read the following selections, you will note that each entry is followed by the name of the person who said it and a number. As oral histories are donated to the Archives, they become part of JOH 003 Savannah Jewish Archives Oral History Collection and are assigned a number by which they are catalogued and stored. Researchers can locate an oral history in the collection using either the interviewee's name or this number. Please see Appendix C for a complete listing of all oral histories included in this publication.

Every image represented in this book is accompanied by a citation including any identifying information necessary for researchers to locate the original in the Archives' collections.

VOICES OF SAVANNAH

Selections from the Oral History Collection
of the Savannah Jewish Archives

CHAPTER 1: THE OLD COUNTRY AND IMMIGRATION *

POLITICAL UNREST AND LIMITED OPPORTUNITIES

You have to understand that most of these people, and my parents definitely included, had terrible lives in Europe and they did not talk about a thing. What little I know about them is very little. **Anchel Samuels, 86**

[My family came to this country from Germany prior to 1860.] Germany was not a confederation at first, or an empire, but the kingdom of Prussia overpowered all those little duchies, and I remember my grandfather hated the Prussians as much as he hated the Frenchmen. They used to, they had no rights or anything, and they were all poor. The only chance they had was to emigrate. **Aaron Guthman, 12**

We were Germans. . . . Papa was in America already. . . . We had a couple of horses, some cows. . . . [Our house was blown up by bombs,] our cows were gone and all we had was a few chickens. The chickens laid eggs and had little biddies. Here comes a hawk and catches one of the chickens in his paws and flew away. My brother, Meyer, ran after him for miles until the hawk dropped the chicken and he brought it back. I said, "What the hell'd you run for? What are you going to do with it now? You can't eat it." He said, "Oh, well, it gives me the satisfaction of being there." And that's the way we lived.

In 1921 . . . we were hungry, had nothing to eat. We begged for food, went around and got peelings of potatoes. My mother used to fry them in the sunshine, put them between two stones and grind them up and make bread out of it. We enjoyed it. We ate it. . . .

My mama, my two brothers, and my sister all came to America in 1921, March 1921. My mother was sick already . . . and my father took her to old Dr. Johnson. He checked her out and says, . . . "She's got about ten years to live." We came here in March 1921; mother died March 6, 1931. . . .

---

* As you are reading, be aware that political unrest may have caused place names to change and national boundaries to shift over time.

We got passports to come to America. . . . To catch the boat we had to go pick up a train, . . . like a cattle train, box cars. We traveled to Warsaw. . . . We had to stay there quite a while, about a month or more, until our passports cleared. . . . Then we finally came to America. And Mama handed my father $500. He was broke. He thought it was like a million dollars. **Ralph Tenenbaum, 58**

Immigrant Couple, c.1890
Feter Mayer and his wife during the late 19ᵗʰ century.
JVM 35 Itzkovitz Family Collection, Folder 1, Item 1

I was born in 1929 in the town of Arolsen [Germany]. My father was a merchant. He had a dry goods store in Arolsen and my mother came from a family of about nine. Her maiden name was Katz and they were in the horse-trading business, . . . in the '20s, [that] was still a big business in Germany, sort of like a car dealership would be in the United States today.

We moved from Arolsen to an adjacent town called Mengeringhausen. . . . My dad had a store in Mengeringhausen. In Mengeringhausen there were only three Jewish families. We were one of the three. . . . I started kindergarten in 1934 and then went into the first grade in 1935. And in 1934 and '35, I still had my buddies in school, my friends. During that time, from the time that Hitler took over as Chancellor of Germany, . . . virtually each month new edicts were proclaimed as to what Jews could and couldn't do. Initially, they weren't allowed into universities and they weren't allowed to hold public office. Then they weren't allowed to work for the government, and . . . each year from '34 on, being a Jew in Germany became more and more difficult.

From my own personal experience, there was a tremendous transition between . . . first grade . . . and . . . second grade. . . . When I went into the second grade, I couldn't sit with my classmates anymore; I had to sit in the back of the room. They were not allowed to talk to me. They could, however, kick me, spit on me during recess, or anything like that. And some did, some didn't. And so we were isolated. I guess there were four Jewish kids in the entire school because my sister and I were from one family and, I believe, another family had two kids. Near the end of '36, . . . my father had fully had enough of being in Germany. Fortunately, he had an older brother that lived in the United States - Fort Pierce, Florida - whom he had written in 1935 so that we would have a place to emigrate to. Quotas were enforced in the United States so that only so many thousand people could be taken into this country from each country and no exceptions [were] being made for Jews in flight [from] Germany.

Of course, you had to have immigration numbers to leave Germany. When your number came up in Germany, if you didn't have a place to go in some other country, then, obviously, you couldn't leave. Because of my father's foresight, we had the immigration numbers over in this country coincide with the emigration numbers out of Germany. That took place in May of 1937. . . .

At that time the German ports were already closed [to Jews emigrating]. We had to take a train to France. . . . We went to Paris, from there to Le Havre, and we took a Cunard, Inc. British liner ship over, the *Britannic*, and seven days later we landed in New York City. That was all pretty exciting for me and my eleven year old sister, while it was heartbreaking for our parents.

An organization known as HIAS took us under their wing. . . . I think we were there for a day or two days. . . . And then they put us on a bus, which was a two-day ride from New York City to Jacksonville, Florida. In Jacksonville, Florida, my uncle Fred [Meyerhoff] greeted us and then drove us down to Fort Pierce. . . .

My dad was a very religious man and he [soon] realized that in Fort Pierce where there were only very few Jewish families, no synagogue, that he wanted to move to a larger city because he wanted his children to be brought up in a synagogue and that type of an education. So in 1938 we moved to Jacksonville, Florida, and it took a while for the Jewish community in Jacksonville to accept German immigrant refugees, because really, at that time, many people in this country had no realization of what was going on. . . . *Kristallnacht* in '39 changed all that. . . . The Jewish community in Jacksonville helped us rent a very large house, it had maybe four or five bedrooms, and some of the first and earlier immigrants stayed in those bedrooms as boarders. And that's where . . . my mother, who was a cook, but certainly not in the catering business, started with this fixing meals for boarders. **Eric Meyerhoff, 18**

My father was born in Berlin. The name Kreh is not a Jewish name at all. There are no other Krehs in Italy. . . . My father came to Italy as a youngster. . . . We grew up in Genoa, and Papa was one of the leading citizens, really, in Genoa.

. . . He was a quite prominent person in business, and naturally he was a German citizen. At that time he traveled to Germany. He came back. But he didn't realize that if you didn't return to your native country within five years, you were losing your citizenship. That's what happened to my father. He didn't go back. . . . He lost his citizenship. . . .

We grew up in Genoa. We had very good years where the Jews had nothing to fear. The law of the land was that the religion of the state was the Catholic religion. . . . In school, for instance, the teachers were priests and nuns paid by the government. . . .

In school, we did feel it because there was anti-Semitism. . . . Easter Sunday, for instance, when . . . we came out of the *shul*. . . . The Jewish people would dress better than the others, so they would start throwing dirt at us and all that kind of stuff. So, we felt it. But otherwise, in business, no. . . .

Communism started developing. Times were bad. . . . This movement created the Fascist — rough people, killing the Communists, giving them castor oil, torturing them. . . . Slowly the Fascists got a bit better. . . .

[In] I think '33, Hitler had already come up [Mussolini joined with Hitler]. . . . They kept the Jews in Italy. They couldn't go to school anymore, the children. They couldn't do this, they couldn't do that. . . . We knew what was going on and I figured out it was time to leave. . . . I was blessed because at that time I had started already to do what I had to do. . . . I had a wonderful connection over there, high-ranking Fascist, in Genoa. . . . He knew I was Jewish and I said, "I need a passport.". . . [The next week] I called him and he said, "Your passport is on the way." After two days, I got my passport. . . . I told my family, "I'm leaving. I'm going to Frankfurt." "Don't go, don't go," they said. . . . I said, "What can happen? I have an Italian passport. Nothing is written on that I'm Jewish. I don't look Jewish, my name is not Jewish. I don't speak but Italian.". . . And, in fact, I had no trouble. **Marcus "Max" Kreh, 59**

I was born . . . [in what is now Poland]. It used to be German, Breslau. . . . The Nazis took it over. I was there until 1938. In 1938 I was married and my husband lived in my parents' house for about three to four months. . . . And we got a telephone call . . . from the Gestapo . . . that my husband should come over; they want to see him. Which was very dangerous because you never get out again. We had papers from New York, from my cousins. My husband had cousins here in New York. They were in the jewelry, the diamond business. They sent us an affidavit that we could come over; that means they vouched for us, that if we come, they will help us. . . .

My father thought I should not go with him. I said, "I'm married now. I go with my husband." So I went, we both went to the Gestapo. There was a man standing in front of the door and he said, "It is very easy to get in, but very hard to get out." Oh my God, my tears came and I started to cry. . . . So we got in and as soon as my husband started to talk, we heard a voice. It says, "You, Warner." It was a friend, a school friend . . . of my husband . . . who heard the voice of my husband. . . . He recognized his voice, called us in his office, stamped everything and we could get out. . . . My father bought tickets for the *President Harding*. It was the last . . . American ship. I was terribly sick on the boat. We had terrible storms. The piano went out into the ocean. . . . We went to New York. My sister was at the boat and my cousins were at the boat, too. When we arrived, I was very thin. I must have lost ten pounds. I never ate anything, from the beginning to the end, ten days, no food. **Herta (Sanger) Danziger, 83**

German Kindergarten Class, n.d.
Herta (Sanger) Danziger, born in Breslau, Germany (now Poland) in 1911,
(center of photograph, marked with "X") may be the only individual in
this photo who survived the Holocaust, during which she lost both her
parents.
JVM 039 Herta Danziger Visual Materials, Folder 1, Item 1

Just prior to World War II, approximately 1937, Mr. Samuel Tenenbaum of Savannah, father of Meyer, Albert, and Ralph Tenenbaum – his wife had died in the past several years – and he discovered that his childhood sweetheart from, what we call the "Old Country," which happened to have been Kobryn, Poland, was a widow with two children. And the situation was not getting any better in Europe, and he got on a boat and went to Europe and married my mother-in-law,

Harriet's mother, and brought Harriet and her brother, Paul Birnbaum, to the United States. **Albert Ullman, 33**

The family lived in [a place] which is . . . sometimes Polish and sometimes Russian. They lived on an estate and they managed the estate for a gentile family. When they started having pogroms and so forth in Russia, my family moved to Brussels, Belgium. Then they scattered all over the face of the earth. Like I said, my oldest uncle went to Palestine. The next uncle went to Australia. . . . They finally came to Savannah and opened a grocery store on Berrien and Montgomery streets. **Albert Mazo, 50**

My father, innocently I would say, because he was not political, got involved with some students who were friends of my uncle's, politically. One of the people whom he got out of jail escaped, and my father was immediately apprehended and he was sent to Siberia. . . . His [the escapee's] crime was a big one. He was caught in soldier's clothes distributing revolutionary literature in the barracks. Well, there couldn't be a bigger crime in czarist Russia. . . .

My father paid a big price for this. He was sent to Siberia, at hard labor. He never did a piece of hard work in his life, and my mother didn't leave a stone unturned, and she had legal counsel. She went to . . . Petrograd, and she got a change of sentence from Siberia, out of the country, and it was called "Zagrinitsa" meaning "beyond the border." And so he came to this country. He came to Savannah because the Levys were here already. My mother's sister was here already. **Pearl (Spivak) Levy, 44**

My mother was an orphan. My dad was an orphan. My dad was born in Odessa, Russia. My mother was born in Cleveland, Ohio. My father lost his entire family in a pogrom when he was only . . . nine or ten years old. He lost them and the only way that he was spared, that he was spending the night with a friend of theirs that had a little farm. . . . He lost his entire family; his mother, his father, two sisters, and two brothers, that [the Russian Cossacks] slaughtered. . . . My mother lost her mother and father in a fire. She was an orphan at four years old.

So my dad . . . stayed with some people there. They weren't relations. . . . In Russia at that time, when any of the Jewish boys, or any of them, became thirteen years old, they were conscripted into the army, to the Russian army, . . . not in the army as soldiers, but laborers and all. It was just like being in a prison or something, he said. Anyhow, . . . an uncle of his from New York had been writing to his folks and he didn't hear from them so he found out what had happened. So he wanted to get my dad out of Russia if he could. This was about a year or two later, he said. He was going on his . . . thirteenth birthday and they would take him in the army. So they smuggled him out of Russia, . . . and they got him on a ship and he came to America.

When he came to Ellis Island, . . . he had a tag on him with a number, . . . and . . . somebody was calling out his number. . . . This man that was his uncle picked him up. He said that was about four o'clock in the afternoon, and he said [his uncle] picked him up and he said that was the last time that he saw daylight for weeks. His [uncle] had an old sweat shop . . . on the East side, right off of Mulberry. And he took him . . . right to the shop and put him to work. . . . He said he had a little room in the attic, it was a little house. . . . He worked there he said for about a couple of years.

But my dad was very outgoing and he was smart. . . . He was talking to one of the fellows there . . . [and] asked him, "Where can you get a job anywhere?" So [the fellow] told him that he heard in Brooklyn they were hiring steel workers. Dad said, "What is a steel worker?". . . . To make a long story short, my dad got up, he said, about two o'clock in the morning . . . and left the house. . . .

So he made his way to Brooklyn. . . . It took him a whole day to get there. . . . He came to the . . . shipyard, where . . . they were doing steelwork on the ships. . . . He didn't know one piece of steel from another. Anyhow, he got him a job and he went to work there. Then he stayed with these people for years, but he had to travel wherever . . . the company was putting up a building, building ships, or building a hospital. . . . And my dad traveled practically all over the whole of the United States working there. **Reuben Schneider, 28**

My family came from Russia, . . . my father and mother and my oldest brother, Mose. Mose was three years old when they came . . . [and] immigrated to New York. We had some cousins there. . . . When he was in Russia, [my father] was . . . an assistant to the rabbi. . . . He had a beautiful voice and he helped with the services and helped with the synagogue there. The reason they came here was because they were putting all the Jewish men into labor camps and into the army. A lot of them cut off fingers and toes so they could get out and come back as an invalid. I don't know how Pop got out, but he had nothing wrong with him when he came out.

When he got to New York he got a job on a street gang that built all the streets in New York. . . . Pop talked to some relatives and found out we had family in Richmond, Virginia. This cousin in Richmond, Virginia, had a shoe repair shop. He said, "Come here, work with me." Pop didn't know too much about making shoes . . . so in scouting around he found the fellow in, what we call now, the metals business, but it was actually a junk shop. He worked in there and worked himself up to be a buyer, and finally they asked him would he travel? And he agreed to do it and that's how we came to Savannah. Pop came to Savannah several times and found the Jewish people here so welcome to him. They started him off, he didn't have anything but his clothes and his son and his wife. **Benjamin Portman, 20**

Young Child of Early Immigrants, n.d.
Despite the fact that Frances (Platzblatt) Weiser was born (25 June 1900) while her mother was on a trip in the northeast, she lived most of her life in Savannah.
JVM 003 Savannah Jewish Archives
General Photograph Collection, Item 2284

When my father left Russia, I was just about three and a half or four years old [circa 1903], and he came to America at the request and with the help of his brother who was living in New York at that time. He had just completed four years of service in the Russian army and had become free of service for about six months when Russia became involved with Japan, and there was talk of another war and they were recalling as many of the men as they could obtain who had served before.

At that time, my father realized that there was no future for him in Russia and he had an opportunity to leave for the United States, so he made plans. They sent him a passport from New York and he packed up what he could, obtained a private wagon driver with a horse who took him across Russia through Germany to Holland. Obviously he must have left either by Amsterdam or some other port, and he came to America. After he was here about three years, he sent for the family - my mother and three boys.

He first came to New York and spent a little time with his brother, and then obtained a position as master machinist with a railroad company who had established one of the largest shops in . . . Fernandina, Florida. . . . My mother unfortunately couldn't stand the climate there, number one, and secondly, she became ill because she kept a strictly kosher home and it was impossible to obtain kosher food in a small town like Fernandina. . . . The doctor told my father, "You either will have to make arrangements to provide her with the food she is accustomed to eating (which would be strictly kosher food) or move to another city where you would find it more suitable for you to live."

So my father immediately made plans to move to Birmingham, Alabama, and they told him, "If you're interested in a city with a large Jewish population, go to Savannah, Georgia." He had also gone to Augusta and they also told him, "If you go to Savannah, you will find people that you are acquainted with from your city of Kobryn, Russia," where we came from. And that's exactly what happened. He came to Savannah, he found people that he knew from the "Old Country" and we settled in Savannah. As I say, it was 1905, and we remained ever since, spanning almost one hundred years in Savannah, Georgia. **Louis Silverman, 29**

[I was born] in Lithuania. . . . We came to the States in 1908 . . . through New York. Of course everybody, most everyone, went through Ellis Island. . . . I remember passing through there. . . . I was about nine. . . . The boat ride took fourteen days. It was a long, slow trip. And I'll give you the name of the ship - the *Korea.*

My father was here in the States before we were, the rest of us. . . . It was the early part of the century, 1901, '02, '03, '04, right about at that time, Russia was at war with Japan. And it was not a pleasant thing, or situation, you might say, to be in the Russian army. Especially a Jew. Because the Russians did not like Jews. . . . They made pogroms in small villages. They would burn a whole village down if there were Jews. Or they would sack, go on a rampage and kill Jews. **Fred Rotkow, 27**

My father, during the first World War, was a medical officer in the Austrian Army. He had one year to finish medical school but never had a chance to complete it. He was captured by the Russians. On weekends the Russian people would take in Austrian officers on a weekend pass. My mother's family took in my father as a guest for the weekend and after a number of visits they fell in love and became married. After the first World War, my mother's family moved to China. . . . [They] lived there until 1926 at which time they came to the United States. Of course, they came through Seattle, not at Ellis Island, but Seattle, Washington. **Charles Becker, 64**

When we come to Hungaria, being refugees in our own land, . . . the state took care of us. . . . They gave us rations, they gave us flour. . . . We were really refugees in our own land. . . . It wasn't our land because we were Austrian-Polacks, Polack-Austrians, and this was Hungaria. But Hungaria was under the Austrian, Franz Josef, . . . emperor of all Austria-Hungary. . . . So we used to get a whole lot more flour than we could use and we had nothing. We had flour. We had chickens. So they used to take the stuff and smuggle it from there into Vienna. You know how? . . . She used to wear a corset with tubes in it. They filled these sacks with flour and she put on a dress . . . and . . . [went] to Vienna and delivered her flour to the relatives and [brought] back things that we needed. **Abe Javetz, 78**

My father came to America from England. He was born in Romania, and like most of the young Jewish people, they probably left Romania to avoid military service which was brutal and dangerous. He followed family . . . to Manchester and from there he came to America to escape religious persecution in 1908. The persecution was that the family was so religious he couldn't stand it, so he came to America. He landed at Boston . . . then moved to New York, and went into business with a friend in the button business which was very short-lived, and then [he] moved to Savannah because the Segall family, Max and Julius Segall, were from the same town in Romania. **David Rosenzweig, 25**

ARDUOUS TRAVEL

My grandfather and my grandmother . . . left Odessa, Russia, by foot. . . . They walked from Odessa across Europe to Le Havre, France, where they would catch a boat to come to Canada. . . . Before they got on the boat somebody stole most of the money they had with them, and God knows how they did it, but they got on the boat and probably slept on the deck because I doubt whether they had accommodations, for they had little or no money, and landed in Canada. From there they migrated to Utica, New York. **Herman Cranman, 36**

Tintype of 19th Century Family, n.d.
JVM 005 Congregation Mickve
Israel Photograph Collection, Item 0012

There is a newspaper article which . . . tells the story of . . . my *bubbe* and my *zeyde* coming with the eight children to Ellis Island. . . . He had sold his entire possessions in Russia and had the equivalent of five or six hundred dollars. At Ellis Island someone stole his money. So as a result, the cousins in Savannah, the Weitz family, had to send money for them to be able to come to Savannah. So that's the way they got to Savannah. In debt, before they even got here! **Albert Ullman, 33**

You know how bad things were in Europe, even in the '20s, early '20s? Well, they were trying to get out of Europe and they wanted to come here, but Fayge Radetsky [was going to have] a baby and they were afraid that the baby may not be able to make the trip. The trip was so treacherous to come across the ocean. So the baby, who was Sam Radetsky . . . was born in August of 1921. They waited on him to come. The other interesting thing is that the family passport when they all came was not Sam's picture, because you realize how difficult it was to have pictures made. So they had a picture made, before Sam was born, of a baby. What difference did it make? A baby! **Anchel Samuels, 86**

[In] 1922 I came to America. . . . At that particular time we was waiting all along so [my father, already in America] could get through. He couldn't get through. So . . . he sent a fellow by the name of Apple. . . . Different people had commissioned him to bring their families. He was supposed to come and help us get started with the papers and the immunization and all that, but he didn't. The next time we met him was in Warsaw. Warsaw, Poland. And that's when we got our papers and everything from the HIAS there. . . . I remember the street we lived on in Warsaw . . . right in the ghetto there.

But he was supposed to see that we got first class accommodations, but, hell, he left us on our own. Say, for instance, he took two or three thousand dollars from each of them and he didn't do two hundred dollars worth of work. We did everything ourselves. . . . We stayed there a month in Warsaw and then we got on a train and we were going to Cherbourg, France. And in Cherbourg, France, they deloused us. You know, put us in these steam baths and gave us some more shots and then they put us on the boat. . . . The boat's name was *Imperaga* and we came to America. **Abe Javetz, 78**

SETTLING IN SAVANNAH

My family has been in Savannah since the first group of Jewish settlers came to Savannah in 1733. . . . My ancestor was Benjamin Sheftall - he and his wife Perla were of that group of forty-two Jewish colonists who came here, and with the exception of a year or so when Savannah was under siege by the British and Mordecai Sheftall, Benjamin's son, was captured and his wife and family took refuge in Charleston, the family has been here ever since. **Marion (Abrahams) Levy Mendel, 17**

My Grandmother [Leah] Weil, I understand, was very observant. She had come from Germany, or Austria actually. The Friday night candles were always lit in the Wachtel home, and I have those silver candlesticks, which I treasure to this day. **Barbara (Smith) Levy, 19**

My father was one of four brothers, . . . [and] they had three sisters. . . . They all came here with their mother and father from Vitebsk, Russia, about 1908, and came into Baltimore on a ship, and then came down to Savannah. . . . The reason they came here was that my grandfather had a half-brother or stepbrother, I'm not sure which, who was Calmon Mendel's grandfather, . . . Solomon Raskin, who came to Savannah in the 1800s and had a large family here. **Sidney Raskin, 23**

My father was born in Germany. He left there as a young man. As a matter of fact, he ran away from home when he was about fifteen or sixteen. He ended up in South America, I think it was, and then worked his way up to this country. He joined the army and possibly, I don't know this for a fact, was stationed at Fort Screven. Maybe when he was discharged [he] just decided to stay in Savannah. **Walter Lowe, 54**

My mother and father were both from Latvia. My father . . . lived in Riga and my mother lived in Schoenburg, just thirty or forty miles away. They were second cousins. My mother came to the United States first. She had a brother, Jacob Hirsch, that lived in Atlanta, and he was the reason most of my relatives came over and most of them lived in Atlanta.

My father . . . came a few years after Mama was here, and they became engaged and got married. My father worked with Uncle Jake in Atlanta who was in the wholesale tobacco business, and we stayed there until I was eight years old. . . . My mother had a brother in Savannah who was in the wholesale grocery business. During the war, this was 1918, towards the end of World War I, Uncle Ben [Hirsch] who was in Savannah . . . asked for my father to move here and help him with his business. . . . We came to Savannah by train and that was a very exciting trip for us, my sister and I. **Samuel Hirsch, 52**

My mother . . . was born in Poland and came to this country with her father and the rest of her family when she was around eight years old. . . . They settled in New York where my mother lived until she was a young woman. . . .

My father's father, Sam Friedman, came from . . . one of the nearby countries that was occupied by the Russians. He was a young man, he was in his teens at the time, late teens, because he was in the czar's army and decided that there really wasn't much future there for a young Jewish man. . . . My grandfather . . . went to Philadelphia . . . [then] came to Savannah because he had a sister living here. **Karl Friedman, 85**

Levy Family in Savannah, c.1912
Family patriarch Aaron Levy established Levy Jewelers, carried on by his son, Jack M. Levy, and grandson and namesake, Aaron Levy, and later by Lowell Kronowitz, a great-grandson. Left to right: (front row) Rosaline (Levy) Tenenbaum and Jack M. Levy; (center row) Rachel (Gold) Levy, Dorothy (Levy) Wexler, and Aaron Levy; (back row) Ida (Levy) Barnett, Sarah (Levy) Buchsbaum, and Matthew Levy.
JVM 003 Savannah Jewish Archives General Photograph Collection, Item 2152

My [mother was] Irma Ginsberg. Her maiden name was Eichholz. She came from Germany in 1929, and came to Savannah because her uncle Zeke Eichholz was here and he was her sponsor. She went to Philadelphia after that to live with a cousin of hers and eventually came back to Savannah and that's where she met my father.

My father was born in Russia. He came to New York, and after a year or two his mother died. He was quite young, maybe three years old, and eventually his father remarried and they came to Savannah, possibly because some of the Ginsbergs were here already.

My mother came from Niederelzugen in Germany and my father came from what we think is Ivya, Russia. **Suzanne (Ginsberg) Kantziper, 84**

My mother was born in what was then Palestine. . . . My mother's family left Israel because of the . . . eye disease [trachoma], . . . they moved to Australia. And then they came over here when my mother . . . was . . . between twelve and fourteen. **Helen (Levington) Spiers, 73**

[My father and mother] were both from Minsk, Russia. . . . My father came over with his mother when he was seventeen years old. We came across her passport the other day. She was thirty-nine years old and he was seventeen years old. . . . [It was] 1907 when they came over. **Irvin "Sonny" Rubnitz, 49**

My father was Simon Goldin. He was from Kosovo, . . . which was in Grodno Gubernia in what was sometimes Poland and sometimes Russia. . . . My mother's name was Bertha Friedman and she was from Bialystok, also in Grodno Gubernia. . . . My father was the first to come here. He came to Savannah in the late 1880s, probably aged somewhat around fifteen. . . . He had come for the reason that he had a brother who lived in this area. . . . He landed in Philadelphia at an immigration center called Castle Garden. . . . He didn't have any money to get from Philadelphia down to Savannah, so he had to stop there. . . . After the six weeks period when he did work there at something, there was enough money for him to come to Savannah and he stayed here.

My mother, in Europe at the time, also was encountering very difficult times. Her father had died. Circumstances were not good. It is my presumption, but it is only a presumption, that there was a *shiddach* that was made. . . . I do know that my mother came around Shavous time which would have been around June, probably in 1903. Apparently she liked what she saw and my father liked what he saw. . . . The wedding actually took place in November. **Doris (Goldin) Lukin, 88**

We stayed in New York for one year. . . . We asked where we should go. . . . One lady said, "All right, if I would be you, I would go down South . . . Savannah, Georgia, for instance.". . . . "Savannah sounds very nice," I said. "That's where we go." So we packed our things, we didn't have too much. . . . We took a bus. . . . We got out in Savannah, Georgia, . . . [and] there were three ladies standing there from the three synagogues. . . . I really wanted to be Conservative, but there was a lady standing there. She was so beautiful, so gorgeous looking. She said, "My dear child, you are Reform, aren't you?" And she put her arm around me, and I said that was the nicest thing I ever had. I vote for them. From that time I was in the Mickve Israel. I've never regretted it. **Herta (Sanger) Danziger, 83**

THE EXISTING COMMUNITY SUPPORTS NEW MEMBERS

People that came over in the late 1800s, 1885 to 1900, 1910 - there was tremendous immigration into this country and into this community. All the new-comers were taken care of. There were societies, [and] they had every facility that a Jewish community would have. They had a *mikveh,* they had synagogues, they had daily services, they had kosher meats, and *shochets,* and butchers, and what-ever was necessary for the community. Charleston and Savannah were really the outstanding Orthodox communities and outstanding Jewish communities in the entire South. Seventy-five or one hundred years ago the Atlanta community was very small and certainly not anywhere near as strong as the Charleston or Savan-nah community. Jacksonville and Florida communities were also comparatively small. **Benjamin Garfunkel, 9**

My husband was stationed in Seattle. He was invited to a home and there was a gentleman there who heard that Benny was from Savannah. He said, "Oh, I had an experience in Savannah." He said, "When I got off the boat," was how he put it, "I was given some ribbons and laces to go peddle. I was arrested for not having a license." And he said, "When I was told that they wanted to see me," he was sure that he was going to be put up against the wall and shot. Instead, he hears this man say, "*Sholem aleichem.*" And it was my father-in-law [Charles Garfunkel] that was Chief of Police and was welcoming him to Savannah. Strangely enough, the man that had given him the ribbons and laces was Morris Slotin. **Charlotte (Shipper) Garfunkel, 37**

[My grandfather and father were] very active after World War I in the cam-paign and drive to take care of the Jews and to bring Jews over, and did the same thing during the '30s before World War II. . . . They gave affidavits that they would not be a financial burden and all that sort of thing for anyone wanting to come over. Once they got here, [they tried] to find them a job or a means of livelihood or something to do. They were . . . the political leaders of the Jewish community all through that time.

My uncle Abe [Garfunkel]was chairman of the finance committee of [Savan-nah City] Council for, I guess, twenty or thirty years, and I know even after he passed away, if a Jewish man was operating a small business or something and was not able to pay the full amount of a city license or something, why, he would always get the amount of license reduced for him, or taken care of. **Benjamin Garfunkel, 9**

NAME CHANGES

My father came from Romania from a little town called Vaslui, and his family name was Schecter. In crossing the waters, escaping Romania, I guess, and on his way to England, the family somehow picked up the name Rosenzweig. It's a German name meaning rose twig, but none of us were German. **David Rosenzweig, 63**

My father came over to this country from Russia . . . [and] sent for my mother who at that time had four children. And she came over from Russia on the boat. It took them six weeks until they got here. The family name . . . I was told . . . was Shane or something, they weren't sure. But when they got off the boat there was a sign . . . that said Steinberg & Company or Steinberg Brothers. And the name probably appealed to them so they took the name Steinberg. Like you say, I'm glad it wasn't Shaughnessy or something. That wouldn't have gone so well, would it? **Sadye (Steinberg) Rabhan, 22**

Three Generations in Russia, 1911
The three generations of the Javetz family, shown before moving to this county from Kopyczynce, Russia, include left to right: (front row) Leib and Abe; (back row) Fannie and Juda.
JVM 003 Savannah Jewish Archives General Photograph Collection, Item 1760

My father came over in 1902 from Russia. Also tried to escape from the military. . . . His name was Rachmalovitz, and when he came over he changed it to

Richman. . . . He left a wife and two children in Europe, and two years after he got here he sent for them and they came over. . . . He had one brother who lived in Beaufort, South Carolina, and he did go to Beaufort but preferred Savannah which was a little larger city, and had two brothers living here in the grocery business. And so he came to Savannah and went into the grocery business like all the other immigrants did. **Ethyl (Richman) Rosenzweig, 25**

THE LANGUAGE BARRIER

Of course [language] was a barrier. It took them a long time to learn. . . . With the children it was different; the children catch on right away and it don't take too long and they know it. But for the grownups it was really sad. . . . I know that there were Jewish communities where Jewish people got together . . . and then we came to Savannah we found . . . that there was a similar thing here.

Those who were Jews stuck together and brought others in so that we would be known. . . . They had a *shul*, a synagogue, and that's how they learned how to read and how to conduct everything, 'cause you had to. **Minnie (Bronitsky) Feinberg Robbins, 24**

I'm sure everybody has always heard the story about the days of the old Savannah Theatre [that] was owned by the Weis family. . . . My *bubbe* and my *zedye*, . . . this is the way that they learned to speak English. What little English they spoke was going to the movies. **Albert Ullman, 33**

Aunt Semi [Semita Rosolio] came from Spain . . . or Morocco, but she spoke very little English; she spoke fluent Spanish. My grandmother spoke very little English but she spoke *Yiddish*. I can remember very well, on Gwinnett Street, Aunt Semi coming and visiting us. And Aunt Semi and Grandma would sit on the front porch and talk to each other. They would tell each other *bubbe mayses*. My grandmother spoke in *Yiddish* which Aunt Semi didn't understand. Aunt Semi told her *mayses* in Spanish, which my grandmother didn't understand. They used to sit and talk for hours and they got along fabulously. Nobody ever had an argument. **Murray Bono, 68**

My mother and father spoke Jewish between them, but we spoke English. And then they soon learned the language. But for some reason, it looked like they all learned real fast, the European Jews. . . . Some of them did go to night school, but my parents didn't. They just learned by being in business. . . . First thing you know, all the Russian Jews were talking English. They slowly and surely learned it. **Lena (Feinberg) Rosenzweig, 26**

My parents only spoke English. My mother spoke it perfectly. My father spoke broken English all his life. . . . My mother came over when she was twelve years old. By the time she was seventeen she was working as a stenographer. That generation of people were very ambitious and when they came to this country, they wanted to be . . . American. . . . They would not speak *Yiddish* or Hebrew in my house. **Albert Mazo, 50**

My mother was an orphan and went to live with two uncles in Augusta, two bachelor uncles. They didn't know what to do with her, a little child; she and her sister, Mrs. [Ida] Berman. They ended up making a deal with the nunnery, Sacred Heart Convent, to take them as a day student. I laughingly refer to my mother as the only woman in the world who could say the "Hail Mary" in Yiddish. **Harris Slotin, 55**

I went to school at Montgomery Street School. At that time my father used to take me there. He used to sit in on my first grade class and my second grade class, and he picked up the alphabet and he taught himself how to read. His writing was quite limited but he learned how to read by learning the alphabet while I was going to school. **Samuel Radetsky, 45**

I remember coming downstairs one time; I was about eight or nine years old. My father was very autocratic and you always tried to please him. And he said to me, "I'm leaving now." At breakfast he says, "If Mr. [Levy] Rentz [the heating man] . . . comes to check the heating system, tell him to make sure he checks the went." So I said, "Okay, Daddy, I'll have Mr. Rentz make sure he checks the went." Whereupon my daddy gave me a clop. Everybody came running in. My father says, "He's mocking his father." Well, my father meant to say "vent". That was the last vestige of that. **Harris Slotin, 55**

I was born in Europe, in Russia. . . . I came here a little over eleven years old. . . . It was a very trying experience for me 'cause in Europe I went to school already, naturally. I spoke the language. I spoke Russian and *Yiddish*, but Russian better than *Yiddish*. When I came here I was speechless. It had a terrible effect on me. I wouldn't go down to play with youngsters, who made an effort to be friendly, until I learned how to speak. My mother couldn't get me down in the street. I wouldn't go 'cause I couldn't communicate. And I suffered terribly. I had a very bad time. **Pearl (Spivak) Levy, 44**

The earliest recollection I have, of course is when . . . I started going to school, and in the main the Irish people, who were the majority of the population in the Old Fort [section of northeast Savannah], were very nice to Mother. And they would lend her a hand when she needed something, if she had to buy something and didn't know how to express herself. **Benjamin Silverman, 29**

SUPPORTING THE FAMILY

I do want to mention the fact that when the immigrants came to Savannah, the easiest thing that they could do without knowing much of the language and without any money, was to start out as peddlers. At the time my father came, as I said before, in the late 1880s, one of the Garfunkel ancestors had a wholesale business, and the young men were furnished with a basket, with notions such as pins and needles, maybe a little sewing thread, and they carried the basket and walked and peddled these penny or pennies items.

I know that my father had a regular route that he went on and even went to Skidaway Island once a week or so. He had hired someone who had a boat who would pick him up in . . . Isle of Hope, where he could get to on the streetcar, and row him to the island, and he did his peddling on . . . his route there, and then he would get rowed back to the mainland. I think eventually he upgraded himself to using a bicycle and maybe even at some point was able to perhaps hire a horse and wagon, but that was his start in the retail business when he came to Savannah. **Doris (Goldin) Lukin, 88**

[My father] came from Poland. . . . [He] was a peddler . . . in the 1800s. . . . My father peddled with Mr. Straus of Macy's, Mr. Leopold Adler of Adler's of Savannah, Mr. B. H. Levy, Sr. of Savannah, Georgia. I don't know where the others went. I only knew that my father wound his way down on foot because he had no money to buy an animal to pull a wagon or a buggy. And so he traveled around the country until he got himself established, but this was out in the woods. . . . When he became more affluent, he was able to buy a horse and wagon and that was when he traveled, peddled. **Frances (Ehrlich) Rabhan, 21**

Herman Traub [my grandfather] was from Germany, as was his wife, Leila Traub. They came over to America. Well, they really didn't come over to America, they were sent to America by their families. So many families in Europe at that time, I understand, sent their children to America to live with relatives because conditions were so terrible in Europe. They still are, but nothing like they were then.

My grandfather, Herman, was sent to live with relatives in New York as a teenager. He didn't know my grandmother at that time. They later met in Savannah. But she also was sent over as a teenager to live with relatives in New York. He was later sent to live with relatives in Savannah. They at one time lived in

Bainbridge, Georgia. Of course, I guess, as most immigrants in those days, they probably came over to the United States with their underwear and something on their backs, but they certainly didn't have any worldly goods and worldly possessions.

From what I understand from my family, he started off, as so many did, walking with a basket full of buttons and shoelaces and so forth, and walked around town selling those things, and then, when he could, he bought a bicycle. Then he bought a horse, and then he bought a wagon. He gradually pulled himself up by his bootstraps and ended up with a wholesale grocery business, H. Traub's, which was located on what was then West Broad Street, now Martin Luther King, Jr. Boulevard, and Broughton, on the west side of the street between Firestone Service Stores on one side and Scarbrough House on the other. He was able to purchase that land as he progressed.

I think one of the interesting things he did, [on] the front half of the land he built a two-story red brick building that he used for his warehouse for the wholesale grocery business. . . . On the back half of the lot he built sixteen little two-bedroom houses, very, very simple. The remarkable thing to me was that he was so grateful for what he had been able to accomplish in the United States and what he was able to do in this new land, that he built these houses and let other immigrants come over and stay in those houses free until they could find work and get settled. **Herbert Traub, Jr., 79**

The Wexler Family, 1921
Pictured left to right: (front row) Sanford Wexler, Jeannette (Wexler) Shiffman, Rose (Wexler) Jacobs, and Dorothy (Wexler) Mirsky; (back row) Harry Wexler, Fannie (Schwartz) Wexler, and Louis Wexler.
JVM 003 Savannah Jewish Archives General Photograph Collection, Item 2187

Daddy went and peddled bananas on the street. I remember I went with him one time, and I was nine or ten years old. . . . We went way out on the Louisville Road and there was a factory out there, . . . and [the workers] would get off on Saturday about twelve. And he would pick his spot, and after they got paid they came out and he said bananas were five cents a pound, or two cents, or whatever. And I remember I worked with him. After that he promoted himself to a horse and wagon. He had a grocery store. **Nathan Karnibad, 41**

He [Pop] went and bought him a horse and buggy. [He] knew nothing about horses or nothing else. They gave him a bunch of stuff, I think they got them from Slotin & Company. You know, staples, thread, and pieces of cloth, and maybe some little bits of underwear, and things like that. He'd go peddle it in the country. **Benjamin Portman, 20**

My grandparents immigrated to this country late - somewhere around 1913, 1914. They already had one child in Europe. My grandfather, his brothers and my grandmother's brothers, apparently they were very close in the *shtetl* that they lived in, in . . . Odessa, Russia, before their marriage. The brothers all came together to this country alone, and then, within a year or so, sent for the women. They settled in New York because that was the port of entry.

I've been told that a very distant relative was living or traveling in the South, and got in touch with them and said, "There's work in Savannah." So they came to Savannah. My parents and their family, my mother's family, have been here ever since. I would say they had to be here before 1916 which is what would have been the date of my mother's birth. **Robert Friedman, 38**

We got here in 1922. I came here from a *shtetl* . . . in Grodno, Poland. We arrived here with the help of my uncle, Phillip Kaplan, who was very instrumental in sending over the right papers and what-not so that we can come to America. We got here when I was six months old, and at that time my parents had no occupation at all. . . . We started a small grocery store. **Samuel Radetsky, 45**

CHAPTER 2: MAKING A LIVELIHOOD

DRY GOODS, CLOTHING AND SHOE BUSINESSES

When [my father] got here, the best job he could get here was what everyone did. And that was in the mercantile [business]. There were many Jews involved. **Fred Rotkow, 27**

[My father] did a bunch of things and he got into the wholesale dry goods business [Slotin & Co.]. . . . The business was located in various locations within a block of Broughton and Montgomery. They ultimately built a building on what is now Zubly and Martin Luther King. The building is still standing. . . . They built that in about 1926. **Harris Slotin, 55**

[Joe Levin & Son] had dry goods. They had shoes, and men's clothing, and all the overalls, and ladies' clothing, and hats. And just everybody, all the boys growing up, worked there; Murray Arkin, Irvin Warshaw, Alex Scheer. I can name just about every young man coming up worked in that store. Alex and Irvin were two devils. They were bad. They even locked one of the men that worked there in the store in the window one day. They were fun. **Audrey (Galkin) Levin, 89**

On Bryan Street you had merchants there who, we used to call them second-hand clothing stores, today they're called consignment shops. But the second-hand clothing stores of the years gone by, on Bryan Street, the merchants there would get the . . . old army shoes, old army boots, old shoes, and they would put new soles on the shoes. They would shine the shoes and put them on a string and then hang them on a stick outside their stores for sale.

I've seen my mother, *alav ha-sholom*, by herself 'cause my father died when I was ten years old and he was usually the shoemaker in the store, but when he died my mother took over the shoemaker duties. I have seen this little woman cut a half-sole to fit a shoe with just a knife. No machine or anything like that at all, but cut the sole to fit the shape of the shoe, by hand with a knife, as well as shape the heel, the rubber heel. Mom would go on the train, the *Silver Meteor* or the *Champion*, to New York to buy the shoes and also buy clothes and things of this type for the store. And then she would have these items shipped to Savannah by steamship. Came on a boat to Savannah and then she would have these trucks bring it into the store. She would then fix the clothes, sew them or whatever that she had to do to fix the clothes, the suits, and fix up the shoes as well. **Irvin "Sonny" Rubnitz, 49**

[My dad] came back to the bank, and then he went into the jeans business with Mr. Alexander. Mr. Alexander had no family here. He and the two brothers [Maximilian and Sigmond Alexander] had started this business on Broughton Street . . . between Abercorn and Lincoln, on the south side of the street, where Levy's Department Store was. . . . Later on they moved out on Bay Street. . . . My dad worked there the rest of his life, and then I went into the business. **Julius Edel, 35**

I started on West Broad Street, right opposite the Union Station. The store at that time was called General Store, but I changed it into an army store and I eventually called it the Old Army/Navy Store. . . . From there I moved up to Broughton Street; I had two stores. Then I closed one. And then I took another store on Broughton Street, blocking other competition. **Meyer "Johnny" Becker, 70**

Union Dry Goods, c.1947-1952
Meyer "Johnny" Becker's first store was located on West Broad Street.
JVM 003 Savannah Jewish Archives General Photograph Collection, Item 2226

I worked at the S. & G. Men's Shop on West Broad Street. It was owned by Max Gordon. . . . The stores did not have hours then. One store stayed open until the store next door closed, which meant that the business stayed open until, oh, ten-thirty, eleven o'clock. This was particularly on Saturday. However, . . . I never stayed until the store closed. I usually left somewhere nine to ten o'clock. **Karl Friedman, 85**

When I left Kahn & Company I wanted to go into business for myself. I bought out a place called Bottom Dollar . . . which was really a dinky little store. . . . We grew there and we had a big business, but I will say that I think every woman now that's married that I know of practically worked there. Because the mothers, all the mothers used to call me as soon as they got out of school, when they were sixteen. "Reuben, my daughter would like. . . ." "Send her down," [I said]. . . . We had a fifteen foot store to begin with and I never will forget, one Easter I had so . . . much help in there the customers couldn't get in. **Reuben Schneider, 28**

My grandfather had a little shoe shop on West Broad and Perry, . . . Southern Shoe Factory. . . . As many immigrants, they were poor. . . . [My mother's] sister, Celia Hirsch, who was a Scheer, was born in the back of the store, that's how poor they were. My childhood, early childhood, I used to come here. By that time, you know, things were great, things were better. They lived in a big house, 410 West Bolton Street. They were living high. I used to come. I used to be in my grandfather's shoe shop all the time. We spent days together. They would just drop me off and leave me there at three, four, and five years old. I began to see the world through his eyes. **Robert Friedman, 38**

My father and his brothers operated shoe stores on Broughton Street in Savannah for many years. And their sisters had stores on West Broad Street around Union Station. And I used to, as a very young kid, have free access to, as it was then called, West Broad Street, all hours of the day and night. It was very quiet and peaceful. Of course, Broughton Street was like home to me, and the City Market. **Sidney Raskin, 23**

GROCERS

[Regarding the wholesale grocery business.] We had immigrants move to Savannah – Jewish people, Greeks, Italians, Syrians, all nationalities – and they wanted something to do. We'd give them a stock of groceries, about five hundred dollars worth of groceries was all we could supply, store plenty of stuff for that. It was easy to go into the grocery business in those days 'cause you didn't have to have the freezers and refrigerators and all of this display stuff. You had one pair of hanging scales for weighing the meat and produce.

Most of the families . . . worked seven days a week and at night, too, if necessary. They didn't go fishing two or three times a week, play golf and hunt and that kind of thing. They worked and they lived in back of the store or upstairs from the stores. They'd fix them up as they made progress. They paid the bills off pretty quick. Worked hard and saved their money until they were able to do better things. All those families are very wealthy now. **Samuel Hirsch, 52**

From what I know, my grandfather had a corner grocery store on Gwinnett and Burroughs, as I believe. I can recall going there. They lived next door to the store. The little apartment that they lived in . . . opened into the store area. It was a very small place, both the apartment and the store, but it had an upstairs and they had a large family at the time. **Herman Cranman, 36**

We started a small grocery store . . . in Yamacraw. And we lived over the store . . . [on] Fahm and York [streets]. My father got himself a job outside and my mother took care of the store and me. She'd be holding me in one arm, and the customers that would come into the store would point out on the shelves what they wanted, because my mother did not know English and neither did I. . . . [My father] had several different jobs. He worked for [Phillip] Newman the tailor making buttonholes. He also had another job, at a little grocery store, a bigger store. And from there the grocery store that we had started getting a little bit bigger, so then he put all of his efforts into that store. **Samuel Radetsky, 45**

When my mother and daddy first got married they ran that store [on the corner of Anderson and Habersham streets] and they lived in a house above that. Again, all this was rental, this was not owned. But they got married on January 19, 1930, and sometime in the summer of '32 they bought the property one block south, which would then be 31st and Habersham. They moved there and moved the store there. . . .

They had a regular grocery store. . . . My daddy cut meat and I remember when they first got frozen food, you know, that was a big deal. They had a freezer like a chest, where they kept frozen food. I also remember in the store when that thing came out, a new thing called "margarine." The federal government would not allow them to color it, so the margarine was white. But it came sort of like in a plastic bag and in that bag was . . . a little pill or something. And that was food coloring. So if you wanted your margarine to look like your butter, you'd have to, I guess, squeeze it to get the color. **Anchel Samuels, 86**

There were mostly little corner grocery stores, and of course the first supermarket as I remember it in Savannah was the Bargain Corner . . . at the corner of Jefferson and Bay streets. . . . Also David Rosenzweig's father had a quite large store out on Bull Street. **Albert Ullman, 33**

[After high school] I worked for Abe Samuels in his grocery store. I recall we used to go to work at eight o'clock in the morning and get off about seven o'clock at night. Saturday it was about eleven to twelve o'clock at night. I made a big twelve dollars a week. I started off with seven dollars. When I got married, he gave me twelve dollars. And what did I do? I used to buy groceries for the twelve dollars. I never took any money home. **Celia (Scheer) Hirsch, 1**

A. Buchenholz, 1900
Owner Abraham Buchenholz is shown in front of his notions shop on West Congress Street.
JVM 003 Savannah Jewish Archives General Photograph Collection, Item 2270

There was a little store across the street from us on East Broad and St. Julian that was known as Hellman's. It was a German family and they ran a grocery store. Of course we didn't buy meats or anything that was non-kosher. But we, the kids, frequented the store to buy crackers and cakes. They had a little store adjoining the grocery store in which they sold beer. And we would take a little pail from the house, or a pitcher, and go across the street and for a dime they would fill the pail or the pitcher. And we would take the beer back home to our father who would like to have his beer. **Benjamin Silverman, 29**

My grandfather was H. Traub, Herman Traub, and when he came to Savannah he opened up a wholesale grocery, feed, rice, hay, oats, canned goods, and so forth, on West Broad Street. West Broad and Broughton. I used to go down there as a kid and play on the sacks and chase the rats, 'cause there were a lot of them, you know, you can imagine in those days . . . back in the late '20s, 1920s. . . . Then my grandfather brought his two sons in and it was H. Traub & Sons. My father, in the 1930s, became interested in having a private brand, private label, and got involved with W. L. Stickney in Chicago, a very fine person. . . . They developed a private label, all kinds of canned goods, called it "Pleezing". . . . They're still manufactured today and even sold up in the East more than anywhere else. . . . That didn't really take off like Heinz. **Stephen Traub, 32**

One of the things that happened there was that Pop opened up a little grocery store . . . a block above River Street. When the seamen came in, they traded groceries for *schnapps*. And Pop had some of the finest *schnapps* in town and everybody knew it. . . . Underneath the house . . . Pop had a little cave or something dug out, and Mama and I, I was still a little boy then, Mama used to come under there with a lantern. We'd crawl under there. She'd pull the hatch cover off and drop me down in there and point out what kind of whiskey they needed to sell, to bootleg. I can just picture Mama crawling under there.

We had dogs and chickens and just eveything; in fact, we used to sell milk. Pop used to sell milk from there. We had cows in the yard all the time, and we used to hire these black kids who would take them across the canal . . . and they'd keep them a few hours and they'd come back, and we sold milk and everything there. **Benjamin Portman, 20**

There was an elderly Jewish gentleman here who sometimes helped conduct services in the synagogue. He had a beautiful voice. His name was [Wolf] Sutker, and he ran a little shop on the corner of Montgomery and Bryan Street. . . . Whatever he sold there was kosher. He didn't sell deli meats and things like that, but one thing that I remember very well is that he was a *shochet*. He slaughtered according to the dietary laws, and we would take chickens there, live chickens, and he would slaughter them. And we would bring them back home and our parents would pick them and clean them and prepare them and salt them and soak them in accordance with the Jewish tradition.

And I remember Mr. Sutker would come to the house every Sunday with a little notebook and pencil and take Mom's order and write it down in *Yiddish*. And if we needed a *shmaltz* herring, I would go over to the store where his shop was. And he always wore a coat and was a real gentleman. He would take and push his sleeve up above his elbow and dig his hand into the barrel of brine, and come out with a *shmaltz* herring which he proceeded to wrap in newspaper to keep it sanitary. **Benjamin Silverman, 29**

My father went to the University of Virginia and graduated as an attorney. . . . I don't think he practiced law long. And he went into my grandfather's business, A. Leffler & Company, wholesale grocers, on Bay Street, right where the

[Savannah] Morning News is now. And right next to that was Ehrlich & Company, another Jewish wholesale grocer that sold the same things that my father and grandfather did. And on the corner of Barnard and Bay Street was Cooley's Laundry, that was another Jewish operation.

[My father and grandfather] were cotton merchants; they sold whiskey in the barrel, they sold groceries, they sold - I remember down in the basement of this place on Bay Street - great sides of fatback. And vinegar, I remember barrels of vinegar. They would take out half the vinegar and then add water to fill up the barrel again. **Martin Leffler, 14**

We [the Georgia Market] had a full line. We had fresh vegetables. We had canned things. There were [other] things too, washing powders, jellies, jams. There was a full meat department with a cooler for the meat and a display case. And they sold paper goods, anything you could buy today, just in a smaller variety. . . . They didn't sell frozen things. The only thing I recall that was frozen was . . . [a] case for ice cream that would be for frozen foods. And they weren't selling frozen foods like you find today, like boxed or bagged frozen things. Mostly fresh vegetables. . . .

My parents sold mostly bread from Holsum Bakery. There were bakeries on Waters Avenue nearby where you could get fresh baked goods. So people could do either one, but the grocery stores only sold the packaged breads. . . . At one point, I remember, they did sell . . . live chickens so the people themselves would take them home and they would kill their own chickens. . . .

[My father] went to the City Market and he would buy greens and different vegetables. But he also had people coming to him, a farmer from Claxton or nearby towns would come by and bring vegetables. People . . . would come by every week and deliver these things. So they had to know how to buy as well as sell because they had to know how much they could sell. . . .

They opened in the morning and sometimes they would go home for lunch if they had good help. . . . The hours were long. They closed maybe as late as seven or eight o'clock at night and they worked seven days a week. On Wednesday afternoon they closed and on Sunday afternoon they closed, and they always closed on the Jewish holidays. Today very few people are able to close on the Jewish holidays. **Suzanne (Ginsberg) Kantziper, 84**

There wasn't much of a weekend, 'cause you worked about six and a half days in those days [1930s and 1940s]. But there [were] Wednesday afternoons and Sunday afternoons. **Norton Melaver, 15**

My father owned a small grocery store. Well, my father had two jobs. He was a pressman for the *[Savannah] Morning News* as his lifetime work, and then he wanted to go into the grocery business and he . . . bought a store on 31st and Burroughs Street which is on the west side of Savannah. Mom helped him run the grocery store. . . . The larger stores came in and the supermarkets and . . . the only things that the small stores were used for then were [for] the people who couldn't afford to pay cash, they would buy on credit and pay it off. It got to be too much for the small little business owner. The supermarkets ran out the small little business owner. **Maxine "Midge" (Lasky) Schildkraut, 81**

Richman's Market, c.1920s
This Zubly Street store was operated by Mendel and Morris Richman.
JVM 003 Savannah Jewish Archives General Photograph Collection, Item 2219

I remember on the corner of where we lived, there was next door to us the Langs. They had a grocery store and they lived above the grocery store. They were German. I used to shuck beans for her for a nickel, a whole peck for a nickel and a big bellywasher, . . . a big old drink. **Gertrude (Scheer) Barr, 1**

Our store was on 41st and Burroughs, and we'd have customers that lived right around the corner in the lane, 40th Lane. There was no electricity. They lived really in shacks. By the way, the neighborhoods were integrated in those times. . . . I still remember the huge wash tubs out in the yard where they boiled the clothes and they made their soap. . . . I did work. . . . You did what you had to do and what you had to do was work very hard. I'll never forget – my mother wasn't a mean person, she was very sweet, as a matter of fact. But I was trying to cut some meat one day, the knife slipped and cut my finger almost off. I wrapped a towel around it, got on the bicycle. And the reason I mention Mother, she was worried to death about it. I had to cycle all the way up to Dr. Levington, Henry Levington's, to sew it back. My mother's words to me were, "Be careful and keep that towel wrapped around your finger real tight and get back here as soon as you can because we've got orders to deliver." Now the reason that we were so concerned about delivering the orders and taking care of the customers was because there was a store on every corner. If you didn't satisfy that customer you would have lost your business and you just couldn't afford it in those days. **Walter Lowe, 54**

I think there was a lot of friendship between the owners and the buyers because . . . a lot of times the customers would invite us to come over, like on a Sunday afternoon to fish at their place or, we went once to the country to the man who used to deliver the greens. So there was an interesting camaraderie between the owners and the sellers and the buyers and I still, today, and it's been over maybe forty years since I've seen these people in the neighborhoods where my parents had the store, and they still remember. It must have been a good memory or they wouldn't stop me and speak to me. **Suzanne (Ginsberg) Kantziper, 84**

DELIS AND RESTAURANTS

We had at the time, in 1911, 1912, five delicatessens. . . . Yes, five Jewish delicatessens. They were Gittelsohn, Rundbaken, Singer, Sutker, and Rotkow. **Lena (Feinberg) Rosenzweig, 26**

There were already established four Jewish delicatessen stores. There was Rundbaken, there was Gittelsohn, and there was Rotkow, and there was Hirsch. Four Jewish stores, all selling delicatessen and other items. **Louis Silverman, 29**

Gittelsohn had a delicatessen, I think the Rotkows had a delicatessen, and there may have been others. . . . Gittelsohn was on Broughton Street between Montgomery and West Broad. **Samuel Plotkin, 8**

I remember we had Hirsch's Delicatessen on Broughton Street. . . . It was between West Broad and Montgomery. . . . And we had the Rotkow family . . . and that was the second deli, . . . then the Hirsches sold out to the Epsteins. . . . And all this was kosher. Years later Gottlieb's opened on Bull and, I think, 35th. **Selma (Greenberg) Dunn, 7**

[My father] opened up a delicatessen . . . in 1934. I recall going with my father down to the Merchant and Miners Steamship Company. It was a boat that came to

Savannah from New York twice a week . . . and they had refrigerators, big walk-in coolers on that ship, and you could receive a refrigerated shipment of cheese, meat, delicatessen meats, fresh meats, and stuff like that. So that's how we got it here. . . . The first store he had in Savannah was on 34th and Bull. **Alan Gottlieb, 40**

The Epsteins had a restaurant on . . . Broughton, upstairs. Well, downstairs was the deli and upstairs they had like a room where they could serve people if you wanted to be served upstairs. **Bertha (Plotkin) Freedman, 8**

Mrs. Epstein's Restaurant, 1940
Mrs. Epstein was one of the chefs to cater to the Jewish community, and her restaurant was a popular meeting place for lunch and celebrations like this anniversary party. Shown in the picture (left to right): (front row) Sally (Levy) Pitofsky, Barbara (Lowe) Brown, Abram Rubin, Phyllis (Lowe) Lustick, and Millicent Melaver; (center row) Madeline (Sadler) Rubin, Fannie (Levy) Lasky, Eva (Levy) Sadler, Sara (Levy) Lowe, Esther (Lublin) Levy, Oscar Levy, Annie (Levy) Melaver, and Hilda (Levy) Broome; (back row) Irving Rubin, Annette (Lasky) Yesner, Walter Lowe, William Lasky, Bernice (Sadler) Elman, Barney Sadler, Robert Lowe, Minnie (Weitz) Levy, Hyman "Scribe" Levy, Isadore Melaver, Norton Melaver, Ursula "Sula" (Director) Broome, and Sidney Broome.
JVM 003 Savannah Jewish Archives General Photograph Collection, Item 2217

My mother's store was really like a little meeting place. Mother would serve meals, but she only wanted to buy kosher meats. She wouldn't buy anything but kosher meats to serve. That was good. Down the street was a ten cent store run by [Nat] Daub. He would come in, go in my mother's refrigerator, cut off a hunk of salami, and eat it. Also, a Gottlieb used to deliver rolls every morning. Bagels and rolls at that time were two for a nickel. They would come in and have one and ask my mother to put the other one up 'til they could come back.

I remember one day a non-Jewish person walked in and sat down and saw one of those beautiful-looking water rolls that Gottlieb used to make, and he had his little drink and he wanted one of those, and he picked it up and bit into it and was very disappointed because he thought it was a cream puff. Not too happy. . . .

We had to have the phone upstairs because that was less expensive, because if you kept the phone downstairs it was a business phone. So every five minutes that phone would ring and [I] had to go flying upstairs. And there would be a husband of one of the wives on the phone. "If you don't mind, would you please send my wife back to the store? We need her." One day I got a call. Next door was Sol Feinberg in the little National Tailor Store they had then. And Sol was married to Rosie. They had no children. The phone rings and I go flying up the steps. "Audrey?" "Yes." [Rosie said], "You know, Audrey, it's awfully cold outside. Would you mind? Go down and tell Sol he should button his sweater." So I went flying down and told Sol to button his sweater. **Audrey (Galkin) Levin, 89**

I lived on the corner of Congress and Montgomery Street in an apartment upstairs . . . where they used to bring the horses to teach them. . . . That's where Mama had started with her kitchen, so to speak. She served lunches to the Jewish people who wanted to come to eat. We had quite a few gentlemen that worked in the stores on Broughton Street, used to come to Mama to have their lunch. . . . That's where, how she made a living. **Minnie (Bronitsky) Feinberg Robbins, 24**

The way I got in the restaurant business, a very good friend of mine, Jim Casey, . . . didn't like what he was doing and I detested what I was doing. . . . At that time there were no drive-ins in Savannah. . . . We didn't know a darn thing about restaurant business or food business. . . . Anyway, one day we were kidding around again about a hamburger stand and then we said, "Why not?" We started thinking about it seriously. . . . This was 1943, during World War II. Restaurants here were few and far between. So we decided, "Yeah," we'd give it a whirl, and then we tried looking for a location. . . .

William Morrison owned a big piece of property on Victory Drive and Skidaway Road. . . . The only thing that was on the corner was a little English architecture building, built along the lines of a typical country English house. . . . This place [was] way out of town. . . . There were no buses, there was nothing out there. In fact, I don't even think Skidaway Road was paved at that time. . . . I remember the first time we walked up to the building, the weeds and grass came up to our shoulders. . . . After a lot of negotiation and talking [David Morrison, father of the owner] agreed to rent us this building as was. . . . We built a kitchen, we put the restrooms in . . . and we were able to get a lot of second-hand . . . equipment. . . .

We . . . finally hit upon the name of "Our House.". . . We finally opened on July 4th, 1945. We were so busy, so jammed, . . . it's a wonder we survived those few days. . . . But it was a new thing for Savannah, a drive-in. Although, we did have a little one hundred seat dining room with a big fireplace. It was real cozy. But this was in July, so you wouldn't use a fireplace. It wasn't even air conditioned in those days. . . .

I have to tell one little funny story that happened at "Our House" that always amused so much. I was standing in the kitchen one Saturday night and this carhop came up to me and handed me her order pad and the pencil and said, "Mr. Traub, would you write this order for me, please." And I said, "Sure." So she gave me the pad and I asked her what she wanted and she told me, I don't remember what it was, a couple of hamburgers, milkshakes, whatever it was.

I gave it back to her and I said, "Why'd you want me to write this for you?" She said, "Well I don't know how to write." I said, "You don't know how to write? How long you've been working here?" And she said it was over two years. She'd been working over two years. I said, "You mean to tell me you've been working here for over two years and you don't know how to write? My Lord, what've you been doing all this time?" She said, "Well, I've been asking my customers to write my orders for me and it never has been a problem. You know, they'd write what they want and I'd turn it in and take it back to them." I said, "What happened this time?" She said, "Well, they couldn't write either." She met her match. We always laughed so much about that. **Herbert Traub, Jr., 79**

In 1950 I married Lucy . . . and I went into business with my father and my mother. . . . Their store was on Whitaker and Duffy Street, and it was a good location at the time because Whitaker Street was a one-way street; most people came home from business driving down Whitaker Street. . . . We wanted to get close to the bakery, 'cause everybody went to the bakery, it was a big attraction. . . . So we opened a store on the corner of 33rd and Bull Street. . . . After that we bought a piece of property . . . a block away, on 32nd and Bull Street. . . . Gunn and Meyerhoff built us an eight thousand square foot beautiful, magnificent facility. . . . It was the last word in delicatessen and fancy foods. . . . We enjoyed a lot of nice business there in that store. . . .

Two years later we . . . doubled the size of that store. . . . Apparently it became too large. The overhead was bigger than what we were taking in and we had to close that store. . . . I went back into the catering business on my own, and I've been in it ever since. . . . For many years we have been making kosher meals like T.V. dinners; . . . we provide them to all the local hospitals. . . . We are constantly being called by the big hotels in Savannah and in Hilton Head. . . . On several occasions we have even gone to . . . the Hyatt Hotel [where] we would *kasher* the kitchen, *kasher* the stoves . . . dishes and silverware, and we've catered conventions at the Hyatt. **Alan Gottlieb, 40**

Gottlieb's Kosher Delicatessen, n.d.
Gottlieb's was located at Whitaker and Duffy streets, before moving to Bull and 32nd streets, and was one of several locally owned Jewish delis.
JVM 003 Savannah Jewish Archives General Photograph Collection, Item 2123

One night . . . the phone rings and they call me to the phone. It was Mr. [Hansell] Hillyer. He says, "Herb, I just wanted to ask you something." He said, "Mrs. [Mary] Hillyer . . . wants to convert the Pirate's House Museum into a tearoom. We just thought maybe we'd like to talk to you and Jim about operating it.". . . Anyway, we met Mr. Hillyer down there and he told us what he wanted and what they'd like to do. It sounded interesting because I loved that old place and felt it had a lot of potential because it was something real. It wasn't built and made to look old, it was old and had a lot of charm and we decided it had a lot of potential. . . .

We thought it might be a good idea to maybe try that. I didn't want to run a tearoom and neither did Jim, but we made a list of things that we felt would be required there, like a suitable kitchen, suitable restrooms and . . . more dining space. . . . Mr. Hillyer agreed to build . . . the Buccaneer Room between the Pirate's House and the Herb House, which is our biggest dining room there. . . .We gave all the rooms names just to make it more interesting instead of the room; the Jolly Roger Room, the Treasure Room, the Captain's Room, the Pirate's Den, the Buccaneer Room, just to create some interest. . . .We opened and people thought we were crazy to go down there, but we did and we had what we thought was an unusual menu.

It just so happened we were able to employ someone who had been one of the managers of the Pink House, Frances McGrath, who had been working the Pink House. She came and decided she wanted to come and help manage it for us. We hired Frances and Frances came in and got us going. . . . As we became better known we were blessed with many, many awards and many, many articles in national magazines and newspapers. **Herbert Traub, Jr., 79**

BAKERIES

When my grandfather and grandmother got married, I think it was in 1887, they decided to open a bakery. I don't know why. My grandfather was not a baker, but he had previously owned a barroom, a bar, where they sold liquor in Savannah. . . . I understand there are people living here right now that remember when he used to ride around, he would deliver the bread in a horse and buggy. He had a horse and buggy and he would take it out; the horse knew the route. The horse walked up and down the streets, downtown around Congress Street and State Street, where all the Jewish people were living in those days. That was before 1900.

He would ring a bell; he had a big bell, a big brass bell. He would ring the bell and everybody would come out to buy bread. He used to sell it five loaves for a dime. . . . People tell me that he was a very charitable man. They said everybody had bread whether they had money or not. He had bread for everybody. He . . . sold tickets five for a dime and you'd pay him with a little blue ticket. I remember the ticket. If people didn't have the money, he'd say, "Forget about it. It's okay. You'll pay me when you have it." **Alan Gottlieb, 40**

Gottlieb's Bakery, as far back as I can remember, was there on 32nd and Bull. And in those days you didn't have to go to the bakery to buy your bread; it came, they came into the homes. They used to come with their wagon or truck and they would ring a bell and the people would come out and buy the bread. Irving, Buster, and Elliott used to go out and people in the neighborhood would come out of their homes and buy the bread. **Samuel Plotkin, 8**

Washington Pie was a thick bread pudding. They would cut up all the [leftover] bread. . . . They'd mix up eggs and sugar and whatever and pour it over the bread and bake it in a real thick pan. . . . Why did they call it Washington Pie?

Because they would cut a great piece of it, and isn't it Washington that's on the nickel? . . . And they got this huge piece for a nickel. **Isser Gottlieb, 92**

When my grandfather and grandmother had opened up the bakery, I heard people talk about the fact that they would do the cooking for weddings, and then they would take the food into the J.E.A. [Jewish Educational Alliance] where the parties were held. . . . So they did cook food in the bakery oven. They were the only ovens that were big enough to do that in Savannah and be kosher. **Alan Gottlieb, 40**

The breads were always the big selling item until Ava and I came up with the Chocolate Chewy. . . . We used to sell eleven thousand chocolate chewies a week. . . . The Chocolate Chewies' original name was "Come Back Cookie,". . . 'cause people would buy it and come back for more. **Isser Gottlieb, 92**

BUTCHERS AND CITY MARKET

The City Market was a big, big building and had steps to go up to, to get in, but inside I see big shelves and counters with fruits and vegetables and all. And then on the wall, one wall were all the butchers, the butcher shops with the different butchers. There were kosher butchers and we had, I think, two or three kosher butchers at that time, besides the others. That's how big it was. It took up a whole square. . . . There was that much activity going on. And people used to come there from out of town with their merchandise or to buy their merchandise. **Minnie (Bronitsky) Feinberg Robbins, 24**

As far as the kosher butchers are concerned, the ones I remember were in the City Market. It was Mr. Sam Friedman, and there was a Mr. [Morris] Levine who was a kosher butcher. I remember those two butchers. **Samuel Plotkin, 8**

The old City Market is where [the family] had their wholesale meat. . . . I worked as a cashier there. . . . Oh, it was wonderful and it smelled terrible, but it was great. It's a shame they ever tore it down. Everybody had a stall there. They had poultry, they had meat, they had vegetables, and all the produce. People would come with these gorgeous baskets and would shell their peas and everything in them. The Grocerteria was right across the street. . . . The Grocerteria was a big grocery store, and Alexander Grocery Company, you see, was there, too. . . . Mother used to come in from Tybee once a week and do the grocery shopping. She would get the train and she would come into town and she would do her grocery shopping and come back out to Tybee with the groceries for the week. **Adele (Meddin) Schneider, 61**

We had at the time, in 1911, 1912, . . . four butchers in the City Market. . . . [They] were Max Cooley, Sam Friedman, and another two. **Lena (Feinberg) Rosenzweig, 26**

City Market, Spring 1954
Many Jewish butchers set up shop in the old City Market building.
JVM 003 Savannah Jewish Archives General Photograph Collection, Item 1826

There was a kosher butcher shop when I got married; Mr. [Israel] Safer ran the butcher shop. . . . It was near the Bargain Corner. . . . In the late '40s . . . they had groups of people coming in from Europe they called the New Americans. . . . One of the men asked to learn to become a butcher and he ran a butcher shop on Bull Street, near Annette's Dairy; it was near Victory Drive. Mr. [Joseph] Golcman had a butcher shop there for years. **Charlotte (Shipper) Garfunkel, 37**

My grandfather was the kosher butcher for the City of Savannah. . . . My uncle Anchel, or "Unchie" as we called him, was a butcher. But he and my grandfather shared for many years a common place of business except that there was a *mechitzah* as it were between them, because my uncle did not sell kosher meat. My grandfather did not sell anything that wasn't kosher. So they kept that separated. **Erwin "Ernie" Friedman, 71**

DOCTORS AND LAWYERS

Billy's [William Weichselbaum, Jr.] grandfather was an apothecary . . . then he became a physician. . . . So many of the children who were delivered at that time, their birth certificates read, "Dr. Jacob Weichselbaum.". . . Billy's father was a dentist and practiced here. And then Billy became a dentist, . . . came back and started practicing in Savannah with his father and Dr. Louis Hohenstein, a cousin. **Mildred (Wolf) Weichselbaum, 51**

[My parents] were married in 1934 here in Savannah at Zeke Eichholz' home on Bull Street. After that they ran a small grocery store on Harmon Street. In 1936 my sister Jane [Rosenblum] and I were born here at the Telfair Hospital. In 1939 my sister Lyda [Parker] was born and they also decided to build their own store which was further down the street on Harmon Street. It was 701 Harmon, Harmon and Wolf.

They ran the grocery business for quite some time and then my mother decided that if my father, who had always wanted to be a lawyer, wanted to go ahead and study, that he could and she would carry on with the business, which they did. They had a butcher and a clerk, and so they had help, and my father studied at night. He became a lawyer in about 1949 and they continued, my mother continued on with the business. He helped her some before he went to his law office.

His offices were . . . in the American Building for a while and then . . . he was with John Jones in his office for a while, but they were not partners, but they shared offices. My mother continued with the business until about 1960. . . . And she then helped my father occasionally, well maybe more than occasionally, in his office. **Suzanne (Ginsberg) Kantziper, 84**

Georgia Legal Services is part of the National Legal Services, . . . set up to give legal assistance to citizens of the United States whose income is less than ten percent above poverty. We do not charge for our service; we are not allowed to charge for our service. We can only handle civil matters; we do not handle criminal matters. . . .

I'm the only full-time volunteer lawyer in the state of Georgia at the Legal Service. We have other lawyers who come in one time, one day a week or a half of day a week, but I work full time. I do the same work as all the paid lawyers do. It's been very rewarding for me. It gives me the opportunity to deal with people and help them. Most of the things are not very sophisticated but they are things that have to be done, like temporary guardianship, custody, adoptions, probate wills, writing wills, and just generally giving people advice. . . . This way, not only do I have a chance to do something, but I feel like I help people. **Albert Mazo, 50**

DRUG STORES

My great-great-grandfather came over from Amsterdam and he settled in Georgetown, South Carolina. . . . One of his sons, A. A. Solomons, came to Savannah in 1845 and that was the beginning of Solomons Company as a wholesale drug company. Having a wholesale drug company in Savannah with the Civil War, and later on the Depression, was quite interesting. I wasn't around for the

Civil War but we have a very interesting document which gives you some idea about the conditions in Savannah after the Civil War. Of course, Confederate money wasn't any good. The economy was shot.

We have some records showing where people out in the country who purchased from the store would make their payment in cotton. We also have a document that they took up to New York to request some leniency on the part of their major suppliers, people like Smith, Klein & French, Colgate, Palmolive, those kind of people; and they did. They gave the company one year of credit until they got back on their feet. Fortunately, they did. **Philip Solomons, Sr., 30**

[Grandfather and father's business] was wholesale dry goods, I believe, and then it went into drugs and they became a wholesale druggist. Columbia Drug Company was located . . . on Lincoln and Bay Street. For many years it was our treat to go down and pick up Daddy at the end of the day and wait for the A.D.T. system to kick in, and then we could leave. Had to make sure it was set off properly. . . .

It was the entire building, and they had a warehouse elsewhere also. They served the Southeast. They were very dependent upon the farmers in the little towns to have good crops so they could pay the druggists in the little towns, so that they could then be paid. . . . I know that there were actually three drug houses in Savannah. There was Reeves-McTeer and Solomons and Columbia, and eventually they were all together. They all had merged and been bought out by another company. . . .

I remember loving to go down to the store. It was dark and interesting, all sorts of interesting things. Because in the early days Dad had huge bottles of Coca-Cola syrup which they sold to the . . . drugstores that had the soda fountains. . . . And they had, oh, tons and tons of tissues and paper goods. And they had the wonderful cosmetic lines, the Eli Lilly line. [Dad] used to complain, as marketing became more and more sophisticated, that they came up with so many different varieties of shaving cream, there wasn't going to be room on the shelf to have all the different rich and extra rich lathers.

There were lots of nooks and crannies in the store. There was a place that they called the lockup, that they had the narcotics in, that you couldn't go in. You had to get special permission to get in there. Only one person, I think, had that key. And then there were the elevators and the big dumb waiters to carry the goods down. It was a . . . rather cumbersome arrangement to pick out an order. . . . In those, the early days, you could really get lost in a labyrinth of shelves and pharmaceuticals and all the old-timey things that people relied on, the Smith Brothers Cough Drops and the Lydia Pinkham compounds that were in the heyday. **Barbara (Smith) Levy, 19**

When I started all there was in the field of anti-infectives was penicillin and the sulpha drugs, believe it or not. So in the last forty to fifty years the development of new drugs has been phenomenal. I went into generics and I was, you might say, looked down upon by the other pharmacists in town for using generics. . . . I was the first to really go into the generics and also the chemotherapy drugs. I was the first one to do that. So I was ready to gamble in business. I gambled on going into things and doing things. It was a big gamble. The gamble of going into business any way. But I was happy with the way we were growing and I tried to keep it under control. It grew. I am delighted with what I did. I mean it was twenty-five years, something like that. **Rupert Heller, 80**

INSURANCE AND ACCOUNTING BUSINESSES

[About starting in the insurance business.] I'll never forget, I saw a client . . . and I went to his house. I didn't have a car yet, 'cause I didn't have the money to buy a car yet at fifteen dollars a week, you know. I went to his house and he said, "Let me make an order for a policy. How do you know if you've got disability, etc. You come by." So he let me come by the house with the policy then. I had three or four policies. So he bought, I'll never forget, he bought a twenty-five thousand dollar policy from me. Hey, that's big time, big time! I made $388 commission on that. That's like making an eight to ten thousand dollar commission now. . . .

He said, "Put your books up and come up to my office tomorrow and I'll give you a check for it and you make an appointment with the doctor for an examination." So [his wife] came in and he said, "You got your car outside, haven't you?" So I said, "Sure." I didn't have a car. What I did was, I caught the bus. He lived on 48th Street. I caught the bus at 38th and Paulsen, so I walked ten blocks. At eleven the bus stopped. . . . They didn't have [a] bus after eleven. This was like eleven-thirty or quarter to twelve. So anyway, I didn't have a car, so I felt embarrassed. Here's this guy just bought a twenty-five thousand dollar policy, he's a big man. I was embarrassed to tell him I [didn't have a] car. So I says, "Yeah, I got the car. I'll see you in the morning."

So I put on my coat and I walked slowly down the street and I looked back, and I wanted to see if he might be looking out the window to see what kind of car I got in. I saw he wasn't looking so I started running. I ran for about ten to twelve blocks until I knew I was out of his eyesight. The next morning I went to get the check. **Nathan Karnibad, 41**

My father started in his business world at quite an early age, he said twelve . . . or thirteen. He started as a "go-for" or office boy for one of the cotton brokers on Bay Street, [then] graduated into another job which was a similar job at an insurance agency. It was the John D. Carswell Agency. . . . He stayed there probably for ten years or so before he went into business for himself. **Herman Cranman, 36**

I went to work in the life insurance business, Mutual of New York, in 1930. I stayed there about nineteen years, and then I went to work for Mass Mutual as a general agent for all of South Carolina and half of Georgia. A very interesting thing in those days, national corporations stayed clear of South Carolina because their rules were so strange. When I opened up in South Carolina, why it was an open field, and we did fairly well there. **Calmon Mendel, 16**

I came out of college and like everybody else, . . . went in the family business. At that time in Savannah, Georgia, . . . Broughton Street flourished. It was a no-brainer. You went to school, came back, went in the family business, unless you were going to be a doctor or lawyer or you could choose some profession. But I mean, most of the people of my era came back and went into the family businesses. Slotin & Company was an institution in this city. My father was a mainstay of it. Wonderful businessman. I wish we had been the businessmen that he was. . . . We made errors in judgment probably . . . and in 1963 we lost that business, which was a traumatic experience for us. . . . On the advice of some friends that said, "try the life insurance business,". . . [and] this year I'll be thirty years with New York Life and it's been good to me. **Leon Slotin, 47**

It's an interesting little sideline, when my father first started out in practice [accounting] in 1925, he had a lot of clients, small merchants in the towns around Savannah, in Glennville, Alma, Hazelhurst and Jesup, Ludowici, Waycross. . . . In many cases he would go to their businesses. In those days you didn't have paved roads so it was an all-day excursion to go to Augusta, Georgia, and spend the night, work on the clients, and come back the next day.

Business was a lot different back in the '20s and the '30s. In the 1930s, as we well know, we had the terrible Depression. Interestingly enough, I have some records, some business records of my father's in which his fees dropped from about eight thousand or nine thousand dollars a year to about four thousand dollars in the depths of the Depression. But I guess four or five thousand dollars was a lot of money to make in those days. **Martin Karp, 42**

PAWNSHOPS

In the pawnshop business we had Mr. Harry Blumenthal, Mr. George Richman, and one time a fellow by the name of [Louis] Goldberg. The Sutkers had a pawnshop, Benny Litman I think . . . had a pawnshop. At one time . . . after Pop had passed, we had thirteen Jewish pawnbrokers here. And the pawnbroking business is altogether different than what it is now. Now it's like . . . making a sale instead of a loan, and the legitimate part is altogether different. We couldn't do some of the things they do today. **Benjamin Portman, 20**

B. & B. Pawnshop, 1918
Pictured in front of the West Broad Street storefront are (from left to right) George Richman and Harry Blumenthal with an unidentified employee.
JVM 003 Savannah Jewish Archives General Photograph Collection, Item 1851

[The pawnshop owners] were all Jewish, and what they did was, if somebody needed some money, they'd bring in a suit of clothes, sewing machine, a gun - guns were big - and they'd get a certain amount of money. The pawnbroker would allow a certain amount of money, so they knew they could always sell it and make a profit. I think they kept things on pawn for like six months, if the people paid the interest on the money. . . . They kept them until the people didn't pay. When people didn't come in for a length of time, I think it was six months to a year, . . . they'd take them out and sell them. Great business. **Rupert Heller, 80**

[My father] went into the housewares, chinaware, and glassware, all such as that . . . and then he got in with a Mr. Kaminsky, Louis Kaminsky, from the pawnshop on East Broad Street, and they'd go in partner and they'd buy out stocks all over. . . . The Central of Georgia would have what they called house sales. . . . They would go down and they'd bid on different things. One time my father came back and he had fifty cases of Post Toasties. I don't know what he was going to do with them. . . . I don't think we knew what Post Toasties were back then. **Beryl Bernstein, 67**

BOARDING HOUSES AND HOTELS

In Yamacraw . . . my grandmother had a boarding house and that's how she eked out a living, I'm assuming. . . . Having a kosher home and what have you, . . . her boarders were Jewish because a lot of men in those days came to this country to work and send money home, and they brought their family over, one or two at a time. So I'm just assuming, but the only boarder whose name I know was Simon Goldin, who is the father of Doris Lukin. He was a boarder in my grandmother's house. **Selma (Greenberg) Dunn, 7**

My mother's maternal grandparents were Bernard and Jennie Dub, and they came to Savannah. They ran a hotel called the Screven House at the corner of Bull and Congress where the Manger [Hotel] was later built. . . . My mother lived there in the hotel, her parents lived there until she was twelve years old. . . . She always told me that one day Grampa Dub came home and said to his wife, "Jennie, I've bought a new hotel." And this was not really a hotel, I guess it was a glorified boarding house, at 3 West Gordon Street. Beautiful house on the corner of Bull and Gordon. And I don't know how long they operated an establishment there, it must have been quite a few years. **Marion (Abrahams) Levy Mendel, 17**

MISCELLANEOUS BUSINESSES

Most [immigrants] went to the business that . . . took the least amount of capital to go into. They started out . . . buying junk and reselling it, or having a tailor shop. Those didn't take much stock. **Samuel Hirsch, 52**

I went to public school up to the eighth grade, then I had to quit school to go to work. I was going from job to job, whatever you could get, six-fifty, seven, seven-fifty, eight, nine, ten dollars, whatever you could get you made. You had to give your family money. Even the colleges I played [ball] against offered me scholarships, but at that time . . . very few of our people went to college. They couldn't afford it. **Harry Eichholz, 57**

When I got out of high school my salary was thirty dollars a month. First job I ever had, thirty dollars a month. **Sanford Wexler, 48**

I started off with ten dollars a week. Well, that was a good salary then, you know. And then I divided it. I gave my mother five dollars and I kept five dollars.

. . . When I became engaged she handed me back all the money that she had saved from me. I'll tell you, she was something. **Sadye (Steinberg) Rabhan, 22**

In helping my brother David, I worked for nine dollars a week. I worked at a place called Eckstein's [dry goods store]. They were going out of business. . . . And I worked there, and every Monday when I got paid, I went into Hirsch's Delicatessen and I bought some cold cuts and things like that. That was my, I gave them a treat at the house. And then two dollars a week I sent to my brother 'cause he was going to Georgia Tech and my brother never forgot it. **Evelyn (Center) Goldberg, 10**

[My father] had a job as a watchman in the stables at the foot of River Street . . . and he was also a night watchman for the coal company that owned the coal yard. . . . He . . . looked after keeping these colored boys or any of them from coming down with buckets and filling up with coal. . . . They told him he had to have a gun because [the boys] could overpower him. . . . So he got . . . a pearl-handled .38 caliber pistol. . . . He never used it. . . . But that kept the robbers outside. We didn't have any problem. **Sam Steinberg, 31**

My father's cousin, Julius Ulman, moved to Savannah and opened a dairy on the old Ogeechee Road. . . . Mr. L. Weitz had sent him to college and he studied agriculture. And he had the dairy for a number of years and served the Jewish community delivering milk. **Albert Ullman, 33**

[My grandfather] was fairly successful early on in his business and he did a number of other things. He operated an ice house in Savannah . . . and he had a farm. My father and his siblings actually grew up kind of on the farm. The farm was located right on Tremont Road, right where the railroad station is now. That was the farm, and they had horses and he raised cattle.

He also, early in his career, he used to go around buying cattle. He bought and sold cattle. Later he went into business with the Meddins to create a slaughterhouse in Savannah for cattle, which he later got out of, and they stayed in it for many, many years after that, the meatpacking business. **Erwin "Ernie" Friedman, 71**

Daddy really started as a real merchant veteran during the Spanish-American War, selling pots and pans – very successful. **Leon Slotin, 47**

Mother took care of the hardware store and Dad went out to work, to pick up jobs. He sold pots and pans, and they got holes in them. And then my father found out that you could buy some sort of a long piece of metal. And he melted the metal and could apply it to the pots where the hole was. And then slowly and surely people asked him to do roof work, and he started taking care of roofs and stuff. **Lena (Feinberg) Rosenzweig, 26**

At the age of fifteen I applied to J. C. Lewis Motor Company. . . . At that time my brother had a store on West Broad Street, and I told him what I was going to do. He said, "Don't go like that. You got the long black stockings on and you're going to go like that and ask for a job? Come back here, I'll fix you up." So over the stockings I put on long trousers. That's supposed to make a *mensh* out of me! So from there I went right directly for the interview with Mr. Lewis. . . . He said, . . . "Tomorrow morning is Saturday. Be here at eight o'clock. You got a job.". . .

I found that anytime I found something that I wanted to suggest I hated to suggest it, because I figured that all that did was just to put more work on me. . . . Every time I suggested we do something, "You do it." . . . I've been with the company now for eighty years. I started when I was fifteen, and I just recently celebrated my ninety-fifth [birthday]. **Sam Steinberg, 31**

My dad arrived in Savannah right after . . . World War I, and he actually went into the bank. Herman Myers had passed away at that time, and Sigo Myers, his brother, was running the bank. And my dad went to work for the bank. The bank stood on the corner of . . . Broughton and Bull. . . .

Mr. [Henry] Blun was going to build a building on the corner, right behind his, on the corner of Bull and Congress. . . . Anyway, Mr. Blun said he was going to build his building . . . ten stories tall so he could stand on the top of it and you know what on Mr. Myers' building. When Mr. Myers got wind of that, he built his taller than Mr. Blun did. **Julius Edel, 35**

[My father] worked . . . with his father in his grocery store. At one point, family legend has it, . . . he had a bar, and my grandmother didn't want him in the bar business, so she trumped up a deal with . . . Charlie Garfunkel who was Chief of Police, to put him out of business on trumped up charges. **Harris Slotin, 55**

My second father, Morris Horovitz, . . . got into the cork and label business with his brother [whom] they called "Chief" Horovitz, his real name was Abe. I don't think anybody ever knew his name. He was always called "Chief."

Anyway, this developed into the barber supply business, and then when . . . the beauty business got a little larger, it developed into mostly beauty supplies, selling to the beauty shops. We were located on . . . Montgomery and Bryan Street, right on the corner. We stayed there for quite a number of years. . . . I grew up working in the store. . . . The name of the business was the Savannah Beauty and Barber Supply. **Arthur "Bubba" Horovitz, 77**

Cranman's Sporting Goods was a unique store for its time. It competed with no other. Customers came from everywhere. Dad even had a regular customer in California who requested merchandise mailed to him. Dad's clientele was from all walks of life, and everyone loved and respected him. His store was a real man's store. Two good friends of his, one a minister and the other an ophthalmologist, used to volunteer as salesmen on their days off just to be amongst the upscale rifles, camping equipment, fishing gear, and so forth. . . .

My husband relates a true story about the time we became engaged. Workmen on the construction sites where he visited as architect would tease him about finally getting married. "But I'm marrying Ed Cranman's daughter, of Cranman's Sporting Goods." They would stop teasing and talk about how they envied him being associated with the store and the owner. **Harriet (Cranman) Meyerhoff, 96**

Cranman's, c.1945
Edward Cranman's store specialized in sporting goods and hardware, and was a favorite spot for local men.
JVM 003 Savannah Jewish Archives General Photograph Collection, Item 2312

I was on the newspaper in school and got articles in the newspaper. I never wanted to be a writer. . . . I was gonna be a teacher and I really was not going to write. . . . At college . . . I was editor of the newspaper and editor of the yearbook. . . . [Later] I joined the staff at the newspaper on the *[Savannah] Evening Press*. . . .

It was a fun job to be on the newspaper. . . . I covered the police beat. . . . I was the education editor and did an education page every week for a long time. I enjoyed doing that. . . . I was able to do almost every beat. . . . I'd met Herbie Schildkraut at a singles affair in Pennsylvania and we decided to get married. . . . Then we lived in Brooklyn, New York. . . . I got my job in New York at *Good Housekeeping Magazine* where I was a medical editor. . . . I was there for fourteen years. . . .

When I got back to Savannah in '84 I thought about the *[Savannah] Jewish News* and I had talked with Millie Melaver about editing it. Paul Kulick was the editor. . . . Paul left town, . . . must have been around '86. But I assumed the job then of the *Savannah Jewish News* editor. . . . I work really out of my home and I have a mailbox here [at the J.E.A.]. . . . The *[Savannah] Jewish News* is owned and operated by the Savannah Jewish Federation. It is often called the Jewish, J.E.A. newspaper, which is entirely wrong. It is strictly a Federation-published newspaper. **Maxine "Midge" (Lasky) Schildkraut, 81**

BUSINESS DISTRICTS

BROUGHTON STREET

At one time on Broughton Street when the Jewish holidays came, Rosh Hashanah and Yom Kippur, Broughton Street in effect was closed up because seventy-five or eighty percent of the stores were Jewish owned. But the people who came to America from Europe, most of them were not educated. They were intelligent people, they were hardworking. Therefore, they all became merchants of one sort or another, whether they had stores, whether they were peddlers, or . . . salesmen. So most of the merchants . . . from West Broad and West Broughton and up to the middle of Broughton Street were Jewish. Even going back maybe a hundred years. **Martin Karp, 42**

During that era . . . we lived above the store 'til '29. . . . I remember the block from West Broad to Montgomery Street. There was Uncle Sam's Pawnshop on the corner, next door were the Krafts. The Hirsches were there, the Lennoxes had a restaurant on the second floor of the building there, it was open to . . . mostly Jewish transients. Come on down. Joe Cohen was on the corner. That whole block was, I think everything other than maybe a shoe repair shop, I think was all Jewish merchants on that block. You know, things were tough and they were really in competition with each other, but they always got along fine. You know, they had business during the day, at night they were friends, they played cards together. . . . The communication and the contact between the people were good. I mean they, everyone realized the situation and sort of pitched in. **Marvin Arkin, 76**

My grandfather on my father's side lived on Gaston Street, and he had a tailoring firm. I think it was Standard Tailors, on Broughton Street. That's where my father worked until he married my mother. Then they opened a store on Broughton Street, Bob Bono's. They sold fine men's wear, men's haberdashery [dealer in small wares, such as hats, linens, trimmings, and small articles of dress]. He died at thirty-three; I was four years old. The business was sold to Morris Levy who continued operating it. **Murray Bono, 68**

At twelve [years old], my first job was with Joe Cohen's Department Store. And we worked all day from nine in the morning 'til midnight for a dollar. . . . On Montgomery and Broughton, Joe Cohen's Department Store. **Benjamin Silverman, 29**

Our family business was B. H. Levy Brother & Company, begun by my great uncle Benjamin Hirsch Levy and his brother, my grandfather Henry Levy; later run by my father and my father's first cousin, Arthur Levy. The other department store in Savannah and also on Broughton Street was Adler's, run by the Adler family. For many years Adler's and Levy's were the only two large department stores in Savannah. Up until World War II most ladies going downtown, as Broughton Street was referred to, put on hat and gloves for the trip. **Elizabeth "Libby" (Levy) Price, 69**

BRYAN STREET

You can start from . . . Barnard Street . . . and Bryan and work your way down. On Barnard and Bryan there was Kolgaklis and the tobacco company. . . . Then across the street from there on the corner was . . . the Silver Moon Bar. . . . Then there was Ben Berliner's store, which was again, a second-hand clothing store with shoes hanging outside on the stick and everything. Then after Ben Berliner's store there was Max Platock's store, the same type of store. . . . After Mamalakis Restaurant there was the Kaplan's Shoe Repair Shop, right there in a . . . like a little hole in the wall. . . . And then there was Morris Rubin's store, which was wholesale, but it was new type of clothing. . . .

And then coming west there was [Morris] Moshovitz, not Movsovitz, but Moshovitz. This was Benny Pike's uncle. And after the Moshovitz store there was the Steins'. . . . After the Steins' store there was the Rubnitz store. . . . They had like a kitchen and a bedroom in the back of that store. I remember eating *challah* back there in the kitchen. . . . From the Rubnitz' store you went again west and then there was Mr. [Nathan] Greenberg's store. Now Mr. Greenberg had a wholesale dry goods store, he traveled and sold out of that store. He didn't open the store for sales right there on the street but he would travel around with merchandise in his car. . . .

And then coming further down there was Friedman's Shoe Store. This was wholesale new shoes. My mother's store was on the northwest corner of Bryan and Jefferson Street and we lived upstairs over the store on that corner. . . . Further down from them was Kirschner's Furs and Skins. . . . They would skin the alligators in the lane and take the skins and sell them and things of this type down there at Kirschner Furs. **Irvin "Sonny" Rubnitz, 49**

The second place where my father had a [grocery] store—we always lived over the store— was on Bryan and Montgomery streets. Actually, in those years Bryan Street was known as the Jewish street. . . . As an example, I forget the term, but the gentleman who would cut chickens and make them kosher and so forth [the *shochet*], was on the corner of Bryan and Montgomery streets. My father's barroom and grocery store was directly across the street. There was also Gottlieb's Bakery in that block and Nugent's Bakery was there. All the other businesses, including second-hand clothing stores and so forth, were owned and operated by Jews. **H. Sol Clark, 5**

WEST BROAD STREET

When I first came to Savannah . . . West Broad Street was THE street. . . . It was person to person, body to body on the street Saturday night, because [Union Station was] there and then you had the Central of Georgia came in also. The small town people came in from the small towns on Saturday night there, . . . 'cause West Broad Street was the shopping center then. The two big merchants then were Yachum & Yachum, one, and Lang's, number two, and then they had L. Weitz & Company and Gordon . . . and Joe Levin. **Reuben Schneider, 28**

West Broad Street was predominantly Jewish merchants, and a lot of high school students would work on Saturdays. They worked at Yachum & Yachum and they worked at Lang's and they worked at Joe Levin's. . . . Across the street from Joe Levin's there was a little luncheonette and it was run by the Galkin family. **Selma (Greenberg) Dunn, 7**

We used to live on West Broad Street; we had a business and living quarters upstairs. . . . We all helped. You see, the store was like this room, and at the back there was a big room that was our dining room, and you walked up like three stairs and you could look in the store and see if a customer came in. And that's the way we managed. **Anne (Lewis) Buchsbaum, 2**

[My wife's] father was a tailor on West Broad Street, which was a famous tailor that all the *shvartzes* used to go there to have box-back suits made. At the same time all the railroad men used to go there. Anybody that wanted a real tailor-made suit would go there. There were other Jewish people here in town that did tailoring. One was Mr. [Herman] Blair . . . whose family also had a shoe repair shop. And another one was Kolman, [Philip] Kolman the tailor. . . . There are other tailors, too, but the . . . best known . . . was National Tailors which is the Odrezin family. **Benjamin Portman, 20**

Georgia Awning & Canvas Products, c.1939
Established in 1924 by Ben Shoenig, the company's buildings on West Oglethorpe Avenue were replaced by the Greyhound Bus Station, though the business carried on through Ben's sons, Norman and Alvin, and family until the 1990s.
JVM 003 Savannah Jewish Archives General Photograph Collection, Item 2122

My father's store was on the 400 block [of West Broad Street], and next door to him was Mr. [Sidney] Paderewski the tailor and Mr. [Aaron] Malitz' jewelry store, and on the corner was the Odrezins' National Tailors. Now down to the right of Papa's store . . . on the next block, was Joe Levin . . . and everybody worked for Joe Levin, that's where you started out. Across the street from Joe Levin was the B. & B. Pawnshop, and of course Mrs. [Minna] Galkin's delicatessen there where everybody went to eat. Everybody went to Mrs. Galkin's. That was the meeting place for West Broad Street. **Bertha (Plotkin) Freedman, 8**

[Our furniture store was] right across the street from Union Station, and we loved it. We spent all our eating time over at the station. It was beautiful. . . . A hurricane came along in 1939 or '40 . . . and it just demolished our store. So we moved down the street, right on West Broad, two blocks down, and that's where we were for the rest of the forty years we were in business. We were right next door to Minna Galkin. She was a treasure of Savannah. She had a little restaurant and everybody used to gather there. **Lena (Feldman) Solomon, 82**

L. Weitz & Company Department Store, n.d.
L. Weitz & Company was once located on the busy commercial corridor of West Broad Street (now Martin Luther King, Jr. Boulevard).
JVM 003 Savannah Jewish Archives General Photograph Collection, Item 2333

THE GREAT DEPRESSION

At that time my father and Morris Slotin went in business together and they moved up to the 200 block on Broughton Street and they opened the United Department Store. Well, they opened in August of 1929 and, you know, in October the bottom dropped out and it was real scary because they had invested a lot of money, they'd even put in an elevator in that store. I remember it was fifteen thousand dollars for the elevator.

Everything changed. The dresses were short. All of a sudden, by the end of October, the new style, all the dresses got long so all the merchandise in the store became obsolete. It was a bad couple of years there. My father and Mr. Slotin decided that one would buy the other out. Mr. Slotin bought my father out. Then [my father] moved to the 300 block of Broughton Street where he remained until he retired. **Marvin Arkin, 76**

I had a very enjoyable childhood and young life. We lived on the corner of 35th and Drayton streets, and I went to Pape School for the first six years, and then public school the rest of the way. I can remember when Drayton Street was a dirt street. I had one brother, no sisters, one brother who was four years older than I. His name was Edwin Leffler, Jr. We [my family] got along real nicely until the Depression when my father lost everything that he had. It was tough going for him since then. **Martin Leffler, 14**

My father, he opened a business in 1910 or '12. It was called Harry Blumenthal's Ready-to-Wear, and then that didn't do too well. So later on he went in with Max Blumenthal and they established the B. & B. Loan Company, . . . pawnbrokers. . . . Max Blumenthal decided to move to Florida, . . . [and] sold his interest to my father, who did well until . . . the Depression . . . [when] he had to sell his share to Sam Blumenthal. **Herbert Blumenthal, 76**

In the early '40s, this was still the aftermath of getting, slowly getting out of the Depression, the company [Solomons' Pharmacy] ran into some financial problems. And a cousin, Harry Alexander, who lived in Atlanta . . . had contact with an oilman from Oklahoma who had been very successful, a great financial person. And he asked Mr. Wolfe, S. E. Wolfe was his name, if he would come down and work with the company and get it back on its feet. Well, he did come down and he was a very, very gruff, efficient person. . . . He [Harry] said, "Now you boys are going to have to live with this. It's not going to be pleasant, but if you want the company to survive you will do what Mr. Wolfe suggests." Which they did and the company survived. **Philip Solomons, Sr., 30**

My grandfather [was] . . . David Amram Byck, Sr. . . . My grandfather's business was known as the M. S. & D. Byck Printing Company. They were located on #2, #4, and #6 West Bay Street, and they had a motto, "The City Hall is next to Byck's." They had a very large printing company. It was the largest printing company south of Richmond, Virginia. They printed and they also had office supplies. It was a very large business and unfortunately, during the Depression years of 1930 through 1935, the business went bankrupt.

My grandfather, D. A. Byck, Sr., David Byck, Sr., had passed away, and my father was left with a defunct business and . . . he and his first cousin, Joseph Byck, who was Moses Byck's son, had to split up whatever part of the business there was, and Joseph Byck took the office supply end of it. Although Dad never had printing presses, he jobbed out all of the work to various printers in town and was sort of like a middle man. He went out and took the orders and sold the jobs and got someone else to do the actual printing.

It was very hard in those post-Depression years on making ends meet, because they didn't have credit cards, and since Dad was in a business that had gone bankrupt – in those days it was very embarrassing to go bankrupt – he had a very hard time struggling to maintain his family situation. But he managed to survive and did a very good job. **David A. Byck, III, 72**

M.S. & D.A. Byck Company, n.d.
Composing room of the printing company located on West Bay Street.
JVM 005 Congregation Mickve Israel Photograph Collection, Item 0093

[During the Great Depression] Minnie Weitz [Levy] had a store on Broughton Street off of Drayton. She had a dress shop and the name of that shop was Minnette's. I worked there when I was about thirteen or fourteen years old as a sales person. I also worked several of the shoe stores, wherever we could find a job. And we worked like from nine o'clock in the morning 'til eleven o'clock at night. That was a day's work. What we earned, I don't remember. Everybody was in the same boat so you didn't feel poor because everybody [was] poor. **Evelyn (Ward) Karsman, 53**

My father was in the jewelry business [in New York] until . . . the Crash. . . . So in 1940 we moved to Savannah, 'cause my father was unable to work and my mother just couldn't make it in New York. Times were not good at that time, and she knew she could open a grocery store, so she came to Savannah and opened a grocery store. . . . We came here in the summer of 1940. And I think one of my aunts had a place at Tybee, and the rest rented places at Tybee, and we'd go out and spend a lot of time at Tybee on weekends or whenever we could. **Norton Melaver, 15**

The Depression was bad, but it didn't affect me very much because I was married already, and my husband had opened up a supermarket and was able to sell cheap. Where other people couldn't sell, he was in a position, by buying volume, he was able to sell cheaper than other people. And at one time I think we were the most popular store in the city of Savannah. It was called the Bargain Corner. It was on Bay and Jefferson. **Lena (Feinberg) Rosenzweig, 26**

SUCCESS STORIES

Julius Kahn . . . was born in 1890 in Lithuania, and he immigrated to the United States. He probably came through Boston in 1906. His name was changed at immigration from Kancipovitz, I think, to Kahn. He went to work in a bar as a bartender that was run by a cousin, Mr. [Julius] Weitz. The bar was at where the Crystal Beer Parlor recently was, at Jefferson and Jones Street. Then Papa went to work at Frank & Company, a wholesale dry goods firm run by a German Jewish family. It was at 217 West Broad; the building is still there. It was built in 1906 as well.

In 1929 Papa left Frank & Company to open his own dry goods business, and it was located at Congress and Jefferson Street. . . . During World War II, Kahn & Company was located at 38 Montgomery Street. . . . In 1946 Kahn & Company was incorporated, and Julius . . . bought the old Frank & Company building himself and went back to work in the building he had started in the dry goods business with. I think that's an American success story if I've heard one. **Jane (Guthman) Kahn 93**

Julian [my brother] and I opened a little shoe factory on River Street. We made these canvas shoes called plow shoes. In a certain area in Georgia they were very good. In plow season we just could sell everything we could make, but that only lasted for a couple of months. And outside of this particular area where . . . there was red clay, it was no good. Nobody wanted them. . . . Eventually we closed the factory, the shoe factory, and . . . [we went] into the wholesale business. . . . [Then] we found a location in Vidalia, Georgia. We opened a store there and sure enough, we bought shoes for six months and paid for it the next six months after we sold the shoes. It worked out that way, and we opened another store, and another store, and another store, and finally we gave up the wholesale business and went into the retail business pretty exclusively. . . .

Our wholesale business was Savannah Wholesale Company. We maintained the Savannah Wholesale Company name for buying purposes, . . . originally it was Allied Outlet Stores. Then we got high class and we started calling it Allied Department Stores. . . . It was a nice little business, it prospered. . . . Finally . . . we sold it and we took contracts for five years to operate the business. . . . We had seventy-two department stores when we left. **Murray Bono, 68**

My father . . . went into business with a man by the name of . . . Hirsch Wolson. . . . He was in the rag business down on River Street. . . . My father stayed in that business for a few years, saved his money, and then he went to New York University and studied and became an accountant. **Erwin "Ernie" Friedman, 71**

B. H. Levy, c.1914-1915
Mr. Levy, founder of Levy's Department Store, was photographed during his term as President of the Jewish Educational Alliance (1912-1915).
JVM 003 Savannah Jewish Archives General Photograph Collection, Item 1673

My sister went to college for two years and she had to quit so the boys could go to college. It was considered important for the boys to go to college because they had to make a living. . . . Slotin & Company had a big building on Broughton and West Broad Street. The partners in Slotin & Company were Morris Slotin and his brothers and his brother-in-laws; . . . Morris Slotin was the oldest and the leader of the business, and my father whose name was Abraham Mazo.

There was Morris Berman who was married to Ida Berman. Mose Berman's wife was Morris Slotin's sister-in-law. Both Berman and Morris Slotin married sisters. Then there was Louis Slotin. Then there was Freddie Ehrenreich who married Lena Slotin. Then the youngest was Louis Slotin.

They worked as a team throughout the Depression and became very successful. They had built a big dry goods business and had a chain of five and ten cent stores in southern South Carolina and Georgia, . . . called United Five and Ten Cent stores. My father was in charge of them. He traveled most of his life, five days a week, taking care of the business in the stores. At one time they had as many as fifteen or twenty stores. **Albert Mazo, 50**

My [Cornell University] graduation was in 1930. Fortunately for me, I went into the office of one of the greatest men I have ever known. He was not Jewish,

Gordon Saussy, who was then mayor of Savannah, and he had graduated from Cornell, so I had the temerity to ask him for a place in his office. In those days you were not paid a salary, but you were given office space, a secretary, and so forth, free of charge. And I went with Mr. Saussy, and two years later he became probate judge, and I was invited by the firm of Hester & Lewis to join them as a full partner. It was a very happy relationship, of course. Emanuel Lewis had always been one of my guides and gods. **H. Sol Clark, 5**

We sold our house and made enough to live for six months and stock my drug store, little hole in the wall. I was just going to do prescriptions and do my friends and relatives, you know. Well, evidently I'd learned pretty good, so it took about two years to get to a very substantial business. People lined up, which was wonderful.

You know, I was enjoying it. I enjoyed the whole thing. It was a real excitement. Patsy helped me. Within two years I had hired my second pharmacist, so I finally got some time off, which was wonderful. Then in another year I hired another pharmacist. So within another few years we were probably doing forty or fifty percent of the prescription business in Savannah, which was big, major business. . . . Finally, at the end, I worked up to seven stores in Savannah. That was in 1992. **Rupert Heller, 80**

CHAPTER 3: POLITICAL AND SOCIAL RELATIONSHIPS

POLITICS

My grandmother was a [sister] of Herman Myers who was the mayor at the turn of the [twentieth] century. . . . He was the longest mayor in office up until John Rousakis. . . . He dug the first artesian wells here. He built the City Hall and they all thought he was quite smart because he built it without any tax increases . . . and he paid for it out of the going budget. . . . They used to write the minutes of the city council meetings in a little book, and evidently Herman Myers got hold of one of these books and was reading it. And it was describing how he had built the City Hall without any tax increases or without any assessments or what have you, and it raved about him. He put a little postscript on the outside of it, "Smart Little Jewish Boy." **Julius Edel, 35**

There was a Mr. A. J. Garfunkel, who was the vice president of what was known as the Exchange Bank, who was really the political representative of the Jewish people. . . . There were twelve aldermen; religiously you always had two Jews, one Orthodox and one Reform, on the board of aldermen. You always had on the county commissioners one Hebrew.

Now the railroads always had an alderman. There were three elements known as the Cracker, Irish, and Hebrew. . . . My partner Joe Hester died, he was serving as Assistant City Attorney, and Mr. John Bouhan, who was the Irish leader, and Mr. Spence Grayson, one of the Cracker leaders who was City Attorney, wanted me to serve out the remainder of Joe Hester's term as Assistant City Attorney. And at that time the only thing they could say was, "No, this is an Irish job, we cannot give it to a Hebrew." And I must mention that the same thing was true over in the county where there was a certain sheriff job that had to be Hebrew. . . .

So when they named me, a Jewish person, had taken a Cracker job, . . . that it was just something that was unusual. I served out the term but it was one of the main reasons why there was an opposition ticket to what had been the machine which had controlled Savannah politics for so long, was the fact that a Cracker did not get a Cracker job, but a Hebrew named Sol Clark. **H. Sol Clark, 5**

City of Savannah Inauguration, January 1929
The new city slate included Mayor Gordon Saussy (front row, fourth from
left) and Aldermen Albert Blumberg (back row, center), H. C. Brinkman,
George S. Clark, S. M. Dutton (back row, second from right), Howard T.
Exley (back row, far right), H. Lee Fulton, Jr. (front row, second from right),
George L. Googe, William J. Hardwick, P. J. McNamara (back row, second
from left), J. F. Sullivan, H. E. Wilson, and Edgar L. Wortsman (front row, far
right).
JVM 003 Savannah Jewish Archives General Photograph Collection, Item 1408

You remember they had on the city council, they had a Jew, an Irishman, a
Greek, I mean, everybody was represented. . . . The Jews took care of the Jew, the
Irish took care of the Irish. I mean, if a Jew came to town and needed a job, Max
Hornstein would give him a stick with a nail on the end and send him to Forsyth
Park to pick up trash. I mean, that's true, . . . everybody who had a problem went
to Max Hornstein. I mean, where else? I remember those days very well. Johnny
Bouhan was the big boy. Those were the days. I don't know whether I'd want to
go back through them again. **Murray Bono, 68**

Before the Justice Department dictated that the city elect aldermen from
districts, we ran as a team or slate, and we all ran at large. So far as I can remember, this team concept always had a Jewish representative in the slate, and in 1969
Johnny [Rousakis] asked me to be part of his team. I was elected for five consecu-
tive four-year terms with him. When we were first elected to office, one of the
men that John asked to run with us was Bowles Ford, the first African American
to serve since Reconstruction days. He was an outstanding alderman who was
responsible for many miles of city streets being paved. Bowles unfortunately passed
away during his second term. . . . The present city council [c. 1997] is the first one
I can remember that does not have Jewish representation. **Leo Center, 4**

Savannah during the '20s and '30s . . . was a very laid-back city. . . . The politics of the city were real interesting during those days. We had one Jewish mayor, Herman Myers. And then, as I remember my father telling me, the political jobs in our city were handed out on the basis of so many Cracker jobs, so many Irish jobs, Jewish jobs, and so on and so forth. It seemed pretty equitable, but there were no black jobs, we were highly segregated. The boss of the county was Irish, and the county was controlled by the Irish. **A. J. Cohen, Jr., 6**

I think from a political standpoint it's interesting to know that the Jewish people in Savannah, for certainly the past hundred years or up until perhaps the last twenty or thirty years, . . . more or less controlled the political destiny of whatever took place in Savannah.

The political representatives years ago, before the women were allowed to vote, the blacks were not allowed to vote, there were probably seven or eight thousand voters in Savannah. In those days there were about maybe three thousand Protestants and three thousand Catholics and about fifteen hundred Jewish voters, and as a result the Jewish voters were able to hold the balance of power and were able to obtain, justifiably so, almost anything that they wished in the way of political power or influence.

There were many Jewish people that had problems or [were] seeking work or employment that were almost immediately given positions with the city departments. We had Jewish policemen, Jewish firemen, Jewish workers in offices, Jewish workers in all of the various departments. . . . My father was superintendent of police for four years, from January 19, '03 until 1907, which was strictly a political appointment. **Benjamin Garfunkel, 9**

I don't think that possibly the Jewish overt presence is as great as it used to be. Although I would imagine the Jewish people have a great deal to say about what's going on because Jewish people, as a rule, are just quite interested, extremely interested in community affairs. So I think they want to be involved and I think it's to the credit of the city fathers and it's for the betterment of the community that everybody's involve[d]. . . .

When I said it's not as prevalent as it used to be as far as numbers, at one time we had a Jewish mayor, at one time we had some Jewish people who practically, from what I understand, that's before my time, ran this city, were like the bosses of the city, involved with the non-Jewish people to running the city and gave out patronage and all the things that used to happen in the days. **Norton Melaver, 15**

Right after World War II, in the late '40s, we got together, and the Jaycees [members of the Junior Chamber of Commerce] fought very hard for council-manager form of government. I was really active in the Jaycees. . . . Political "ins" fought it tooth and nail, and they really threatened us at the polls . . . but . . . it passed. . . . Since then the city has progressed and we became one of the All-American cities and honored in a number of different ways. **Stephen Traub, 32**

On the one block on West Broad Street where there were four stores with families living overhead, . . . from that block of only four families, the three Jewish families produced the judges. I happen to have been the first Jew in the history of Georgia to be named as an appellate judge and I'm very proud of that. My appointment came from Jimmy Carter when he was [governor]. I served as I was supposed to 'til retirement at the age of seventy, then returned to practice. **H. Sol Clark, 5**

Georgia Appellate Court, January 1972
H. Sol Clark, the first Jew in the history of Georgia to be named an appellate judge, was sworn in by Governor, and future United States President, Jimmy Carter.
JVM 003 Savannah Jewish Archives General Photograph Collection, Item 2291

Different things my grandfather, the Judge [Arthur Solomon, Sr., Chatham County Commissioner, 1914-1958] did: He developed Victory Drive as the road to the beach. He also put the white line on the roads on the outside line . . . because he was having trouble seeing by then. And he also developed the Park and Tree Commission here in Savannah, as well as Mosquito Control. **Sue (Solomon) Herman, 94**

When I was asked to run with the Republican slate, . . . Curtis Lewis ran for mayor. . . . I remember the closing date for the entry was the first day of Shavous. . . . The day before I said, "You better make up your mind whether you're gonna run 'cause tomorrow I'm not gonna be available, and I'm not gonna be able to qualify."
So Jay Gardner called Shelby Myrick who was the Ordinary, and . . . he said, "Shelby, you know, Benny's not gonna be able to qualify. If we get a ticket he'll run with us." Shelby said, "I'll tell you what, you tell Benny to come on over and I'll let him qualify, and he'll give me his check and I'll give him the oath and I'll

put it in my desk drawer. If the rest of you qualify, fine, and if you don't qualify, I'll just tear it up." So I went over the day before anyone else. . . . I didn't know until I got the newspaper that afternoon that . . . I was running because . . . the others qualified but no one had told me. . . . We were supposed to be inaugurated in office on the, I think it was the third of October, it was 1966. And that was the first or one of the last days of Succoth, and I told 'em, "Well, you go ahead and have your inauguration, but I won't be there because it's *yom tov*." All the others, the mayor and the other aldermen, were all not Jewish, but they insisted, over my objection, that they were gonna postpone the inaugurations from the third until the fifth of October so that I could be there. **Benjamin Garfunkel, 9**

Savannah Jews have always been a force, an economic and a social force in this city, and we have always participated in everything that went on, business-wise, banks, social activity, real estate, and there's always been a very nice relationship between the communities of the Jewish businessmen and the gentile businessmen. Now, we've been excluded from certain things but we've managed to make our own way. We are a force in this city and I hope we will continue to be a force. **Martin Karp, 42**

ANTI-SEMITISM

An interesting thing, my coming to Savannah, as compared to living in St. Petersburg, and if there was this much anti-Semitism on the west coast of Florida, what in the world was I going to expect in Savannah? And then I come to Savannah, and much to my surprise, the entire Broughton Street is filled with Jewish merchants, and on the high holiday, they didn't close the stores on just one day, they closed the stores for two days for Rosh Hashanah. Broughton Street was virtually just closed for Rosh Hashanah and Yom Kippur. I was just amazed with that. **Eric Meyerhoff, 18**

We've always had a great relationship. We never had any problem, . . . none that I can recall in the way of anti-Semitic feeling. We knew it was there, of course, it's always going to be there. It's not going to change. But . . . we always had Jewish aldermen. In fact it was Jewish aldermen that helped build the present City Hall. I think his name was [Herman] Myers. He was mayor at the time that that was done. So we've always had a great relationship with the Christian community. Never had any problems. **Sanford Wexler, 48**

I never in my whole life, I never suffered with anti-Semitism. . . . I always went with Jewish people, therefore I didn't know anything about anti-Semitism. In those days we didn't know anything about things of that sort. **Evelyn (Ward) Karsman, 53**

As far as anti-Semitism goes, I think that the individual brings an awful lot of it on himself. I have never run into it. I have never hidden from the fact that I was Jewish. I never went around advertising it, but I never denied it. And I think I have gotten along pretty well with everybody. I have a lot of Christian friends. **Martin Leffler, 14**

I think we always felt there was an underlying aspect of anti-Semitism, but that overall the Savannah Jewish community had a very healthy relationship with the general community. **Norton Melaver, 15**

I think at times there's snide remarks, or little undercurrents or something like that. But we never picked anything up and made a big issue of it. We always tried to conduct ourselves in a very mannerly way. **Mildred (Wolf) Weichselbaum, 51**

Being a Jew in Savannah was not really a problem that I ever knew about except one day when a kid came up to me in the park and said, "You are a Jew, aren't you?" I said, "Yes." He said, "Y'all killed Christ, didn't you?" I said, "Well, I really didn't know that we had killed him." But other than that, we really never ran into much anti-Semitism. The community was a nice place to live. **A. J. Cohen, Jr., 6**

The only time I really remember anything, was that there was a dirty little girl who came by and wanted to play with us, with the children who were playing in the neighborhood, and we didn't particularly want her to play with us. . . . She called me a "dirty Jew." And I looked at her and could not believe that, as clean as I was, and I was never very clean, but she was much dirtier. **Beatrice (Heyman) Goodman, 39**

I remember my brother, Jake, and Billy Beckworth used to fight practically every day after school. . . . He was always starting up with the Jewish kids. . . . I really never had any problems, and when anybody would say anything . . . I would disregard 'em. I would never give 'em a second thought. **Bertha (Plotkin) Freedman, 8**

I don't know whether you would call it anti-Semitism, but right there adjacent to the synagogue, there were a lot of people living there, young fellas, who I guess they just didn't like the *Yiddish* boys and girls. This was right in front of Liberty Square there, and I know that on holidays there would be many a time fights would break out in front of the synagogue.

They would throw rocks and many times our boys would get out there and beat 'em. But they were a bunch of young ones. I don't know whether in those days they called it anti-Semitism, but they just were Jew haters or whatever you want to call it. But they were young fellers and they'd always pick a fight, especially around the holiday season. But we came through that pretty good. I remember we used to give 'em some good fights. **Samuel Plotkin, 8**

The tough kids that grew up around the B.B. Jacob *shul* were just harassing the Jewish kids. I mean, walking the street they'd taunt you and they'd pick a fight and everything else. Somebody said we'd better teach these Jews how to fight, how to do something. [The Jewish kids picked up the sport of boxing]. **Murray Bono, 68**

When I was in high school, I was once taken to the yacht club, the Savannah Yacht Club, and was having a lovely time with friends, and was asked by the manager who my parents were. They knew I was not a member, and I felt very uncomfortable then, and made it my business not to return for a number of times. **Barbara (Smith) Levy, 19**

Anyway, in junior high school, I was walking home one day - I have to tell you this story - with a girl that we always walked together with in eighth grade. She said to me, "Bunny, I'm going to put your name up for D.D. Rats." I said, "Okay, what is D.D. Rats?" She said, "Well, it's a sorority, you know, a junior high school sorority." I said, "Okay. Fine."

She came back the next day and she said, "Bunny, I'm really sorry," she said, "but the president told me that we've just never had Jewish girls. Therefore, I'm not going to be able to put your name up." I said, "Oh, that's okay. It doesn't matter to me." Well, little did I know that I was being discriminated against because of my religion. I had no idea. **Phillipa "Bunny" (Sherman) Cohen, 90**

In my early childhood, when I was pre-school, my family used to go to Highlands [North Carolina] for several weeks in the summer. Dad was an avid and champion golfer and he would take us up there . . . and we'd stay for a couple of weeks. . . .

When we went back to the same club [after World War II] we were not wanted. We felt it very strongly and I think it was quite a blow to my dad that we were no longer accepted; . . . it was sad and I remember his dismay. We . . . never went back as a family there. **Barbara (Smith) Levy, 19**

I don't remember any incidents. I do remember other students calling us "Jew baby" or "Jew," making slurring remarks like that. I remember that very well. They used to say, "There's that Jew baby" or something. . . . That's the only thing that I remember that was discriminatory. . . . The teachers were very nice to me. I was very close to the teachers. **Alan Gottlieb, 40**

In school I was called "Jew baby" all the time. . . . But I studied like crazy because I had to be better than they were and I was. But there was a lot of animosity I would call it, because I was Jewish. I used to have to bring a note from home saying that I was absent because of a Jewish holiday and they didn't believe me. . . .

It was hard. It was very lonely. Very lonely schooling. . . . I guess that's why I'm so quiet sometimes, you know, I had to. I was afraid to open, pick up my hand to answer a question, 'cause everybody would just look at me, you know, "What you think you know, you Jew girl?" "Christ-killer." I took all that. It wasn't fun. I guess it left its mark on me." **Gertrude (Scheer) Barr, 1**

The only time we experienced anti-Semitism was the children when we went to school. If the kids were angry with us, they'd say something like "dirty Jew" or something like that. But in the business we didn't see much. I guess there was such a variety that you could go to so many stores, that if you didn't want to patronize a Jewish business you didn't have to. **Suzanne (Ginsberg) Kantziper, 84**

I was the only Jewish child in the school, and of course there was some anti-Semitism but nothing really bad. They would call me things like "Jew baby" and that sort of thing. But it was not, it was not unbearable. We never had fights. We never did anything like that. **Anchel Samuels, 86**

We went through a lot of the teasing by the gentile people about being Jewish. In school I had many fights because I got called "Jew baby" and things like that back then. At B.C. [Benedictine High School] it wasn't like that. The Catholic boys who were predominantly at B.C., of course, were very friendly to all the Jewish boys. As a matter of fact they were, we all were good buddies. We are today. **Rupert Heller, 80**

There were some teachers in school who didn't like Jewish kids, and they would favor the non-Jewish kids. . . . There were some teachers who were known . . . to spank a Jewish child, a Jewish student. . . . Some teachers were known as anti-Semitic. . . . We had a governor [U. S. Representative] of the state . . . who was as anti-Semitic as anyone could be, and his name was Tom Watson. **Fred Rotkow, 27**

I remember not coming to school for a certain reason because it was a Jewish holiday. And I didn't come, and she [the teacher] was upset over the fact that I had missed a test or something. And she said to me, "Well, why can't you push your holidays up to Saturday or Sunday?" And I was so upset I started to cry. I was very naive and shy and I wouldn't speak up to anything, but I'll never forget that woman as long as I live. **Bess (Eisenman) Center, 3**

Savannah Patriotic Celebration, n.d.
Members of Congregation Mickve Israel joined in a festive gathering. Shown left to right: Joseph Solomons, two unidentified men, Frank Traub, Sr., two unidentified men, and Joseph Byck.
JVM 005 Congregation Mickve Israel Photograph Collection, Item 0078

[Anti-Semitism] was there but we thought nothing of it. We thought it would falter. We never did, our group, get too friendly with gentiles. I can say that I've lived in Savannah for eighty years and I cannot think of a gentile friend. I mean, they're all my friends, but I mean I don't have any closeness with them. . . .

But as far as anti-Semitism, I felt like it, you know, it's out there, but we seem to get along as a community pretty well. The only time when we were younger around the B.B. Jacob, Montgomery Street, when we'd play outside, there was a little square over there and it had a bunch of rednecks over there and we didn't get along too well with them. . . .

When we were at the public schools, most of the Jewish kids would get off in a little corner at lunchtime and that's the way I remember, you know, going through junior high and high school that way. It even held over to Armstrong [Junior College]. **Marvin Arkin, 76**

The *goyem*, the Christian kids, . . . as soon as we got out of school, we had to start running and they'd come after us. They used to take our lunch away. **Benjamin Portman, 20**

When I first went to Waters Avenue School . . . approximately 1938 . . . I do remember a lot of times I had to go down the alleys to get home because they would always want to fight me. . . . They [my parents] did their best to explain . . . that we were special chosen people and certain things that are going to happen in our lifetime. It was sort of a taboo back then. It was going on everywhere, but people sort of overlooked it.

I managed to cope with it and I made a lot of non-Jewish friends. I guess I was pretty smart because I got this boy, Johnny Groover, who was the biggest boy in the class, he became my best friend; so nobody would mess with me or Johnny Groover would take care of them. **Lewis Kooden, 91**

I was the curly-headed Jew boy on the block and we had a couple of yokels who used to give us a lot of static, but it wasn't anything major and it was nothing that couldn't be handled. **Samuel Radetsky, 45**

I never was even aware that I was different. I wasn't at all aware. There was no dividing line for me. When we got in high school and the questions of sororities began coming up, and this was not a sorority only for my school, but for all the schools in the area, they may have had some rules and restrictions, but they changed them and allowed me in. And I even became president of Entre Nous [high school sorority], which was mostly made up of girls, at that time, from St. Vincent's. . . . I was fortunately very well received by my classmates. **Barbara (Smith) Levy, 19**

I remember there were some Catholic people that lived on the corner, and the little girls were my good friends. Understand, I'm like first, second grade, and they were my good friends. . . . They used to run up and down the street and say, "Damn Jew, damn Jew," in front of my house. Now, they only knew, . . . I'm sure, that's what their parents said. "Those damn Jews live down the street.". . . They didn't know what that meant. **Harriet (Kanter) Konter, 43**

The Irish, the billy-goat Irish as they were referred to, and the Jews lived downtown. . . . They still had their differences and they still would scrap and fight individually, . . . have rock throwings and different things occurred from time to time. Then as they got more respect for one another, I think that sort of eased off. . . . Philip Cranman . . . got into some scraps with the people, but eventually they became his just dearest friends. He sang in the Cathedral choir as a young boy. . . . His father said, "What are you going to be, an Irisher?" But he enjoyed the camaraderie. **Stephen Traub, 32**

People ask me whether they tried to convert us at Benedictine. Au contraire. They told us if we were Jewish to be good Jews. They would not allow us to go to school on Jewish holidays. We were not permitted to go to Catholic church when the other kids did. We were treated very well. **Albert Mazo, 50**

If I had any anti-Semitism, I didn't know about it. It might have been behind my back, but I think I had more at Savannah High School of that kind than I did at Benedictine, 'cause I was extremely friendly with people in my class. When we had the school, the class dances, and so forth, I had my Jewish date, they had their Catholic dates, and we all got along fine. **Herman Cranman, 36**

We had a Jewish mayor at one time. . . . It seems to me that the political machine was through favors to different ethnic groups. That was before blacks were even voting. So we had Jewish Chief of Police, I think at one time. But there was a lot of anti-Semitism. Lots of it. And the Ku Klux Klan was pretty strong back in those days. . . . They were more anti-black than anti-Jewish, but they picked on Jews along with it. **Samuel Hirsch, 52**

They used to say, . . . "Don't worry about Jewish identity, the *goyem* won't let you forget.". . . I recollect that I've never felt at all any threat to being Jewish. **Harris Slotin, 55**

[Leo Frank, who was falsely accused of murder] worked for my brother-in-law in the pencil company, and also his wife was a cousin of my wife's. . . . We were down in Savannah when that . . . trial took place. And when we went up to visit Atlanta . . . I went to jail to see him. I talked to him through the bars. He stood up to the bars and I talked to him about it. That fellow wasn't guilty. . . . There was always a latent bigotry against the Jews. The Jews rarely got into trouble. Whenever they could get one that was in trouble, they never let up on him. **Aaron Guthman, 12**

I went in the service, . . . one guy came up to me and he said, and I remember just like it was yesterday, he said to me, "You know, the little town I came from in Pennsylvania, we didn't have any Jews." I said to him, "Well, that's the reason why where you came from was a little town." **Harris Slotin, 55**

One day somebody noticed that one of the houses had the cross on there and they got excited, thought that that was a Christian image. So they talked to some of the Jewish leaders and they went to see the lady and she said, "Yes, that's a cross out there." And she said, "Let me show you something." They walked outside and she said, "Look over there on that house. There's a Star of David. Now, are they discriminating? So why do you come to me and accuse me of discriminating?" And they laughed and it was all straightened out and that was it. **Sanford Wexler, 48**

What he [my father] preached to us, you're always going to have somebody saying, "That damn Jew." Don't let that worry you. You've got to make sure the playing field is level. If it's not level, then do something about that. But don't spend any time worrying about who's calling you a damn Jew or *kike* or anything like that. **Harris Slotin, 55**

RACE RELATIONS

A black entertainer told me one time, he says, "You come South and you see a restaurant and you want to go in, it says, 'No Blacks' so you didn't go in." But he says, "that was segregation." But, he says, "You go into New York and you see a fancy restaurant and you go in there and they take your order. It was two hours before it got to you." So in the same way they were segregated up there, too. It was a little more subtle there than down here. **Sanford Wexler, 48**

B'nai B'rith Book Donation, c. February-March 1947
The local chapter of B'nai B'rith presented several volumes to predominantly African American Georgia State College (now Savannah State University). Pictured left to right: unknown individual, David Rosenzweig, Rabbi Louis Youngerman, Benjamin Silverman, Emanuel Lewis, Sidney Raskin, unidentified individual, Abram Eisenman, and two unidentified individuals.
JVM 003 Savannah Jewish Archives General Photograph Collection, Item 0194

Every time there was a big band, well-known black orchestra in Savannah, we went. I think about how segregated things were in those days. The whites, the few whites that attended sat in the balcony. **Walter Lowe, 54**

I remember segregation in a very modified kind of way. The black community and the white community interfaced but they certainly did not mix well. I had a nursie and my mother would serve her at the table, you know. She certainly ate the same food we did, but she took her plate into the kitchen and ate at the kitchen table. That was, no one would have thought to invite the servant to eat at the table with you. . . .

Desegregation was only announced when I was . . . a junior in college, 1953. Eisenhower announced it. The first time I ever sat next to a black person . . . I was coming back from Vanderbilt to Atlanta to have the high holidays with my family. Sat next to a black person on the bus and I thought that was a wonderful phenomenon.

But . . . it turns out the first experience I had riding next to a black person was when I was playing with Herman [Friedman]. We must have been ten years old or so, ten or eleven, and they had a very nice house and a lot of servants. Herman told the gardener's son, John Henry, that we would take him home and he said, "You just get up on Jack's handlebars.". . . Herman rode behind me on his bicycle just laughing. . . . That was actually the first time I "broke" the color line. . . .

I remember when my mother saw in the newspaper that a black family had been burned out. She gathered things in this house for us to take over there to give to the family. . . . There was a kindness between people, even black and white then. It was not equality but there were considerations in both directions. **Jack Golden, 74**

This community——I've always had a love-hate relationship with the community. It's closed, it's cliquish, yet it's open to new ideas. . . . I knew I wanted to come back. I knew I would wind up here. I would wind up here for two reasons. . . . One reason was that I have always felt a sense of, a positive sense of obligation to the Jewish community, and I've always felt very proud to be a Savannahian. . . . The other reason . . . was because . . . as a Jewish person who grew up in the South, I have always been concerned about Jewish-gentile relations and Jewish-black relations. . . .

When I was a kid, I mean I couldn't have been more than eight years old, . . . I just simply could not understand or accept the attitudes of people on the bus or the bus driver when a black woman came on and was forced to go to the back. . . . I got off the bus. I was very, very upset by it, became actually physically ill. . . . I just felt a great need to know more and to respond to the black community. **Robert Friedman, 38**

We had a very peaceful integrated process here in Savannah, compared to many of the communities. . . . But back in 1960 there was no such thing as a black cashier in a supermarket in Savannah, Georgia. Black customers would shop at a supermarket, as well as white customers, but it was understood that the position of cashier was held by a white woman. Some of the black leaders came to me and said that the time had come to put black cashiers in. And it was a very difficult experience because I felt that they were one hundred percent right, but I also had a business to run, and there were no black women who had been trained to be cashiers. It was a very difficult time. I asked if they had any people to recommend and they said no, they would not do that because that would not be in keeping with what they were trying to do; they would not put themselves on the line as to recommend some specific people.

So I went out and recruited, through the black churches, I recruited one person. I finally winnowed it down to one person, and took this young woman upstairs in our store on Habersham Street, and worked with her for hours and hours until she learned how to be a cashier. She finally went to work as a cashier. We were met with a lot of resistance by the white customers. But it took hold after a while, and some of the other stores started in doing it, but I'm pretty sure that we were the first one that had a black cashier.

Another incident which was an extremely, extremely traumatic experience was around 1971. Betty and I signed a petition, and there was a full-page ad pleading with the Board of Education here to get on with the business of teaching our youngsters, and that if busing was what was needed to bring about the integration process, that the courts had ruled was the law of the land, that that's what we needed to do; we needed to bus the children and get on with educating our children. Well, it was a full-page ad, and the most visible, when I say that with no sense of pride or other indication, was the fact that Betty and I were the most visible signatures among, I imagine there were one hundred of them or more, because we operated supermarkets and people went to supermarkets to buy groceries.

So the next thing we knew, our supermarkets were being picketed by the white mothers in Chatham County. And we ended up going to court to ask for a stay of this picketing, and make them cease and desist, and the judge ordered that the pickets be halted until we could discuss it in court. And finally we came to an amicable agreement of some sort which was not, it wasn't something that we were very happy about, but it was a very, very tense time for us. The courthouse was packed with angry white mothers who thought that we were trying to destroy their children's education. . . . Our children weren't threatened, but we were threatened. Betty was threatened that if we didn't quit trying to do these kinds of things that something might happen to some of our children. It was a very, very ugly time. **Norton Melaver, 15**

It raised all kinds of issues with me as to what kind of obligations, if any, did Jews have with regard to blacks, with regard to people who are oppressed in general. . . . It continued to direct my efforts in education as I grew up. . . . I found myself studying minority relations and becoming an activist in the Civil Rights movement. Coming to Savannah at one point during the Civil Rights movement, . . . arriving at my parents' home and being told I should leave town immediately because there was a bomb threat. I left and didn't return for a couple of years. **Robert Friedman, 38**

They [Civil Rights protests] broke me. Picketed for almost two years. Just Broughton Street, not West Broad and not East Broad. Just Broughton Street. That broke me 'cause that was a period when I had just taken over next door and I spent a lot of money doing the store over, went and bought a lot of merchandise for Easter. It was unbelievable, my volume dropped eighty-five percent in one year. **Reuben Schneider, 28**

Civil Rights, . . . we had a store on Broughton Street. We had boycotts, we had fire trucks, we had lot of things that went on on Broughton Street when I was in business there . . . that affected business there for a couple of years. . . . That really helped deaden Broughton Street because the Mall had already opened up and Broughton Street began to be a little less important factor in the city. . . . I can remember as a young boy living on Broughton Street, in the evening after the store closed, we'd take chairs out and sit on Broughton Street and take a freeze or something, and I can remember the K.K.K. mess coming down Broughton Street on parade. . . . I guess we just took it in stride. It was there, we were there. They were going to march and thank goodness nothing happened. **Marvin Arkin, 76**

I really don't know what the attitude of the merchants was in those days [during the Civil Rights period]. I would suspect that they [Jewish people] were tolerant because of having been a persecuted people, they certainly would be more inclined to be tolerant of other peoples' persecutions and problems. No-body denies that the colored people, black people were persecuted. **Stephen Traub, 32**

I was, I guess you might say, somewhat instrumental in coming up with the idea of offering our swimming pool [at the J.E.A.] to the inner-city youth. We realized that on Friday afternoon we'd close the building early and the pool, there-fore, couldn't be used. The inner-city youth just didn't have any place to go swim-ming. We arranged for them to use our pool every Friday afternoon. . . . We had some members who were opposed to this. The thing about inner-city was mostly young black children. Some of our members opposed it. But, basically, it worked out, and I am very proud to say that we played a hand in offering these facilities to those youngsters. We also integrated some of our other programs, to start with, something as innocuous as the bridge club, some black people came in and wanted to play. . . . And we said, "Sure, why not." So it became a fact that we were integrated in every which way. That happened during the time I was in office. **Norton Melaver, 15**

The Ku Klux Klan were meeting in the small towns. . . . I began attending the Ku Klux Klan meetings and taking license numbers. . . . They would go out on the edge of town and burn a cross and have a big meeting with their hoods. . . . The meetings were around where I lived [Ridgeland, South Carolina], but I also attended meetings in other areas where they did not know me. . . . I would take notes and send them to Atlanta, to the Anti-Defamation League, about who was attending, from where. And they followed up on some of the leads . . . and they found out that these were people who were prominent lawyers in Columbia, South Carolina, or wherever, and were attending these meetings. I was subsequently threatened, threatened my family, by a member of the Ku Klux Klan who called me a Jew and said that, "You continue your activities and we're going to get you." **Albert Ullman, 33**

I was on Monterey Square, and I lived there for at least twenty years. . . . I was also living there during the time that the integration took place and the first black was admitted to Armstrong [Junior College], and the state patrol were staked out around the entire area for that first week of the integration. **Eric Meyerhoff, 18**

When I moved to Savannah, I became involved with the Civil Rights movement. And my assignment came from the Anti-Defamation League, was to sort of go around town. . . . There were certain times of the day . . . when some activities were going on. I would go up on Broughton Street and . . . in the year of 1961, I was standing on the corner of Broughton and Barnard streets, when the sit-ins were going on over at Kress. . . . I was standing there talking to Dan Rather and . . . we were saying that . . . one of these days this is all going to be history. **Albert Ullman, 33**

Then when they started the business with the integration, which I think may be the late '50s, early '60s, there was a boycott of Broughton Street and many of the merchants did suffer because of the boycott. The boycott ended after about six months, I guess, and the city had very capable leadership in terms of integration. The only bad incident that I can remember, well there were a number of bad ones, but one in particular was the night that Martin Luther King was killed and there were several merchants, businesses that burned on West Broughton [West Broad] Street. Yachum & Yachum burned to the ground. Absolutely . . . there was no reason necessary to pick on him, to pick on the Perlman family, but they burnt the store down. **Martin Karp, 42**

The store that the Perlmans owned, Yachum & Yachum, was burned. . . . [It] was located on West Broad Street. A lot of Jewish people worked there sometimes. . . . So that was a sad loss of a business on that street, [which catered to] the blacks, black people. They sold everything; shoes, clothing. I think they had some notions, too. **Suzanne (Ginsberg) Kantziper, 84**

Throughout my ninety years of life in Savannah, we have not had any difficulty between blacks and Jews. They have always had a good mutual respect, although there was not the use of the facilities, and even though stores like Levy's and Adler's had to be integrated. In the end it was done peacefully without the turmoil that existed in other cities.

We did have one very sad experience . . . when Martin Luther King, Jr. was assassinated. Somehow or other there was this craze among certain blacks to set fire to stores, and so forth, and one of the stores that they burned that night was the Yachum & Yachum Department Store on West Broad Street. This was a store that had served the blacks well, and while it was Jewish owned, it had twenty-five employees who were black, and they, of course, lost their jobs because Yachum & Yachum went out of business at that time. **H. Sol Clark, 5**

I played with black kids. I lived on the four hundred block of Broughton Street. My friends were the little black kids in the lane. Of course, I was a little girl, I wasn't even five years old. What did I know of black, white, or green? I knew it was a little girl back there. **Lena (Feinberg) Rosenzweig, 26**

My best friend was a black girl, . . . she was my closest friend. I had Jewish friends, too. But I learned early on that there was, there was no stigma attached to being black. I was proud to be her friend, I really was. Her mother was a school teacher, black school teacher, her father was a black barber. They lived with their . . . grandmother and another son. But they were the finest people you wanted to meet. . . . We got along fine. We used to write stories, just sit there and write stories and see who could write the best story. She'd read mine and I'd read hers. There were some wonderful stories; I wish we'd kept them. **Gertrude (Scheer) Barr, 1**

My very best friend was a black boy who was of light-colored skin so he was known as "Yeller." . . . [Years later] I was driving into Savannah from Tybee when a bridge opened and I had to stop behind a truck that contained the prisoners from the chain gang. They, of course, worked on the roads in those days. So I was sitting at the wheel of my car when one of the young men in the chain gang group waved to me and said, "Hey, Solomon," that's what I was always called as I was growing up. I wondered who could that be, and I got out of my car and went over to him and I said, "You called me Solomon, who would you be?" He said, "Don't you recognize me? I'm your friend Yeller." Here was my boyhood chum, really, who had been so close to me.

We had never had any further contact during my college years but nevertheless I had obtained an education, thanks to my parents, and the fact that I was able to make loans from people like Morris Levy and Sam Blumenthal, who enabled me to complete my college education. I was a lawyer and here was "Yeller" on the chain gang. I've often told that story because it was an experience that made a tremendous impression upon me in my own life. **H. Sol Clark, 5**

Coming from Russia they [my parents] didn't know too much about the Klan, any of the stuff, the Cracker *goyem* that we had. Her [Mama] best friend was a black family that lived next door. Every *yom tov* she'd bring them all kinds of stuff to eat, and whenever they made anything special . . . they'd call us kids to go have something. Of course, *trayf* Mama wouldn't eat. **Benjamin Portman, 20**

You see, we lived on Broughton Street, and behind every street there was a lane and that's where the black people lived. They never lived in a house, they always lived in the lane. . . . I'm happy that my little friends were all black little kids that lived in the lane because it was convenient for me to play with them. But I knew that they couldn't do this and they couldn't do that. And when I live to be ninety and look at television, seeing how much recognition they get, I just shut my eyes and say, "Thank God, thank God." Because they are smart, they're talented. . . . I'm very thankful. **Lena (Feinberg) Rosenzweig, 26**

Across from our house was an Irish lady, who of all things, I was real friendly with her son, we were little kids maybe six, seven, eight years old. She made the Ku Klux Klan uniforms. What she would do is cut out the patterns and we'd take them and spread them out in the right place, and then she'd come and put them together and sew them up. I never then saw a Ku Klux Klanner. But we had a pawnshop on Broughton and West Broad, they used to march that way and we used to run in the stores where they couldn't bother us. **Benjamin Portman, 20**

WARS

Local Georgia Militia Officer, c.1895
The identity of this soldier in elaborate military regalia is unknown.
JVM 005 Congregation Mickve Israel Photograph Collection, Item 0064

CIVIL WAR

My grandfather was Isaac Roos and his father was . . . David Roos. My great-grandfather fought in the Civil War and his name is on a plaque, David Roos, in Fort Pulaski, because he served with the Georgia Hussars. He's listed out there as a private. **Matiel (Roos) Leffler, 14**

I was one year old when General Grant was first elected President. He was a great general. He had the troops and the war material. The Confederates didn't have anything at the end of the war—they had to give in. But he was magnanimous in his accepting the surrender of General Lee, and I always liked the memory of General Grant for that reason. **Aaron Guthman, 12**

WORLD WAR I

In 1916 I guess, [my father] was stationed at Fort Screven. In those days they sent the soldiers to the camp to be stationed as close to home as possible. . . . He always used to joke about the fact that his mother used to send him hot meals on the train from Savannah to Tybee to Fort Screven. I remember he told a funny story. He said . . . when World War I was over . . . he wanted to get out of the army as soon as he could, he wanted to come home and get married to my mother. So he told the sergeant, "I got to get out of this Army, and if you let me go, I'll send you . . . cakes and pastries like you never saw before. I got to get out soon." The guy let him out and he sent him stuff [from his family's bakery]. **Alan Gottlieb, 40**

It was very, very hard to get anything like candy bars, or things like that, because everything was rationed. If you had an extra card, that was wonderful; you'd get an extra candy bar for somebody. So I always had a lot of candy bars for my husband and myself. Men that worked with him that didn't want candy, they used to give him their ration cards. So I always had a lot of candy, and these kids used to come every day and I knew they wanted a candy bar. **Helen (Blumenthal) Hirshberg, 13**

First World War, c.1917
Isadore Weitz was only one of many local soldiers to serve the United States during World War I.
JVM 003 Savannah Jewish Archives General Photograph Collection, Item 2303

WORLD WAR II

We couldn't understand at first that Hitler, one man, a "*meshugge*,". . . should take and control a whole nation, Germany, who considered themselves lofty and above everybody. But that was a tragedy. That was a pity. **Louis Silverman, 29**

During World War II, my father got a letter from his nieces saying they were starving, could we send them food? My father consulted with the officials and they said no. Any food that you send to Brussels would go to the Nazis. The entire family was wiped out during the *Holocaust*. . . . I had another uncle went to Paris, . . . he disappeared during the war. My aunt disappeared during the war, World War II. **Albert Mazo, 50**

Probably the most unifying experience of all for me in the Jewish community here and everywhere else was during the Hitler years. When Hitler took over Germany, it was just unbelievable. None of us really believed the German people, who are a civilized people, could be performing as a nation the cruelties upon the Jewish people just because of their religion.

Anyway, during those years, the Jewish community just joined together, there was no longer the cleavage that had previously existed between the Reform, and of course, the Conservative began to grow also. **H. Sol Clark, 5**

I was at the movie . . . when they interrupted the movie to announce that we had been bombed in Pearl Harbor. I remember the feeling of my heart sinking. I got so frightened. You know, that they could bomb Pearl Harbor, . . . why couldn't they just bomb Savannah. . . . I immediately picked myself up out of the movie and we ran home.

But I remember that vividly, it was so vivid in my mind. . . . I was about eighteen or nineteen years old. . . . I'd go to the J.E.A. where they had dances for the soldiers. I'd dance a little bit and then go home. . . . That was our social life when the war was on. That's how I met my husband. **Gertrude (Scheer) Barr, 1**

About 1941, Helen and I were dating each other, we had a Sunday afternoon standing date. I'd pick her up and we'd take a ride out to the country and just talk and sight-see. . . . One afternoon, us and another couple were out and we heard on the radio that Pearl Harbor was bombed and the war had started. . . . I think I was seventeen at the time, and all of a sudden became very eager to get into the service. I couldn't wait until I got old enough to get into it. **Herman Cranman, 36**

My toddler years were spent in a four-plex apartment on the 1300 block of East Henry Street. . . . What I do remember about living there was, I used to walk around with my toy telephone and I would call "Pearl Harbor." This was during the early '40s and the war was going on, and I thought Pearl Harbor was my playmate. That is what I remember about the war.

Then I also remember that we had ration books and I still have my ration book. It has my name in it. Each member of our family had a ration book. **Phillipa "Bunny" (Sherman) Cohen, 90**

There was Pearl Harbor, and bingo, off to the service I went! . . . I came home December '45. . . . Sworn in, I lost my independence on Independence Day,

Fourth of July '42. . . . Started in England, and then from there to the beaches of France and across. **Samuel Radetsky, 45**

I grew up during World War II where life was just different and we used to save twenty-five cents a week to buy a war bond. When you saved eighteen dollars and seventy-five cents you could purchase the war bond and it would be worth twenty-five dollars at maturity, probably ten years later. . . .

During the war foods were rationed and gas was rationed, and I've heard recently that maybe saving tinfoil from chewing gum wrappers and rubber bands may not have helped the war effort but it certainly helped the patriotism for people who did these things. . . . You couldn't just go to the grocery store and buy what you wanted. Sugar was a big ration item. **Jane (Guthman) Kahn, 93**

During the war I remember you had ration stamps for shoes, which you traded off to somebody else for something else. **Selma (Greenberg) Dunn, 7**

During the war we had shortages, but then every merchant that had anything on his shelves all of a sudden could sell it for whatever price. So we got through the Second World War, and at the end of the war then the city then began to scramble to get back into a normal pattern of activities, businesswise, social, and so forth. **Martin Karp, 42**

We did have Army here and it was not uncommon for the J.E.A. to plan a program. And we went out to the base which was here and it was an Army Air Force base here, and then we went to Hinesville, and our parents, our mothers, chaperoned us. They had these big dances. . . . A group . . . did the spotting of airplanes. . . . That was the time that women suddenly went into the shipyards and worked, and did men's work that they never had done before. **Harriet (Kanter) Konter, 43**

During World War II when the J.E.A. asked for us to offer our homes to the soldiers for the *Seders* and they used to come from [Fort] Stewart for *Seders*. . . . You never knew how many were going to come in, were going to get passes. . . . We were going to be seated at the table that had to be turned diagonal because that's how many soldiers we had. It was my husband, my son, my daughter and myself, and the rest of the people around our table were soldiers, sailors, Coast Guardsmen, Navy men. We had seventeen people. **Frances (Ehrlich) Rabhan, 21**

I know that Mother was concerned about the fact that there [were] . . . so many soldiers here in town. And I was admonished to go to the movies only if I had three friends, or two other friends to go with me. . . . I remember the tea dances we attended at the U.S.O. Club. It was at the Guards' Armory. We wore long dresses and danced with the soldiers who were so happy to see girls; . . .we thought it was wonderful. We were doing our bit for the war effort. It was fun.

But life did change after the war. The city did begin to change. Streets began to be paved that we'd ridden horseback on. The city began to move as the soldiers came back in. Housing began. Here we are today with all the remains of what happened. All the factories.

I can remember going to a shipyard where we had a new ship being commissioned to go fight for the war effort. And as little ones, I can remember putting on a circus to raise money for the Red Cross. We put that on as children. That was our one dollar and fifty cents for the war effort. That, in addition to saving newspapers and planting a victory garden. **Barbara (Smith) Levy, 19**

Second World War Fundraising, c.1942-1943
Even young children contributed to the war effort. These friends held a circus and raised $1.81 to donate to the American Red Cross. Pictured in costume (left to right): (front row) Kayton Smith, Jr., and Margery (Guthman) Braverman; (back row) Jane (Guthman) Kahn, Betty Ray Fleishel, and Barbara (Smith) Levy.
JVM 003 Savannah Jewish Archives General Photograph Collection, Item 0770

I remember sitting with my grandfather. He had a huge map of Europe on the wall of his shop and there were lots of pins. There were different colored pins for the Allies and the Axis, and where we had family and where others had family. People would come in. . . . They would read the map and keep up with the map, maintain the map and moves of the Allied armies. All his sons served in the war. The girls were active here in the U.S.O. **Robert Friedmen, 38**

Well, I remember that it was very sad. Parents used to pray that their children would come back. Some did, some didn't. We all prayed hard. We hated war. **Lena (Feinberg) Rosenzweig, 26**

I went to Norfolk, Virginia for my Navy boot training. In those days the Navy needed men so badly to man its ships that boot training lasted only three weeks. I was scheduled to be shipped out when Freddy Apostoli, the then middleweight champion of the world, arranged for me to stay in Norfolk to box there for the Navy. . . . In 1943, I was sent into action against the Japanese on a patrol torpedo (PT) boat. I think I am the only sailor who served on a PT boat who didn't claim to have sailed with or met John Kennedy. **Leo Center, 4**

They transferred me to Roanoke, Virginia, where I was drafted. In those days, it was either 1940 or '41, I've forgotten which one, every young man had to register for the draft for one year. I was on my eleventh month when Pearl Harbor came along and I couldn't get out. I was single, had no dependants, and I had no excuses to get out. So I wound up with five and a half years of military service. I was discharged December 22, 1945. . . . I came home and mother told me that the Garfunkels . . . were having a party for returning servicemen, . . . and that's where I met my charming wife. **Martin Leffler, 14**

When I was notified to report to Atlanta for the draft, I talked to Mother about it and said, "Mom, what should I do about the food?" Momma was a liberal, she was strictly Orthodox, very religious, but she said, "You have to do what you have to do in order to sustain your life, and if you have to eat the food that they serve, you do the best that you can; you don't have to eat hog meat, you don't have to deliberately go out to eat *trayf* food." **Benjamin Silverman, 29**

When the war started, they lowered the requirements and you had to take an examination which was a high school equivalency exam, which my parents, for some unknown reason, gave me permission to take. Probably thought I wouldn't pass it. But I passed it and I passed the physical, and I found myself enlisted into the Army Air Corps, and that was in the end of '42. . . . I got called, I think it was in March of '43, for classification into the Aviation Cadet Program. . . . I qualified as a bombardier . . . and I accepted it and was trained as a bombardier. **Herman Cranman, 36**

In January of '46 I got my draft notice. . . . They decided that I was smart enough to go into the Signal Corps or the Medical Corps, so I chose the Medical

Corps. I trained for six months, went to the Philippines in the Occupation Forces, worked for the Tenth General Hospital in Manila. Beautiful city that was so bombed up it . . . was terrible looking. . . . Then I caught malaria, got treated. Then the war was pretty much over. Now we got shot at a few times from . . . the rebels in the Philippines, and they used to raid our barracks for supplies, toilet paper, food, anything they could get. . . . I spent seven months in the Philippines. I came home looking green because I had been taking atamine which turns the complexion green. So I didn't want to go out, but I did go to school in that condition. Very embarrassing. **Rupert Heller, 80**

United Service Organizations (U.S.O.), 1942
The Jewish Welfare Board, one of the U.S.O. organizations, sponsored gatherings between women and servicemen during the war to help keep up the soldiers' morale and make them feel at home.
JVM 003 Savannah Jewish Archives General Photograph Collection, Item 2193

I was thirty-four years old when I joined the Navy. . . . I was very troubled about Hitler—if he ever came over to this country, that we ought to do something to try to stop it. And so I saw an article in the paper one day and they wanted people, grocery and food supply business experience and college graduates to get a commission in the Navy. So I applied for it and I got a commission. . . . I skipped Ensign and got Lieutenant J.G. [Junior Grade]. . . . It wasn't long before I got orders to go to supply course school in Babson Institute [outside of Boston]. . . .

So I went there for a month and got indoctrinated. I went to Morris Levy's and bought my uniform, and they put the insignia on backwards. **Samuel Hirsch, 52**

One night my husband came home and he said, "I've got something to tell you." And I said, "Well, I've got something to tell you, so you go first." So he said, "Well, I've been transferred and I'm going to the Pacific War Theater." I said, "That's great, you're also going to be a daddy." So I followed him, went with him to California. . . . Anyway, we went out on the train, no planes in those days, and the trip took two nights and three days, . . . but it was a wonderful trip, actually. Then he left, so I returned to Savannah. On January 31, 1943, Joseph Armand Price, III made an appearance and Joe did not see the baby until the baby was fourteen months old. **Elizabeth "Libby" (Levy) Price, 69**

When World War II started, I went in as a pilot and got . . . sent to Korea. Ended up in the Air Force anyway as a radio operator/gunner, served in the Eighth Air Force. Then came back to retrain in B-29s at a base in Japan. As a matter of fact, Irving Gottlieb, from Gottlieb's Bakery, was a cook in my outfit. **Meyer "Johnny" Becker, 70**

I was in the United States Coast Guard. . . . Louie Tanenbaum . . . he was recruiting officer. . . . I was 6'2" at the time and weighed 141 pounds. He says, "You're four pounds underweight, I can't take you.". . . He said, "You go eat all the bananas you can and drink the water that you can consume and come back and if you weigh 145, I'll take you into the service." Well, to make a long story short, I made the weigh-in and that's how I got into the U. S. Coast Guard. **Herbert Blumenthal, 76**

As a kid I always wanted to fly. I used to go out to the airport on my bicycle any chance that I had. The airport was Hunter Field, that was the county airport at that time before they opened up Savannah International. I used to go out and just gawk at those airplanes, the few that they had. . . .

When World War II came along, my brother and I tried to get into Cadets. We couldn't because both of us had high blood pressure, so they wouldn't take us. . . . I went on to be classified as a radio war operator and gunner. When I was down in Miami taking basic training they called me off the field and told me that I had an application for Cadet, and I told them I couldn't pass the physical. He says, "You're going to pass the physical now." Of course, I guess they needed people so they led me through the whole thing. . . . I finished up my flying and got my wings and my commission in Valdosta, Georgia. . . .

When I first went into B-24 crew training . . . I ran into Pete Grossman. . . . He says, "What you doin' here, Bubba?" I says, "I'm gonna fly this thing." I said,

"What you doin'?" He says, "I'm a crew chief on this." He says, "You gonna fly it?" He says, "I ain't going." Of course, it was a little joke; but I was so happy to see Pete, we . . . went out whenever we could get off the field. **Arthur "Bubba" Horovitz, 77**

There is one incident which I have to believe an angel was looking out for me. I carried a radio for a lieutenant who was a forward artillery observer. We got to our position one night when it was so dark you literally could not see anything. I was tired but I started to dig a foxhole. But before I had dug very deeply, an infantryman came by and told me he was moving up further and that I could have his foxhole.

Since I was tired and his hole was already dug, I decided to move to his foxhole. But I left my equipment behind. That night the Germans shelled us quite heavily. One shell landed on the spot where I had originally started to dig, just about sixty feet from where I spent the night. My carbine was destroyed as well as some of my equipment which I had left in that spot. **Sol Newman, 60**

Military Service during World War II, 1944
Pictured here is Martin "Maier" Rabhan while stationed in New Guinea.
JVM 003 Savannah Jewish Archives General Photograph Collection, Item 1368

My combat group . . . was the 376th Bomber Group, stationed . . . [in] Italy. . . . We flew missions all over the Balkans, southern Germany, southern France, and northern Italy, dropping bombs on various targets, strategic targets like factories, war factories, bridges, oil fields, oil refineries, and so forth. . . . I managed to fly thirty-four missions. I was on my thirty-fourth mission when I got shot down. . . . We got shot down by a German fighter. . . . We had a fire in the bomb bay with still a load of bombs that hadn't been dropped yet. We had to bail out. . . .

The first thing that these Hungarian farmers who caught me asked me was something about being Jewish. . . . They were standing in front of me with pitch-forks pointed at my belly and all I had to do was say "yes" and I wouldn't be here today. But I said, "no, I wasn't Jewish," and they didn't do anything. All they did was beat me up a little bit. . . .

Incidentally, when I bailed out, I had a *mezuzah* on my dog tags. When I got to the ground I needed to get rid of it. I pulled my dog tag chain out of my shirt and the *mezuzah* was gone! I couldn't find it. I looked all over, . . . it was gone. I guess that was a sign. **Herman Cranman, 36**

[For more information regarding Cranman's P.O.W. experiences, see *A Measure of Life: War, Captivity, Freedom*. Savannah: Herman L. Cranman, 2002.]

United Jewish Appeal Food and Clothing Drive, 15 November 1946
Sponsored by the United Jewish Appeal, local ladies collected food and clothing to be shipped to Jewish survivors in Europe through the Joint Distribution Committee. Pictured left to right: Hyla (Lewis) Hirsch, Elizabeth (Eisenman) Bernstein, Sophie (Richman) Black, and Ruth (Weiser) Silverman.
JVM 003 Savannah Jewish Archives General Photograph Collection, Item 0177

When the war in Europe was over . . . I was coming back with my group to be regrouped and shipped out to the Pacific. . . . We knew we were picking up prisoners of war. . . . I got into the wrong mess hall and I got my plate, went down there and they were dishing out which I would call slop. . . . I grabbed my tray and I was walking along and all of a sudden I hear a little voice in back of me saying, "Bubba.". . . I turned around and there was a skeleton with skin stretched over it. Herman Cranman! If you've ever seen a person like that, I just dropped the whole plate right there. Of course, we hugged and so forth and so on.

Come to find out I was in the wrong mess hall. It was the prisoner of war mess hall. They didn't want to give them any solid foods because of what they had to eat for quite a long time. Of course, Herman said he was hungry. I found my mess hall up on deck and we had two settings to eat. We had a ticket to go in. Of course, I would go in and then I'd give the ticket to Herman through the window and he would come in. That's the only way he could get to eat. It was amazing what a fellow like he could put away in food. He'll tell you to this day that I had never seen a fella eat like he did that time. **Arthur "Bubba" Horovitz, 77**

CHAPTER 4: RELIGION

To better understand the commentary of our oral history interviewees, we have attempted to define the different branches of Judaism. These are the simplest of definitions and are meant only as an aid in understanding the quotes:

Orthodox Judaism requires strict adherence to traditional, biblical, and rabbinic law.

Conservative Judaism refers to adherence to tradition with some departures in keeping with times and circumstances.

Reform Judaism is a liberal approach, eliminating tradition regarded as irrelevant to the present.

SYNAGOGUES

GENERAL

In the 1880s, when the immigration began from Eastern Europe, the members of the B.B. Jacob, for the most part, were of German origin. And they were hesitant, didn't want to accept the Polish and Russian Jews as members of the congregation. My grandfather said, "Well, if they're not good enough for you, I'm not good enough for you." He formed another congregation which later went back into B.B. Jacob.

But an aside to that, I used to be friendly with and wrote some insurance as a young man for Henry Boley, who was from an old family here. He would sit down and reminisce with me, and he remarked to me one day. He said, "You know, everything is almost a circle. The wheel turns."

And he said that he was a member of Mickve Israel Synagogue, which was a Reform Temple, and his parents were from Germany, he was German. And he said that when his parents came, that Mickve Israel was an Orthodox congregation and basically Spanish and Portuguese, and they didn't want to accept the Germans. And finally the Germans got to be members of Mickve Israel. And then later it became a Reform Temple, and the Germans now didn't want to accept the Polish and Russian Jews as members of Mickve Israel.

But he said the funny part is that the Spanish and Portuguese were looked down upon by the Syrians and the Jews from the Middle East because they originally had immigrated from Syria and Persia and those countries to Spain. And those Middle East countries looked down on the Spanish and Portuguese, the Spanish and Portuguese looked down on the Germans, and the Germans looked down on the Russian and Polish, and the Russian and Polish looked down on the Syrian and Middle Eastern Jews, because each one thought they were better than the other, and the whole circle turned around. And I thought it was an interesting comment that he made, and I'd never thought about it that way. **Benjamin Garfunkel, 9**

I think there was a time where the cliqueness was very, very noticeable. For instance, . . . if a girl from the B.B. Jacob went out with a boy from the Temple, that was considered a big honor, many . . . years ago . . . because the Temple held themselves away from us. . . . But as time has gone on, we didn't associate with them. . . . Then all of a sudden, we had no Sunday School at the B.B. or Agudath Achim, there were no Sunday Schools. Everybody started going to the Sunday School at the Temple. I think that started, . . . that had a lot to do with our children intermingling. **Evelyn (Ward) Karsman, 53**

It was really strange, . . . but the Orthodox and Reform Jews did not associate with each other. I went out with Orthodox Jewish girls, never with a Reform Jewish girl, although I married one later. . . . The Reform Jewish synagogue people . . . were mostly German Jews who had come over in the mid 1800s. By the time my folks came over, they were already established and had businesses, they'd become successful.

The Eastern European Jews who came over in the late 1800s, early 1900s, were just getting started, and I think the Reform Jews probably helped Americanize the immigrant that came over, and I think, if I'm not mistaken, they're the ones who really established the Jewish [Educational] Alliance. **Albert Mazo, 50**

Where I was born, in my neighborhood, I lived next door to some very fine Reform Jews. I learned early on that there was a different type of Jew. These people, you know, they were sort of alien, but in terms of observance, they were more observant in the Reform than we were of the Orthodox. . . . But one of the interesting things was, there was almost no social intercourse between the kids in the Temple. The only reason I knew any kids in Temple was because they lived next door to me. **Harris Slotin, 55**

There was not the cohesiveness that I would like to see in the Jewish community despite the fact that I've said there was a family aspect to it. When I was growing up and spent a lot of time at the J.E.A. on Barnard Street, just to be very totally and brutally honest . . . I didn't know too many people who were members of the Mickve Israel Synagogue. I don't know how it came about.

I think, in retrospect, that some of the members of the Mickve Israel Synagogue helped set up the J.E.A., but . . . it was set up for the Eastern Europeans when they came in, and the members of the Mickve Israel Synagogue were mainly descendants from the earlier immigration of German Jews, and they were already part of the Jewish community . . . and therefore were separate and apart in many ways. . . .

I think it's in some ways the Temple and the Agudath Achim and the B.B. Jacob, which are all very strong pillars of our community, somehow did not have the ability to bring together the community. They each have their own adherents and it becomes difficult sometimes. I think . . . the crux of the matter is nowadays from what I understand, is . . . that according to Orthodox tradition, they don't want the J.E.A. facilities to be open on *Shabbat*. The Reform people would like to see it open on *Shabbat*, and that is the outstanding example of some of the things that cause a little bit of dissension in the community at times. **Norton Melaver, 15**

I was a member of B.B. Jacob until Dorothy and I got married, and we had a very strenuous rabbi there at that time. Dorothy had been married before [and he] wanted us to go through a lot of gyrations that neither of us were interested in, and I explained to him that I wasn't a very religious person, but if the synagogue wasn't available to me when I got married and when someone was born and when someone died, why I was really wasting their time and mine. So I went to see Dr. Solomon [Rabbi George Solomon] who was very pleasant, and explained my situation. He married us and I became a member of the Temple, and have been a member since. **Calmon Mendel, 16**

The Conservative *shul*, all those members were members of B.B. Jacob. All of them. They pulled out and they started a thing called the *"Minyan,"* I would say in the '20s. . . . What caused it was that ninety percent of these people were working people. Two things they wanted to do was to be able to go into service, get through with it, get out. They wanted less, to pay less dues. Some of our most prominent people . . . were active in our *shul* and went there. Eventually what they took was a little house that was . . . between York and Oglethorpe . . . . Of course, we were always friends between us all, there was no difference, no walls, no nothing. They'd come and go to our *shul*, we'd go to theirs. It worked out real well.

It wasn't until the Conservative movement came in and that's when the A.A. moved to Drayton Street and had a complete synagogue themselves and a different set of rules. And, of course, when they got to where they went they changed some of the rules and regulations like the other Conservative *shuls* did. We still remain as we were before, separate with the women and so forth. **Benjamin Portman, 20**

MICKVE ISRAEL

We're the third oldest synagogue in America and the only one that is Gothic [Revival] in design. The reason it's Gothic in design is because it was the first synagogue in Georgia and all the architects were building Gothic churches, and who knew what a synagogue looked like? So finally the Temple fathers accepted the Gothic plans and there you are, we're the only Gothic synagogue in America. **Elizabeth "Libby" (Levy) Price, 69**

One of Congregation Mickve Israel's Spiritual Leaders, n.d. Rabbi George Solomon served Congregation Mickve Israel from 1903 to 1945, during which time the congregation completed the long transition to Reform.
JVM 003 Savannah Jewish Archives General Photograph Collection, Item 2184

Both of my grandfathers, Grandfather [Samuel] Herman and my Grandfather [Abraham] Leffler, were on the building committee of the Temple, Congregation Mickve Israel's Temple, which was built in 1874 [1876-1878]. I was confirmed there and the people that were in my confirmation class, they were the ones that I went with socially, and played with them; and then the people that were in my public school class, they were the ones that I played with in the afternoons. I've never had any problems getting along with either one of them that I know of. . . . We always had a Jewish home and we observed the holidays. My father was vice president of the Temple for a good number of years, and my mother sang in the choir and she taught Sunday School, in the Sisterhood and all that business. . . . I'm a past president of the Temple. **Martin Leffler, 14**

There are two Byck windows that we are proud of. One was given by Simon Byck, which was my great grandfather, and the other window on Wayne Street was given by Lehman Byck, which is Sylvan's great grandfather. I think it's just so marvelous that the two brothers were staunch members of the Congregation Mickve Israel and gave windows and contributed their time and money and effort [have windows] just opposite each other. **David A. Byck, III, 72**

In my very young days, Mickve Israel was conducted like an Orthodox synagogue. The rabbi, [Isaac] Mendes, was very strict - he wore a *tallis* and he wore a *yarmulke*, and they read the *Torah* on the Sabbath, and then gradually, little by little, it became a Reform synagogue. So we now have the Reform, the Conservative, and the Orthodox, and the Orthodox still is maintained as the largest group in Savannah. **Louis Silverman, 29**

I guess foremost is the change in Reform Judaism. Because instead of being Classical Reform, our congregation has changed very much, in the last ten years especially. Since new families have joined the congregation, they have brought their customs and their desires into our Temple and it has changed greatly. Not to my satisfaction, frankly. **Marion (Abrahams) Levy Mendel, 17**

There were no *Bar Mitzvahs*, and to think, to even think about wearing a *yarmulke*. . . . We went to Sunday School and that really burned me up because it was held on Saturday morning, and the Boy Scouts used to go on a hike on Friday night. I'd have to get up and leave to come back for Sabbath School.

Yeah, we went to religious school and we were confirmed, and that was in place of a *Bar Mitzvah*. . . . The truth of the matter is, I wasn't exposed to any Hebrew at all. The only Hebrew that I was ever exposed to was during the *Kaddish*, I guess, and a little bit during the regular service. But I think the rabbis and the congregation at the time shied away from as much Hebrew. **Julius Edel, 35**

Mickve Israel was very non-traditional at that time. Nobody wore *yarmulkes* or *tallises*. Of course, practically all the services were in English or very little Hebrew. It had been an Orthodox synagogue 'til about 1880 . . . and then it started going Reform. It was a Sephardic synagogue originally, then it veered off Orthodox. B.B. Jacob Synagogue split off from that. **Samuel Hirsch, 52**

But Temple people were, at that time, had descended from Germany. They were mostly German people, you know, and they wanted a tremendous amount of reform. They've come back a long way, the traditionalism, now compared to what it was. In our day it used to be a standard kind of expression, we used to say, "The B.B. Jacob is Orthodox and they lean along towards Conservative, and the

Conservatives of A.A. lean along towards Orthodoxy" and then they'd finish it by saying, "But the Temple people they're *goyem* altogether.". . .

It's not like that today. It's changed a lot. . . . They didn't [*Bar Mitzvah*] in those days, they had Rabbi Starrels who apologized if a child wanted to get *Bar Mitzvahed*. They did not allow a *Bar Mitzvah* at the Temple. They had a confirmation, but you could not have a *Bar Mitzvah*. That kind of made the kids feel uncomfortable, including the kids at Temple, who felt like they were getting cheated. **Harriet (Kanter) Konter, 43**

When Israel was getting its independence, a lot of Jews in this country were, didn't want Israel. . . . They were afraid that their people would have dual loyalties to two countries. This was a silly way of thinking. A lot of members of Mickve Israel particularly were in that group. Like my father resigned from it at that time.

After Israel started, it was attacked so many times and . . . a lot of people who were *anti-Zionist* became *Zionist*. About that time Mickve Israel started going back to tradition - a lot of people wear *tallises* and *yarmulkes*. A good bit of the prayer is done in Hebrew, about half and half, I guess. **Samuel Hirsch, 52**

I was a member of the J.E.A. and the kids used to go down there, but . . . they weren't really accepted there. In fact, Cathy [(Edel) Solomons] would come home with stories of, "Why are you here? You're not Jewish," or "You're half Jewish." Because I think the Orthodox looked upon a Reform Jew as being not completely Jewish. **Julius Edel, 35**

A lot of the German Jews felt that they were here longer, who had more culture, more Americanized, sort of held to themselves a lot. And a lot of the Orthodox Jews . . . figure[d] that the Reform Jews weren't Jewish enough, some didn't consider us being Jews. **Samuel Hirsch, 52**

The early life at Mickve Israel was a bit unusual. We had a religious school that met on Saturdays and in later years they changed that to Sundays, I think. But when I went there we went on Saturdays. It was more of a playtime, I guess, than anything else. We didn't have much curriculum, although we did sing songs and had discussions in classrooms.

I was always into trouble. I remember going, being sent to the principal more than once. Ruth Stern was her name, and she was so sweet. I remember . . . one day, she said, "Stephen, if you have to come in here any more, I'm just going to have to call your mother." And I said, "Oh, please don't do that. It would just worry her.". . . Reason prevailed and I don't think she ever squealed on me. **Stephen Traub, 32**

We had . . . Saturday morning school. . . . We lived next door to the Mendes family and the girls, the Mendes ladies, went to Temple, and they would walk me home 'cause I'd have to go to Temple with them after . . . Sabbath School. . . . The most beautiful thing was Ruth Byck had just gotten married and she taught us that year. She was a very pretty lady and we thoroughly enjoyed Sabbath School there. . . .

That was the year, in 1935, when the Sisterhood decided to have the silver links made for the confirmation [chain]. . . . I'm on the first link. They didn't do it alphabetically. What they did was according to the service. I had the opening prayer. My name is the first name on the first link of that whole, long silver [chain]. **Adele (Meddin) Schneider, 61**

Congregation Mickve Israel Sisterhood, c.1950s
These bathing beauties represented the Congregation's Sisterhood in a swim suit fashion show. Left to right: Marion (Abrahams) Levy Mendel, Mildred (Wolf) Weichselbaum, Sarah (Deich) Coleman, Bea (Rabhan) Chaskin, Dorothy (Wexler) Mirsky, Shirley (Massell) Solomons, Matilda "Mat" (Shapiro) Clark, Barbara (Traub) Harris, Ruth (Ferst) Byck, Betty Michels, and Josephine (Wachtel) Smith.
JVM 003 Savannah Jewish Archives General Photograph Collection, Item 2242

We had a very large [confirmation] class. Oh, gracious. Of those that were confirmed, the ones who are still around are Libby Levy Price, Herbert Traub, Martin Leffler. There were others that are gone now, I. A. Solomons, Martin Kirschbaum, [Jane] Basch. All I can remember now. **Marion (Abrahams) Levy Mendel, 17**

I went to Sunday School at Mickve Israel and also was confirmed at Mickve Israel, and in those days Mickve Israel was what is known as Classic Reform, which means that we did not have *Bar Mitzvahs* or *Bat Mitzvahs*. We had very little Hebrew in the service. We had only confirmation. It was that way the whole time I went and also when my children were educated in their Jewish religion. Of course, now we've gone back to being more traditional, and all of my young cousins and relatives have been *Bar Mitzvahed* and *Bat Mitzvahed*, and we still also have confirmation. **Elizabeth "Libby" (Levy) Price, 69**

My contemporary group during that period, some are still living, would have been Helen Edel [Udell], . . . Helene Herman Harris, . . . Henrietta Steinheimer [Victor], . . . Adele Meddin Schneider, . . . Jack Coleman, who [are] still living. We were all confirmed at Mickve Israel Synagogue in 1935 in white dresses and white suits. Mickve Israel Synagogue had no *Bar Mitzvahs*, why we don't know, but there were no *Bar Mitzvahs*. Before I was confirmed and after I was confirmed, I attended Temple every Saturday morning. . . .

Rabbi Isaac Mendes who preceded George Solomon in the pulpit at Mickve Israel, the last of the Sephardic rabbis that we had here, had only one child. He had a son named Joe Mendes. . . . Joe and I carried the *Torah* every Saturday morning for years and years and years. My uncle George would be in the pulpit, and our cue would be, "And who shall ascend the mountain of the Lord?" And we would march down the center aisle and up on to the *bema*, and take the [*Torah*] out for Uncle George. We just did it for years and years and years. **A. J. Cohen, Jr., 6**

The confirmation service was really a beautiful, beautiful service. The girls usually wore white gowns, long mostly, as I remember. And the boys wore dark pants and white coats. All the girls carried bouquets, as I remember. For years and years it was just the same. We had an opening prayer and a floral offering and a closing prayer. And I can't even remember the names of all the prayers, which we could learn, of course, by heart, because we couldn't get up there and read. We had to say them. It was really a beautiful ceremony, and then afterwards we would have a reception in the social hall. **Elizabeth "Libby" (Levy) Price, 69**

My three children are fifth generation and their children are sixth generation Savannahians. It's a great tradition, I think, to follow and to be proud of. When my oldest granddaughter, Jessica [Byck], was just *Bat Mitzvahed* in the Temple and the rabbi made mention of the fact that she was sixth generation of the Temple and we felt very proud. **David A. Byck, III, 72**

One of my earliest recollections is going to services on Saturday morning with my mother's mother, my Grandmother [Fannie] Guckenheimer, who always sat in the front pew, right to the right of the *bema*. I would go and attend services there fairly regularly, and that habit has followed me all my life. **Marion (Abrahams) Levy Mendel, 17**

Grandfather [Joseph] Rosenheim was the secretary of Temple . . . for twenty-five years, followed by the next twenty-five as president. . . . The third twenty-five years he was president emeritus. So he had quite an active role in the Temple. I think that this was one of the reasons why, it's just a guess on my part, but I think it's one of the reasons why my father did not follow through with the same interest in the Temple. The result was, as far as I know, we were members of the Temple but we rarely went in. **John Kayton, 65**

I have absolutely no recollection of learning any Hebrew. I guess we absorbed it in services, the *Shabbats*. . . . We had a home-grown choir. I can remember my Aunt Mildred [Kuhr] and my cousin Marion [Mendel], among others, in it. . . . We had a woman, Addie May Jackson, who was the congregation organist. She played for Sunday School, a little tiny organ . . . given by Philip Solomons' uncle or great uncle about 1905, '10, somewhere along in there. Addie May played it in the Sunday School room, and she also played the big organ in the sanctuary until . . . the late '40s, early '50s, . . . until she died or retired. . . . The only holiday that specifically I recall is Succoth. I recall a song . . . we used to sing at Succoth. **Alan Gaynor, 62**

When I was vice president of the congregation, I kept telling the board I wanted to build an archives. . . . Ed Feiler was on the board, and he said that Jane was a licensed contractor. . . . [Rabbi] Saul Rubin and I were talking, Suzanne Danzig [Mendonsa] walked up, she got in the conversation. I told her what I was doing. No big secret. And she said, "I know where you need to put it." She said, "You don't need that stage. . . . Tear up the stage and put the archives there." And I said, "Capital! That's what we'll do."

So then at the meeting I told the board I was gonna do that, and Ed volunteered Jane, his wife, as a contractor, to tear it out. And she did. She cleared it all out, the cases came in. We put the [ancient] *Torah* in there, and the stuff that we had in there, and all of a sudden stuff began to come in. And it was coming from everywhere. Now they've got more things than they can put in there, and they have to rotate. . . . And that was my biggest contribution to that congregation, was to get that archives done. **A. J. Cohen, Jr., 6**

B'NAI B'RITH JACOB

My grandfather was one of the original members of the B.B. Jacob Synagogue. . . . I remember as a kid going down to the B.B. Jacob for the high holidays to sit with my grandfather. He always sat on the side of the *bema* in that first row, right next to the *bema* in the old B.B. Jacob Synagogue on Montgomery and State Street. **Erwin "Ernie" Friedman, 71**

I remember getting up on the third floor there [old building], up on the ceiling practically. I don't know how my mother ever climbed those three flights of stairs. . . . Finally Mama moved down to the second floor. . . . It was hot up there. . . . They put some sort of air conditioning in finally. **Bertha (Plotkin) Freedman, 8**

You could never wear little enough clothes to [the B. B. J.] synagogue in the summertime for the high holy days. . . . There were windows in the building and one of the things that I remember the most was seeing women get up and raise the window and about fifteen minutes later somebody from that side came over and pulled the window down. And then somebody from this side, the other side, raised the window, somebody from that side went over and pulled it down. There was just no being comfortable in the summertime and the high holy days. . . . Synagogue was packed. They didn't have individual seats. They were benches with backs, of course.

And, you know, when you get yourself all closed in to make room so that everybody could sit down, you were lucky if you could breathe. . . . And if a bench would hold eight people comfortably, for the high holidays at least twelve sat there because the mothers came every *Shabbes*, but on the high holidays the children came with them. . . .

If you were there about nine you could have the bench, *daven* almost to yourself, and you could *daven* very comfortably. But as time went on and people arrived with their children, you were lucky if you could breathe by the middle of the service. But it was wonderful. Wonderful to be able to see, be with your family and your friends. And if you were young enough and you could read, then you could help the elderly find the page when they would get a little bit mixed up and they would hand you the *Siddur* and shake their heads as if to say "Please." And a camaraderie is what kept us all together. **Frances (Ehrlich) Rabhan, 21**

The old *shul* was very hot. I remember, I do remember once the rabbi announcing from the pulpit on Yom Kippur, he was thanking the Movsovitz

Company, or Izzy Movsovitz, for donating the ice. Somehow they were using huge amounts of ice to circulate cool air in the building. . . . They must have put a lot of ice somewhere where the fans could blow across that ice and possibly blow some cool air into the *shul*. **Alan Gottlieb, 40**

Congregation B'nai B'rith Jacob, 1961
Rabbi Rosenberg presents the confirmation class of 1961. Left to right: Sherry (Tross) Demberg, Marilyn (Rabhan) Swedarsky, Barbara (Seeman) Gottlieb, Sherry (Safer) Warsaw, Rabbi Abraham I. Rosenberg, Rena (Rosenberg) Jurkowitz, Brenda (Robinson) Wolchok, Eileen (Goldberg) Kalikow, Arlene (Hirsch) Sampson, and Barbara (Roth) Balin.
JVM 003 Savannah Jewish Archives General Photograph Collection, Item 1878

It was hot [at B.B.J.]. You'd fan yourself. Particularly on Yom Kippur, you know, when you were fasting, it was tough. And all the windows were open and finally they put in what they called "air flow" and they would have a place down in the basement where they'd put ice and the fans would blow across the ice and have that come in there. That was the only way you could do it. It may have lowered the temperature two or three degrees, but that was all. It could have been eighty-five degrees or ninety degrees inside that place, or more. 'Cause it was always filled, you know, on Yom Kippur. **Sanford Wexler, 48**

I think I was the youngest member that ever served on the board of B.B. Jacob. . . . My purpose was being on the seating committee at that time. I remember Joe Lesser was in charge of the seating committee and he asked me to work out—we had complications at that time because we had more members than we had seats. So I suggested why don't we put the members together. Well, I really stuck my foot in my mouth because he says, "Over my dead body!" That was it.

So in the meantime, in those days we didn't have air condition, so some members were always putting the windows up and pulling them down. Some people would complain 'cause it was too hot or it was too cold. So we had what you called revolving fans, oscillating fans, like sixteen inches. So that's the only *shul* the people didn't *daven* by *shoklen* up and down. They went . . . side to side because they had to keep up with the fans. **Herbert Blumenthal, 76**

As a child I remember when the old B.B. Jacob was knocked down and the building that is there now, on Montgomery Street, I remember when that was rebuilt. I remember sitting on the ground and waiting for the man to finish up the design on the front door. They would cut the tiles, I remember, and they gave me the tiles and I used them for jackstones. That was about 1911, 1912. **Lena (Feinberg) Rosenzweig, 26**

I was a ring bearer at my uncle's wedding, and for the occasion my dad got me a suit of tails and a top hat. I was about four and a half years old. And then I was at the wedding, and after the wedding they paid off the first [building] mortgage at the B.B. Jacob Synagogue. Since I had the suit, they invited me to carry the mortgage down on a pillow up to the *bema* and they burned it. **Sidney Raskin, 23**

The synagogue was on Montgomery Street, right off Broughton. At that time we were young children . . . when I lived there, and everybody walked to the synagogue. Everybody went to Hebrew school. We'd go to school, and then we would come home, and then go back to the B.B. Jacob synagogue where they had Hebrew school. . . . But that was all we were allowed to do. We'd walk through the square and go straight on down to the synagogue and stay. **Evelyn (Ward) Karsman, 53**

I went to B.B. Jacob Synagogue. I went to Sunday School. I did not go to Hebrew school. . . . We had a confirmation. . . . We went every Sunday to Sunday School and we took the lessons and we had to do, it was like regular school, because we had to do essays and all sorts of things and we took tests. We were confirmed at thirteen. . . . Maier Rabhan was in our confirmation class and so was Sam Berliner. They were the only two boys. . . . They went to Sunday School as well as Hebrew school. They had *Bar Mitzvahs*. **Beatrice (Heyman) Goodman, 39**

We went to Hebrew school in the old B.B. Jacob on Montgomery. . . . They had classrooms downstairs and it was very comfortable. . . . We went to *shul*. My grandmother, Jennie Gottlieb, she encouraged me to go to *shul* every *Shabbes*; in fact, she used to leave money in my father's store; she would give him money every week and that was to encourage me to go to *shul* on *Shabbes*. . . . I enjoyed the Hebrew school. I had a teacher who I was very fond of, . . . Mr. [Rabbi Hirsch] Geffen. He taught me everything I know about how to *daven* and about going to *shul* and what you do in *shul*. He was my favorite teacher. **Alan Gottlieb, 40**

We always belonged to the B.B. Jacob. My grandfather was there. I remember going to *shul* with Grandpa. Of course, I took my *Bar Mitzvah* lessons from [Isaac] Fialkow and Albert Hornstein. We called it Fialkow's Hebrew Academy between us. I guess the best thing we learned at Fialkow's was how to play chess. I mean, if we played a good game of chess, we were good students. . . . At any rate, we got through all right. We got *Bar Mitzvahed*. **Murray Bono, 68**

In my estimation [the B.B.J. downtown] was very beautiful inside and there were many weddings, and they were always very beautiful. Ladies always dressed to the nines. If you did not have a new outfit to wear to synagogue on the high holy days, you were scorned. Everybody came with new hats of all types, whether they looked well or not, it was new. **Frances (Ehrlich) Rabhan, 21**

Where my mother sat in the synagogue on the lower balcony at B.B. Jacob, there were two . . . old ladies who sat in front of where my mother's seat was. And I used to always be fascinated on Yom Kippur because they would come to synagogue with, each of them had an orange that had been stuck all around and all over with whole cloves that they used to smell in order to revive themselves and to be able to survive the fast. **Doris (Goldin) Lukin, 88**

My father, he liked Rosh Hashanah, Yom Kippur. He couldn't go on Saturday 'cause he worked on Saturday, see. But he learned it and he liked it. So I went with him. I'll never forget when we went to Rosh Hashanah and I drove the car. . . . We were driving straight on Broughton Street . . . and Rabbi Rosenberg was walking, and Daddy was sitting by me, so when Daddy saw him he ducked to the floor. He didn't want the rabbi to see him. He was embarrassed, he fell on the floor. I'll never forget it. **Nathan Karnibad, 41**

My mother-in-law was always interested in the B. B. Jacob Sisterhood. In fact, she was the first president of the sisterhood. . . . Prior to that it had been called the Daughters of Jacob. When they changed it over, for some reason which I don't know, she became the first president. **Charlotte (Shipper) Garfunkel, 37**

The problem was we had a *cantor* by the name of Hirsch Geffen. He was there for many years. He was a wonderful *cantor*. It came time for his retirement and we were split like fifty-fifty because some members wanted to retain him and the others felt like he should go. So when it came to the high holidays, there was really a split down the middle. . . . But anyway, we ended up on East Victory Drive, I think it was called First Christian Church, for the services. We brought . . . our *Torah* there, I mean our *Torahs*. We had an assembly, about thirty or thirty-five people.

That's the only time I can remember a real split where they separated from the B.B. Jacob. The main purpose was, . . . the amount of the pension for Cantor Geffen was like a hundred dollars a month. Everybody at that time thought it was too much. . . . I'm talking about the era of like '47, '48, 1947, 1948. In the meantime, after the services and everybody got through the high holidays in separate locations, it became aware that Mr. Geffen was up in age and a hundred dollars a month wouldn't be too bad. In order to get the synagogue back together, they decided to go for that, which was twelve thousand [hundred] dollars a year. . . . To make a long story short, I never will forget, . . . Mr. Geffen lived to be about ninety-two years old, so in the long run he did quite well. **Herbert Blumenthal, 76**

Getting back to the *shul* thing, those numbers sound pretty high. I don't ever remember them giving him [Geffen] twelve thousand dollars a year. Maybe I'm wrong. I think it was like three thousand dollars a year or something like that. I remember later going to Richmond, Virginia, and Mr. Geffen was in a Jewish retirement home up there . . . and we went by to see him. At that time he was well into his nineties and he really wasn't at his best. . . . Even at three thousand dollars a year he was on pension for about thirty years or so. It was a very long time. **Marvin Arkin, 76**

The synagogue, . . . I recall it as a wooden building, in the same location on Montgomery near Broughton as the building exists there now, which was sold to another religious group. . . . We have now a magnificent building that is worth several millions of dollars, and it is very outstanding, and our congregation has always been maintained as the largest attended Jewish congregation strictly under Orthodox rabbinical supervision at services. **Louis Silverman, 29**

[B.B.J.] was cramped on Montgomery Street, and . . . south was the only place they could go. And it was a very . . . difficult task to raise the funds for the building, but it was very beautiful and very worthwhile. I remember the day that they moved, and they only wanted to bring the *Torahs* in a car that was not driven on *yom tov*. And that was no easy task. But they finally had enough cars to bring all the things, all the symbols, etc., to the synagogue. . . . The opening ceremony was so beautiful. You could see the men walking in with the *Torahs*, and the house was just packed. Everyone was so excited. It was such a wonderful and beautiful occasion. Of course, the women were all dressed to the nines, so were the gentlemen, and Rabbi Rosenberg, in his own inimitable fashion delivered the most eloquent address. **Frances (Ehrlich) Rabhan, 21**

Congregation B'nai B'rith Jacob Moves, 15 April 1962
Rabbi Rosenberg leads the procession from the Montgomery Street synagogue to the congregation's new home on Abercorn Street. Those pictured include: Melvin Sutker, Jeanette (Segall) Lipsitz, Sam Adler, Daniel Rabhan, Rabbi Abraham I. Rosenberg, Louis Wexler, Alvin Karsman, Louis Black, and Benjamin Portman.
JVM 003 Savannah Jewish Archives General Photograph Collection, Item 1925

[When] Mr. and Mrs. Sam Blumenthal died . . . they left a piece of property on the corner of Hall and Abercorn, . . . the southwest corner. . . . I guess he left it to the B.B. Jacob Synagogue to be used as a religious school. . . . The new B.B. Jacob was built without one single classroom. They did not put a classroom in that building because they were committed to the educational process taking place in the Alliance. **Alan Gottlieb, 40**

AGUDATH ACHIM

There was another group of men that came after 1900 and they didn't speak English very well and they didn't have much to say about the B.B. Jacob. So they decided that they were going to form their own little synagogue, and that was called the *Minyan*. They bought an empty store and they used to have the services . . . I believe, a block down from where the original first B.B. Jacob was. . . . From there that little group went to Drayton Street, and today it's called the Agudath Achim. It's run by the grandchildren and great grandchildren of these original Jews who built the "Little *Shul*." It was called the "Little *Shul*" and as it changed, it came to be called Agudath Achim. It turned Conservative although it was strictly Orthodox in 1906. . . .

They formed a separate synagogue because they didn't have any say-so with the B.B. Jacob. The B. B. Jacob was run by men who were already here and were established and they had the say-so, and I guess they felt they were Jewish-conscious, but they were what they call greenhorns; they were green, and they wanted to have a say-so, so they formed their own. **Lena (Feinberg) Rosenzweig, 26**

There was a lot of animosity in the B.B. Jacob, I understand. Some people that wanted to be the rulers of the thing and so they had an argument and that's why . . . the "Little *Shul*" was built. . . . It was just the B. B. Jacob first and then the "Little *Shul*" was formed after that. It was just a little *shul*. They had a downstairs and a little balcony upstairs. I can see it as if it was just yesterday. It was a darling little wooden *shul*, right on the lane before you get to Oglethorpe Avenue. **Evelyn (Ward) Karsman, 53**

I know the history of the synagogue but I don't remember my parents talking about it. I just know it through reading it. It was my understanding that we were an Orthodox synagogue when we were founded. Some of the members had become disgruntled with whatever was happening over at the B.B. Jacob and they decided to form their own synagogue and they, first they rented a room and then they rented a little . . . place where there was an auditorium and then they built the *shul* on Drayton Street. It was the first congregation in this area to become a Conservative synagogue. **Maxine "Midge" (Lasky) Schildkraut, 81**

My grandfather, Simon Mordecai Rubenstein was also one of the founders of the Agudath Achim Synagogue. It was called the "Little *Shul*." It was on Montgomery Street near Oglethorpe Avenue. It was on the right-hand side of the street when you left Broughton. **Evelyn (Ward) Karsman, 53**

The Conservative [synagogue] originally started in a very small way in a house about two blocks away from B. B. Jacob Synagogue on Montgomery Street. Then from there they moved to Drayton and put up a beautiful building. **Louis Silverman, 29**

Agudath Achim started several years after we came here. It finally moved to the old Lawton Memorial building which is now the Greek Orthodox Church, and they used that when Rabbi Labovitz was here. They used that for the synagogue for about three years, and then they built the building on Drayton Street. **Samuel Hirsch, 52**

I was *Bar Mitzvahed* in March of 1941 and in September of the same year the Agudath Achim congregation had built a synagogue. That was the synagogue on Drayton and Waldburg. That was their first high holiday celebration there. That's when my family moved from the old Orthodox synagogue and we joined the Conservative congregation. **Karl Friedman, 85**

The A.A. finally moved off of Montgomery Street to their first *shul* that they built when Sam Tenenbaum and the Tenenbaum family were responsible for getting this building up on Drayton Street opposite the Park Extension. From there, of course, they moved on further south. But the A.A. which was Orthodox along with the B.B., they became Conservative. . . . The people that were in the A.A., the members, they became Conservative because the *shul* became Conservative. **Samuel Radetsky, 45**

The benches in our . . . chapel [Agudath Achim], . . . all the benches came from the old synagogue. **Julius Rudikoff, 46**

We were a small congregation and we grew as time went on. Then the neighborhood became less than desirable and the city was moving to the south side anyway. And through the generosity of J. C. Lewis, the land was donated and the beautiful building we have now is the result of that. I have never belonged to any other synagogue. **Selma (Greenberg) Dunn, 7**

The A.A. was looking to build a synagogue. They found this lot on Lee Boulevard facing Abercorn that was available for sale. But they didn't have the money to buy it with. So Albert Tenenbaum . . . [who] was president of the A.A., . . . knew Curtis Lewis owned that lot. He goes to Mr. Lewis and says, "I know something you can do for Sam Steinberg. He's been with you all these years. He's handled everything that you wanted handled. You couldn't find a better employee, and the least you can do is to give 'em that lot to the synagogue in his honor." So he said, "Okay." . . . They raised the money to build the synagogue and I think they finally got it paid off but it took a long time.

Albert goes back to Mr. Lewis to tell him that the synagogue wanted to thank him for the gift of the lot for the new synagogue, but they have to have a parking place for the cars. . . . [Mr. Lewis said] okay, he'll do that too. . . . So he had plenty of land and he was able to, whenever he gave this to the synagogue, he was able to get them appraised and get a tax credit for whatever the value was for a charitable deduction. So it worked out good, for the synagogue and for him. He got the deduction and they got the land. **Sam Steinberg, 31**

Congregation Agudath Achim, 1965
Sam Steinberg (left) presents Mayor J. Curtis Lewis (right) a plaque in recognition of his gift of land for a new synagogue on Lee Boulevard. Looking on are Congregation President Karl Friedman and Albert Tenenbaum.
JVM 007 Congregation Agudath Achim Visual Materials Collection, Box 1, Folder 10, Item 14

The Agudath Achim always, from the inception of that building [in 1940] at least, permitted men and women to sit together. But on either side of the main sanctuary there was a raised section on each side about a foot off the floor, and many of the women sat there. Then there was a small balcony and some of the women actually sat there. . . . My father became president of the synagogue. My brother became president of the synagogue. Eventually I became president of the synagogue. I think we were the only members of that synagogue that had three presidents in the same family. **Erwin "Ernie" Friedman, 71**

The synagogue we belonged to was the Agudath Achim which was on Montgomery Street between Oglethorpe and York, and it was on the west side of the street. It was not a magnificent structure. It was strictly Orthodox. The women sat upstairs, the men downstairs. . . . The earliest religious person that I can remember was Reverend [Harry] Schatz and he was not a rabbi. . . . He could teach, he performed all the duties, but he was not an ordained rabbi. . . . He taught Hebrew School, he *davened*, he performed, he was a *shochet* also. And he performed everything in the synagogue that had to be performed. Synagogues were so poor they didn't have a rabbi. **Selma (Greenberg) Dunn, 7**

We went to Hebrew School and we formed a little group of, a crowd that went to Hebrew School and then also on Saturday mornings we would catch the bus, the Parkside bus was right out my back door, and we all would get on the bus at different stops and save seats for each other. Then we would go downtown to the Conservative synagogue and go to Saturday morning services. After services, we would all, as a group, walk downtown. **Phillipa "Bunny" (Sherman) Cohen, 90**

My father was one of those who was not particularly happy in the Orthodox synagogue, and I'm not really sure why. He was closely related in business and in personal friendship with the Tenenbaum family. Shortly after the congregation, the Conservative congregation, Synagogue Agudath Achim, was constructed in 1940 on Waldburg and Drayton Street, we, our family left the B.B. Jacob and my father became a member of the congregation of Agudath Achim. So my brother Karl was *Bar Mitzvahed* at B.B. Jacob, and I was *Bar Mitzvahed* at Agudath Achim. We have maintained our membership since then. . . .

[Irving] Gordon . . . was the first rabbi in the, what was then, the new building. Agudath Achim had occupied some other buildings but this was the first building that they owned. Had been built with funds that were raised, much of by the senior Samuel Tenenbaum who brought his three sons . . . in there with him. **Erwin "Ernie" Friedman, 71**

One of the founders [of the Agudath Achim] was my grandfather, [Jacob] Lasky. We were always members of Agudath Achim. . . . The synagogue was always a very important part of our lives. . . . I went to Hebrew School; Mrs. [Libby] Levine taught me in the afternoons. . . . The rabbi at that time was Rabbi Isidore Barnett. He asked me if I wanted to be *Bat Mitzvahed* or I wanted to be confirmed. So I chose to be *Bat Mitzvahed*. . . . That was one of the first *Bat Mitzvahs* that was done in the synagogue. We only did it on a Friday night. We did not do it on a Saturday morning and the only things I got to do was lead the service on Friday night and lead the *Haftarah*. . . .

I went to Hebrew School and Sunday School at the synagogue for six years. . . . The other thing, I guess, that I remember the most about *shul* was Rabbi Barnett demanded that everybody be very quiet during services. He would stop the service if people made noise. I mean, totally stop the service. **Maxine "Midge" (Lasky) Schildkraut, 81**

I went to the Agudath Achim Congregation on Waldburg and Drayton Street. . . . That's where we belonged. At that time we belonged to the Conservative synagogue. My father was very active in the synagogue and on Friday nights he always went to services and I enjoyed going with him. I think I got my spirituality from my father and probably also my mother's family in Atlanta because they were very religious and observant. **Phillipa "Bunny" (Sherman) Cohen, 90**

Congregation Agudath Achim's Golden Anniversary, 28 October 1951
Members of Agudath Achim celebrated the congregation's 50th Anniversary with a gala held at the Oglethorpe Hotel. Left to right: (front row) Lena (Feinberg) Rosenzweig, Raymond Rosen, Mildred (Goodman) Rosen, Rose Kronstadt, Sophie (Miller) Bodziner, and Philip Bodziner; (back row) Lee Barnett, Rabbi Isidore Barnett, out of town guest, William Wexler, Dorothy (Levy) Wexler, and Meyer Tenenbaum.
JVM 007 Congregation Agudath Achim Visual Materials Collection, Box 1, Folder 3, Item 6

They really had a wonderful choir and they didn't know Hebrew. I knew my mother had never known Hebrew, but she would sing phonetically, the Hebrew songs. And it was always the Jewish choir. It was not non-Jewish voices. It was Jewish people who always, just members of the congregation who would meet every week and rehearse and then that *Shabbat* they would perform.

Now, usually in that day, in those days, Friday night was the big service. Saturday morning was a service but not quite as well attended. People would go on Friday nights rather than Saturdays like they do nowadays. They had Junior Congregation every Saturday for the kids and I know the kids would get together, and we'd go to Junior Congregation and then we'd walk downtown and have lunch and go to a movie, not very religious but that's what they would do. **Maxine "Midge" (Lasky) Schildkraut, 81**

I think [Congregation Agudath Achim] was an offshoot of the B.B. [J.] The congregation was Orthodox. . . . It was not in the best of shape, and when they decided to build the synagogue and move to Drayton Street, we were still an Orthodox congregation. We still had a balcony, but instead of having all the women upstairs, on the side it was raised up a step, so the women sat on one side and the men sat on the other side. And then when, I think Abe Tenenbaum was instrumental in starting this Conservative movement, it did not work out. He formed, not he, some people formed a congregation called the Yeshurun which is where the present Greek Orthodox Church is. There was a rabbi, Labovitz, and he, apparently for lack of support money, I don't know, didn't work out. Rabbi Labovitz in turn became head of the J.E.A. **Selma (Greenberg) Dunn, 7**

That [Agudath Achim] was like a . . . Socialist synagogue. Those people were really working people and you know, I think we got a workmen's credit union and that developed from those people who . . . generally ran stores on West Broad Street. They were tailors, they were shoemakers, and they were a little, leaned a little towards Communism. You know, they believed this country was good but they thought you should share with everybody as Socialism does. There were very few young kids that went there. It was mostly some of the old people that came from Europe. **Harriet (Kanter) Konter, 43**

[Yeshurun] actually would have been the fourth congregation. . . . That was really the beginning of the Conservative movement. . . . My father was opposed because he was a very Orthodox man. But the majority went out and we became a Conservative synagogue. **Selma (Greenberg) Dunn, 7**

RELIGIOUS OBSERVANCES

KEEPING KOSHER

I knew non-kosher food existed, but I did never partook because I figured if I did I was gonna keel over. **Selma (Greenberg) Dunn, 7**

As far as the Orthodox is concerned, I've lived, as I said, ninety-nine years. In that ninety-nine years I've never had an occasion to go into a *trayf* restaurant and order a meal. I have lived through nothing but strictly Orthodox observances as my mother taught us, may she rest in peace, and my wife Ruth, she observed when we got married and before we got married. It was understood that we would have to maintain our home just as we were accustomed to it with our parents.

Orthodox living, from a religious point of view, does not change. The change is in the individual who chooses to break away and live a more relaxed type of life and not feel that he is rigidly bound down as some do. Those of us who continue to observe don't feel any inhibitions about it. We feel the same freedom as the one that doesn't observe anything. So it is no hardship on us and there will never be any changes from the real strict Orthodox Jew. **Louis Silverman, 29**

I had them [my children] all at home, because I couldn't eat the food at the hospital. It wasn't kosher and I was quite strict about the food. **Lena (Feinberg) Rosenzweig, 26**

We had about four kosher butchers here, . . . late '20s and the '30s, something like that. And we also had about five or six *shochets*. We also had *mohels* here. We didn't have to import a *mohel* for a circumcision. We had them right here in Savannah. . . . That's because everybody that was Jewish wanted to keep a kosher house. **Samuel Radetsky, 45**

I remember Mr. [Moses L.] Kaplan very well, . . . he killed the livestock and chickens to see that they were kosher. . . . He was a *mohel*, . . . he conducted the circumcisions. **Sidney Raskin, 23**

My father used to take the chickens, and took them to the *shochet* in the City Market, . . . Mr. [Moses L.] Kaplan, who was also the *mohel*, and a big treat was to go to the City Market—it was actually a beehive of activity. I remember Mr. [Morris] Levine was a kosher butcher. Mr. [Samuel] Friedman was a kosher butcher. There was a lady, after the *shochet* slaughtered the chicken, then you went downstairs and there was a lady, her name was Mrs. [Yetta] Davis. Mrs. Davis used to pick the chickens.

And then when my father brought the chickens home, of course there was pin feathers, and so you took the chicken and you held it over a flame to sort of get all the pin feathers off. Then there was a board . . . and you had to kosher it. And the same thing applied to meat. Once you brought it home from the butcher, you put it on the board and you put coarse salt. And as children we all ran out of the kitchen. We found it gross. **Selma (Greenberg) Dunn, 7**

I went with Mama to the chicken store on Congress Street, and she'd go in and feel the chickens in the coop . . . feel how fat they were. . . . Then we would take those chickens over to the City Market downstairs and let the *shochet* kill 'em, . . . they would kill 'em a certain way. And then he had somebody there that would pluck out most of the feathers after he killed the chickens. I remember Mama paying him a nickel to kill, . . . then they would wrap it up good. . . . They would finish cleaning them at home and then you had to burn the pinfeathers off on the gas stove. . . . I remember her opening the chickens and getting the little yellow eggs from inside and she would cook the eggs in the soup. Oh, everything was so delicious. **Bertha (Plotkin) Freedman, 8**

My father had *shmiches*, that means that he was considered an Orthodox rabbi. . . . When he came to the United States and he saw so much going on where they would not practice Judaism properly and he was asked to certify certain products as kosher for Passover. When he saw that they weren't properly kosher for Passover and different things, he got very upset with the whole system and he moved away from it and got into business.

We still maintained a quite traditional home. I went to *Talmud Torah* at a very young age and we observed practically, I guess we observed all of the holidays. I was brought up in, what I would call, a very good Jewish tradition, observing the holidays, just a little cycle of holidays, Rosh Hashanah, Yom Kippur, Succoth. **Norton Melaver, 15**

Sabbath Table, n.d.
This demonstration depicts a table ready to greet the Sabbath.
JVM 052 Abraham I. Rosenberg Photographs, Box 1, Folder 2, Item 1

My mother lived with her aunt after her mother passed away and she was always trying to get . . . *Tante* [Etta] Cuba . . . to come to Savannah, and she would never come because we didn't keep kosher. One day I came home from school and I found my mother out in the backyard and she had the silverware in the dirt. I said, "What are you doing?" She said, "Well, I'm koshering the silverware.". . .

I know Jackie Gleason, or one of those guys on T.V., made a story out of this and they said . . . a joke about somebody was outside in the middle of the night doing this and the neighbors called the police, and I thought, well, at least my mother wasn't out there in the middle of the night. **Phillipa "Bunny" (Sherman) Cohen, 90**

We kept a kosher home. My grandparents wouldn't think of eating anything not kosher or letting anything not kosher in the house. Anything that wasn't kosher we ate on the back porch. . . . I got very sick; I was in the hospital for about three months. Which was something that today would be a nothing; they'd give you an antibiotic. But the doctor prescribed that I should have oxtail soup. . . . My grandmother thought chicken soup would do it, but the doctor said it was oxtail soup.

What we did, they bought an extra set of dishes for me, an extra set of everything so they could make the oxtail soup, so I could have oxtail soup and get well. Eventually I got well, so I guess it worked. **Murray Bono, 68**

DEATH

Jews handle their own dead, they prepare them for burial, and having the *[Bnos] Hesed Shel Emeth*, which is the ladies' organization, means that no Jewish female . . . is handled by any men; they are handled completely and solely by the women who wash them, clothe them and prepare them for their last rites. **Benjamin Silverman, 29**

I remember that when people died, they didn't go to the undertaker. They were washed at home and the body was placed on the floor and covered with a sheet. When it was time for the funeral, the undertaker would bring the coffin to the house and the body was put in it. I remember many times it was taken into the synagogue if the person was a religious person. **Lena (Feinberg) Rosenzweig, 26**

The *Chevra Kedisha* is the men's burial society and the *[Bnos] Hesed Shel Emeth* is the women's. . . . They have a committee in the *[Bnos] Hesed Shel Emeth* that will come to the home and arrange a meal for the family after the burial and when they come back, and they'll do everything they can to make it comfortable for them and to let them know that they are not alone. . . . That is one of the finest of services, it is a *mitzvah*; the biggest *mitzvah* that you can perform is to help someone during their time of trouble. **Louis Silverman, 29**

We washed the dead. I washed the dead for twenty-seven years under the supervision of Mrs. Eugenie Garfunkel. She married a Savannah man. She wasn't a Savannah woman, but she did the work and she did it until she died. **Lena (Feinberg) Rosenzweig, 26**

I know now the [death] shrouds are bought from a concern that makes them in New York, but many years ago I remember when they would call me at Sunday or Saturday night or something else if someone had passed away, and I would go down to either Slotin & Company or Kahn & Company and buy a bolt of linen, and then go around and pick up some of the ladies that would help them, Ms. [Eunice] Steinberg, Ms. [Fannie] Rabhan, Ms. Blum. . . . They would sit down and they would cut out the linen and sit there and sew it, . . . [a] shroud for the body. **Benjamin Garfunkel, 9**

At the time Sipple's Mortuary was on the corner of Jones and Bull streets, and the limousine would come and pick up the ladies that were involved and take them there, and that's where they performed the last rites for the burial. When Sipple's moved out here, by that time, unfortunately, there was one of the ladies who had passed away. There were just a handful.

And I wasn't elected to any office, I was "willed" the office. My Aunt Eugenie [Garfunkel] was very insistent. . . . It took a lot of years before she could get me to go with her or even get near it. **Charlotte (Shipper) Garfunkel, 37**

When you're sitting *shivah*, friends come to visit you to limit the grief that you are undergoing and to help you overcome your trials and tribulations, which is a wonderful thing, and that was just as much practiced sixty, seventy-five, eighty years ago as it is today. **Louis Silverman, 29**

The mourner sits lower than everybody else and there are actually mourners' chairs that you can buy that are lower chairs in which they sit, and that is the reason for sitting on a bench or a crate or something like that. . . . But the mourning itself goes way back into the Bible where they tore their garments and they sat in sack cloth, they sat on the ground, and I think it dates further back than we know. **Benjamin Silverman, 29**

[The building at Bonaventure Cemetery] was deeded by a Wilensky family to the *Bnos Hesed Shel Emeth*, that's the women's burial society. It had been terribly vandalized back in 1972. . . . We found out that according to the deed, if we ever tore the building down, it reverted back to the city.

So, with the help of the *Chevra Kedisha* from both the B.B. Jacob and the Agudath Achim, we revitalized the building. And it is used from time to time by families . . . if the weather is really bad. . . . I think that it was used before they used the mortuaries. **Charlotte (Shipper) Garfunkel, 37**

MISCELLANEOUS

There was a *mikveh* on President Street that was very near the B.B. Jacob, just around the corner I would say. The City of Savannah bought up all the property in that particular block so that they could make a parking lot there. When my father-in-law had built the house on Hall Street, he made a *mikveh* for my mother-in-law. . . . Then, when the B.B. Jacob Synagogue was built out in this section, the *mikveh* did not belong to any synagogue as far as I know, but I know that this particular *mikveh* belongs to the *Bnos Hesed Shel Emeth*. That's the women's burial society. We bought the house, we built the *mikveh* in it, and that is the one that is used today. And we will continue to use it. **Charlotte (Shipper) Garfunkel, 37**

My grandfather started the first daily *minyan* in Savannah, and my father told me that when he and his brother were boys, seven and eight years of age, they would go around knocking on the doors at six o'clock in the morning to try to get men together so they could have a *minyan*. **Benjamin Garfunkel, 9**

Tu B'Shevat, 2 February 1958
Planting a tree to celebrate the holiday are Leslie (Gordon) Leland, Barbara (Ginsberg) Tanenbaum, Nancy (Asher) Bracker, Abro Sutker, Sherry (Safer) Warsaw, and Barbara (Seeman) Gottlieb.
JVM 003 Savannah Jewish Archives General Photograph Collection, Item 0567

When my Aunt Eugenie [Garfunkel] came to Savannah as a bride, her father . . . saw that there was no public *mikveh*, went back to New York to his own family, got funds to build a public *mikveh* for the women in Savannah, and the first *mikveh* was built on Zubly Street. **Charlotte (Shipper) Garfunkel, 37**

I remember when we moved to Gwinnett Street and my grandfather couldn't walk so well and we wanted to go to *shul*, but in those days you don't drive to *shul*, you walked to *shul*. If you drove to *shul*, you stopped two blocks from the *shul* — you'd get as close to the *shul* as where you could walk in. So . . . my mama would drive us to maybe Broughton Street and Barnard Street, and we would walk the rest of the way. **Murray Bono, 68**

When he [my husband Benny] first went into the service and they'd fall out for reveille, he would always go back into the barracks to *daven*. He was the only Jewish fellow in that barracks and a couple of the fellows wanted to know what he did. "Why don't you go to breakfast?". . . And he had them open their own Bibles to show them where and what and how he was praying.

From that time on, as long as he was stationed there, as soon as reveille, as soon as they broke to go to the mess hall, these boys stood guard outside so that he could *daven* and they waited for him. **Charlotte (Shipper) Garfunkel, 37**

I remember, when we lived on the four hundred block of Broughton Street, there was a Jewish doctor. His name was Fischer, and he lived in Yamacraw, on Fahm Street. He didn't have a car. He'd come in on a bicycle to the four hundred block, and the mothers would bring the children, and he would vaccinate us. . . .

Mothers gave birth, but they never used a doctor. Most of them, the majority of them, used a mid-wife. . . . Of course, when a bride was going to get married, I remember that all the brides fasted the day of their wedding. . . . There were one or two that married out of the faith. . . . And when they did marry out of the faith, the family would sit *shivah*. **Lena (Feinberg) Rosenzweig, 26**

We had a double wedding. So we got married in December of 1956, . . . here in Savannah at the old B.B. Jacob Synagogue. And I think it was one of the few double weddings they've ever had, and it was some custom that the older one had to get married first. So I got married first and then the time elapsed so, somehow, it was after dark and so it would mean the next day. So I was the matron of honor for my sister, at her wedding, right there in the same spot. . . .

Our reception was in the new J.E.A. It was open only about a year or so before we had our wedding reception at the J.E.A. That was a nice occasion. All of my family came in from different places. All of my aunts and uncles from Chicago and different places so we had a very nice weekend. Then we all went back to college. **Suzanne (Ginsberg) Kantziper, 84**

We observed the holidays, positively. The fact is, in the very beginning we used to have non-Jewish friends come in at night to turn off our lights or turn them on. No, turn them off before we went to bed. That's how, really and truly, we followed the laws in those days. . . . We weren't *shomer Shabbes*, because after all we had to make a living. **Samuel Radetsky, 45**

We kept a kosher house, but my father worked on Saturday, as I think everybody else did. But we walked from 35ᵗʰ Street to Broughton Street on holidays. . . . I don't think we were as observant as some of these young people now are getting, and I admire it. **Betty (Blumenthal) Cantor, 66**

At that time [1911, 1912], the majority of the people were . . . strictly kosher. . . . Most of the mothers attended the *mikveh*. . . . On the block where we lived, on the Sabbath, only two stores closed Saturday. It was Gittelsohn's Delicatessen, and my parents always kept the store closed on *Shabbes*. **Lena (Feinberg) Rosenzweig, 26**

Never any question about if I was Jewish. [My parents] kept kosher and we had *Seders*. . . . My mother had a, I guess you'd call it a broom closet today, and in that broom closet she had like five or six charity boxes, which they used to call *pushkes* and on *Shabbes*, before *Shabbes*, she would put money in the *pushke*. Well, about twice a year these men would come around to get the money out of the *pushke*. **Anchel Samuels, 86**

HOLIDAYS

The Jewish community was small and it was very much a part of your life style. You know we didn't get diverted. Every kid I know of stayed home for every holiday that was Jewish. If you went, that was the big disgrace. If it was Purim or Succoth . . . you stayed home and the school system understood that. And you did go to synagogue. You were expected to go. **Harriet (Kanter) Konter, 43**

We observed all the Jewish holidays. We always had Yom Kippur and *Seder* at my grandmother's. . . . She had a large house and would have all of her children and grandchildren, and it was really nice. It was lots of fun. **Elizabeth "Libby" (Levy) Price, 69**

My parents always closed [their grocery store] for Rosh Hashanah, Yom Kippur, and all the major Jewish holidays. . . . The cooks, the women who worked for Jewish households, the cooks knew what was coming because they probably prepared the foods, like *gefilte fish* and *tzimmas*. **Suzanne (Ginsberg) Kantziper, 84**

People used to walk to *shul* on *yom tov* and walk back and forth and some of them used to take a place at the hotel for Rosh Hashanah so they wouldn't have to do all that walking back and forth. **Samuel Radetsky, 45**

Many people who lived more towards the Southside, you know, they wouldn't ride on *yom tov* or on the *Shabbes*, especially on the holidays. I know, Rosh Hashanah and Yom Kippur, many of them would stay in the hotel; Savannah Hotel was there on Bull Street between Congress and Congress Lane. . . . They would stay there during the high holy holidays. They would rent a room there and just walk from Bull Street to the synagogue. **Samuel Plotkin, 8**

PESACH

My grandmother was born in Hungary and she was a very, very religious woman, and I grew up in a house that was Orthodox, kosher. We observed all the holidays. My grandmother, about two months before Passover, would clean the house, including [with] the feather, and that you dust, that you took the *hametz* up with. . . . That is a custom, you clean out the corners in case you have missed some *hametz*. . . . We changed dishes for Passover. We strictly observed Passover and we had an icebox that was only used for Passover. Never used any other time of the year. **Selma (Greenberg) Dunn, 7**

[My mother] did Passover and did everything you were supposed to do. . . . She was just an excellent cook. On Passover, I still can see the cakes lined up. She would make these sponge cakes, different kinds, and just line them up on the table. Each one prettier than the other. **Audrey (Galkin) Levin, 89**

While the Workmen's Circle didn't specifically dwell on the religious days that we have in the Jewish religion, we knew by the smells in the house. Passover, we knew that the *gefilte fish* that Mama used to make. We [they] were very Jewish, my parents, although they didn't go to synagogue much. **Gertrude (Scheer) Barr, 1**

Never had a *Seder* at home. But we had the community *Seders* at the Temple and we participated there. So I was introduced to that. Later, as a married woman, [I] was invited to a *Seder* at Rabbi Starrels' home in addition to the one at Temple. Found it such a delightful custom that we always had one after that. **Barbara (Smith) Levy, 19**

I remember getting the dishes and silverware ready for Pesach. We didn't have a lot of silver. You know, we would kosher our silver for Pesach. We didn't have a separate set of Pesach silver, so Mama would have a special pot and we tied the silver up with a cord and dipped it into the pot, the very boiling water, and then you put it under the cold water, and then you'd dry it, with a clean dish towel. . . . Then the dishes, she had two big pans on the . . . dining room table, . . . and we'd bring the dishes in and wash 'em. Now we had separate Pesach dishes, but silverware you could kosher. **Bertha (Plotkin) Freedman, 8**

On Pesach we used to take the pail there [to the Meddins] and they'd put the milk in the pail because it had to be kosher. **Anne (Lewis) Buchsbaum, 2**

ROSH HASHANAH AND YOM KIPPUR

When we had Yom Kippur and Rosh Hashanah, Broughton Street and West Broad Street, which were occupied by the stores that were owned by Jewish merchants, were closed. It was like a holiday for everybody because of the Jewish souls observing the high holidays. **H. Sol Clark, 5**

For the holidays, we lived so far and we wanted to walk, we couldn't walk, so we would go downtown and stay at the Hotel Savannah. All the Jews did that lived far out. You'd go and we'd always buy new clothes and new shoes and new stockings. I mean, everything new. And we stayed at the hotel. That was a big treat for us. **Annette (Berman) Gray, 87**

In my day, Rosh Hashanah and Yom Kippur were very, were observed. If you walked down Broughton Street, every Jewish store was closed. **Selma (Greenberg) Dunn, 7**

When the Jewish holidays came, Rosh Hashanah and Yom Kippur, Broughton Street in effect was closed up because seventy-five or eighty percent of the stores were Jewish owned. **Martin Karp, 42**

We would walk from 36th Street otherwise, but for Yom Kippur [the adults] would come downtown after supper and we would get them into the Savannah Hotel. We'd get a room for them. They never brought anything. They slept, I guess they'd take their dresses off and whatever they had on, and the next morning they'd get up because they didn't eat or wash or – you know, you didn't do that on Yom Kippur. And they'd put their clothes on and walk over to the *shul*. And they'd be in *shul* all day. But for Rosh Hashanah everybody would walk to *shul* together down Montgomery Street, on that rickety brick sidewalk, and think nothing of it. And we all wore high heels. I don't know how we didn't break our ankles. **Bertha (Plotin) Freedman, 8**

My family was Orthodox, and they did keep a kosher home, and all the friends I knew at that time kept kosher homes. And [my father] would say, along with most of the parents, that if you bought your tickets to the movies before Rosh Hashanah, then you could walk downtown and go to the movies in the afternoon.

And that's what, and I'm talking about now, fourteen, fifteen year olds. We would then walk home from synagogue. We had the Rosh Hashanah meal, and then we would meet and walk down Bull Street, all these kids down Bull Street, all the way to Broughton Street, where that's the only place there were theatres. And have our tickets in advance, and go to the movies, then walk back home. And we thought nothing of it. . . .

I can remember when Yom Kippur came, when my parents got older, they would rent a hotel room and that was very common, at the Savannah Hotel, so that they could walk to synagogue. . . . On Bull . . . right off of Broughton, was the Savannah Hotel. It's where the First City Club is now. . . . It was Yom Kippur and they didn't eat, and they would spend the night downtown the night before and stay the whole time until Yom Kippur was over. **Harriet (Kanter) Konter, 43**

I want to make mention of the fact that in later years when many Jews had moved more to the Southside and walking to the synagogue on Rosh Hashanah and Yom Kippur became a hardship, we very often had someone sleeping in our house during the nights of those holidays because our house was still located where people could walk to the synagogue. In those days, of course, those people who lived in the country, towns around Savannah, who did not have family or places where they could stay, they would go to the hotel and sleep over and then they would be able to walk to the synagogue. **Doris (Goldin) Lukin, 88**

Between Rosh Hashanah and Yom Kippur there is a custom and it is called *shlogn kapores*. . . . There were certain prayers to be said and the chicken was swung over your head, yelling and screaming. . . . So all the *kapores* was supposed to be going in that chicken . . . and then that chicken was given away to a non-Jew. **Selma (Greenberg) Dunn, 7**

Before the high holidays Mother used to get live chickens and would tie the legs together and would say a prayer as she waved the chicken over your head. . . . That chicken was supposed to be a sacrifice for you just like in the Old Temple when you brought your sacrifice to the Temple, you brought a sheep or a goat, and that is where the word "scapegoat" comes from because that is the sacrifice. . . . I don't know of anybody that does this custom any more unless it is the rabbis. **Benjamin Silverman, 29**

The only time that we went to the river was Rosh Hashanah, the afternoon of Rosh Hashanah, to throw the stones in the water. **Fannie (Center) Kramer, 10**

When my kids came along they had a thing called the, instead of the Super Bowl, they had the Rosh Hashanah Bowl behind the J.E.A. And they allowed them to do that, and they played touch football and it got to be a big thing. Every kid, when they left synagogue and after they went home and had their dinner, they went over to the J.E.A. that afternoon and that was permissible. **Harriet (Kanter) Konter, 43**

Chanukah

I remember . . . having *latkes* for Chanukah. . . . We didn't get all the presents that they get now for Chanukah, but just having *latkes* with applesauce and sour cream was just wonderful. I don't know, Mama made all the traditional foods that *Ashkenazi* Jews made. **Norton Melaver, 15**

In those days we didn't give gifts [for Chanukah]. The children wore . . . a little cloth sack that had a ribbon go through it . . . and you wore that for the whole time. For the eight days you wore that, and anybody that wanted to give you Chanukah *gelt* would open up your little bag and put money in it. This is what I remember wearing, the little cloth bag. And mama used to make them for all of us, and then, of course, when my children were born, she made them for my children. **Bertha (Plotkin) Freedman, 8**

My grandfather was not a wealthy man. I remember well as a child on Chanukah my brother and I got a gift from him and that gift was a nickel. That was our Chanukah gift. 'Course back in the 1930s and '40s you could buy something with a nickel. **Karl Friedman, 85**

Chanukah was not the commercial venture it is today. No way. There was no such thing as eight presents. You lit the candles and we got nickels, dimes, or pennies, or whatever it was, that was Chanukah *gelt*. There was no, what I call commercialization of Chanukah. **Selma (Greenberg) Dunn, 7**

Succoth

My father used to build a *succah* in our backyard on 36th Street, and my brother Jake used to go out and help him. He would just get slats of wood and put 'em together, and then he covered the top, you know, with the slats. . . . And they put a table and benches out there. Mama, I remember, handing all the fresh fruit. . . . And we always had our meals out there during Succoth. **Bertha (Plotkin) Freedman, 8**

PURIM

We had the services at the synagogue, but then, after that, any sort of celebration like the Purim Ball we used to have every year. I don't remember when it started, but the Hebrew Women's Aid used to have a Purim Ball every year and it was a ball in every sense of the word. They had the Purim Queen, the Purim King, and they had this big affair at the J.E.A., and the Grand March, and everybody came in costume, and it was wonderful. **Frances (Ehrlich) Rabhan, 21**

Purim Carnival, 21 March 1954
Candidates for Queen Esther and her court in 1954 included (left to right): (front row) Arthur Geffen and Harvey Sussman; (center row) Shirley (Lefko) Cohen, Arlene (Gottlieb) Jaffie, Linda (Rosen) Palefsky Cranman, Arlene (Bracker) Lischkoff, Betty Judy (Homansky) Kaye, and Sherry (Kantsiper) Gold; (back row) Abram Rubin, Tanya (Lefko) Berman, Sandra (Rosen) Luxemberg, Deanne (Javetz) Levine Whitlock, Barbara (Tenenbaum) Hacken, Delores (Lehwald) Kaminsky, Ruth (Mincey) Markowitz, Davida (Tenenbaum) Deutsch, Walter Rabhan, and Susan (Reiner) Lourie.
JVM 003 Savannah Jewish Archives General Photograph Collection, Item 0518

YIDDISH SCHOOL

I am Sam Plotkin, and we're going to speak about the Arbeiter Ring *Yiddish* School that I went to when I was possibly thirteen, maybe fourteen, years old, which would have been in 1928 or '29, and we were the first students . . . of the school when it started. It was started by the Workmen's Circle and . . . it was held on West Broad Street, on the corner of Perry Lane, above Mr. I. Center's store. . . . Everything we learned to read and write [was] *Yiddish*, Jewish literature.

We had plays during the holidays and on other occasions. Everything was spoken in *Yiddish*, all the classes. . . . The Arbeiter Ring means Workmen's Circle. The meetings were held also in this building. As far as the school is concerned, I don't recall just exactly how many days a week we went to the school. But I went for at least two, three years, and when I graduated, the school continued—how many years, I really have no idea at all.

Well, it was important to the parents, the parents of this organization, so their children, their offspring, would be educated in reading and writing and whatever other subjects that we were taught in *Yiddish*. Although many of us came from the first generation of immigrants that came to this country, and *Yiddish* was spoken, but reading and writing was something that . . . we had had, and these schools were throughout the country. **Samuel Plotkin, 8**

When I became of school age, there was a choice made that I would go to the Workmen's Circle, to the Arbeiter Ring, rather than go to traditional Hebrew school. I did. It was designed, basically, like traditional Hebrew school in that it was after school. . . . What we did was we basically learned *Yiddish*. We learned the alphabet, which is the same as Hebrew, and we learned how to read and write. As you progressed in school, you were introduced to poetry and the great *Yiddish* writers and . . . small short stories and what have you. . . .

I do want to mention . . . two of the teachers that . . . I had, that was David Rossi . . . [and] Mr. Platt. The reason I mention them and others, like Paul Kulick, who was also very active, 'cause the organization and . . . how they were viewed in terms of being on the periphery, really, of the Jewish community. . . . Many of them were traditional Jews who continued with *Yiddishkeit* and sent children to Hebrew school before *Bar Mitzvah* age. But many of them just never bothered. But also they were very much a political organization. They all read the *Forward* [newspaper] in *Yiddish* every single day. There was always news about this branch in the *Forward* when people were honored here, and they were honored and recognized nationally. It was a major, major center for activity. . . .

I resented people's attitude with regard to . . . what I had been educated into. And there was . . . a lot of criticism by peers about not having gone to Hebrew school, about having a non-*Bar Mitzvah Bar Mitzvah* in *Yiddish*, which I did. . . .

I was *Bar Mitzvahed* in *Yiddish*. . . . I literally got up and spoke before a very large group of people in a restaurant here. . . . We knew Rabbi Rosenberg . . . and [my mother] invited [him]. . . . I must tell you that the only person that showed up was Rabbi Rosenberg, and I will never forget it as long as I live. Not only did he show up, I remember him sitting there with a glass plate eating an egg and having fruit, and getting up at the table and speaking in *Yiddish* to the group. It endeared him to me forever, let me tell you. **Robert Friedman, 38**

Some people used to think that [Workmen's Circle] was a Communist oriented organization. . . . I never [thought so]. We put on plays, all in *Yiddish*, our recitations in *Yiddish*. It was just a study of the language, being able to write it, read it and speak it. . . . My father was one of the organizers and Mr. [Harry] Applebaum and Mr. [Hyman] Hoffman, . . . all of these are Workmen's Circle. We had our affairs, it was our, it was a Workmen's Circle peak. The name will tell you what it was. People of workers. And that's why they thought it was a Communist organization. . . . It was activist. . . . It was Socialism in its finest form, which I agree with. . . .

We had our meetings and our classes above a store, the entrance was in a lane. . . . There was a little stage there and we had guests. It was a regular school. I graduated from there. I was the youngest one in the class. I guess they didn't have enough, I was put in a higher grade. There weren't too many my age. . . . The organization was made up of workers, laborers, a lot of them. Not so many had stores, or they had a store they worked themselves. . . . I think that a lot of them from the Workmen's Circle originated from Russia and they were poor as church mice, very poor. . . . Most of the people that were members of the Workmen's Circle lived in the poorer sections. **Gertrude (Scheer) Barr, 1**

I was born in 1928. I remember attending the *shule*. I started there when I was six years old. The building was over Mr. Center's store. . . . I remember the Jewish typewriter that used to sit on the table right outside the office. . . . Every Sunday night the women, the wives of the men who had children there at the school and belonged to the Workmen's Circle, they used to prepare a Sunday night supper. And there was always this soup, . . . it was a *milchik* soup. And I don't know what they put in it but it was always so delicious. . . .

All the adults spoke in *Yiddish* to one another, of course, but the children, you know, still spoke English. And they had plays for all the holidays, for Purim, for Chanukah. . . . I also remember the picnics, we always had picnics at Tybee. And then there was also like a country club out near Thunderbolt. . . . We moved on my tenth birthday, and we moved out to 36th Street. Well, I didn't want to attend *shule* anymore because it was too far to go. And I tell you, to this day I don't know how I got down there, because Papa used to call everyday when I came from school to make sure that I went to *shule*, because he was determined all of his children were gonna know how to read, write, and speak *Yiddish*, which we all do. **Bertha (Plotkin) Freedman, 8**

Workmen's Circle, c.1950s
Shown left to right are (seated) Becky (Birnbaum) Dinerman, unidentified, Rebecca (Shapiro) Rubnitz, and Dora (Berkowitz) Grossman; (standing) Mary (Cooper) Kaplan Swadlow, Sarah (Dunitz) Dunn, Aaron Udinsky, Sidney Paderewski, Leon Cooper, Rose (Garfinkel) Hoffman, and Annie (Udinsky) Cooper.
JVM 003 Savannah Jewish Archives General Photograph Collection, Item 1827

Now, what was also very special about [my grandparents] was that they were Socialists. They brought Socialism into nationalism with them. Certainly my grandfather did. He hated the Communists because his father had been murdered in their own home and the rest of the family escaped, but he was an internationalist. He . . . was instrumental in the development of the Arbeiter Ring, Workmen's Circle branch here in Savannah, which was an organization that wasn't just international in scope, but it was an organization that was devoted to the continuity of *Yiddishkeit*, meaning the *Yiddish* language, drama, poetry, history.

There was a very large group of people in Savannah, many of whom lived, worked I guess, originally on what is now Martin Luther King Boulevard. . . . We moved here when I was about five. By the time I was school age, I used to join my parents and my grandparents on Sundays; it was a huge communal meal that was . . . prepared by a couple of women in the Workmen's Circle. The organization and the *shule*, the school, was housed above Mr. Center's store. Mr. Center had a dry goods store on West Broad and Perry Lane. **Robert Friedman, 38**

Quite a few Jewish people in Savannah weren't connected with any synagogue. . . . You heard about the Arbeiter Ring? . . . A lot of people in Workmen's Circle who actually weren't supposed to believe in God but still had that little attachment in there. And people who hadn't been here very long or just neglect to join synagogues, they'd get together and some traveling rabbi or *chazan* would come through and they would set up chairs and have services. **Samuel Hirsch, 52**

JEWISH EDUCATION

I went to a young Israel *minyan* to say *Kaddish* in Miami, and there was a man that was very nice to me, . . . and I asked someone whether I could give him something. . . . [I was told] if I wanted to do something for him that I should make a donation to the Hebrew Academy of Miami, that he was interested in the day school they had started in Miami. . . . He said that the only way he would accept the check would be if I would take it to the school. He wanted me to see the school. . . . So we drove down to 8th Street and saw the school, and met a man by the name of Lauer, and he told us that he started the school. He said, "If you want to start a school," in his words, "the first thing you do is kidnap four children and you lock 'em in a room and you start a school." . . .

So we came back home all enthused and we decided we were gonna start a day school in Savannah. . . . Rabbi Rosenberg had been away, and he called my wife . . . and my wife said, "Rabbi, we're gonna start a day school." And he said, "Yes, someday we'll have a day school in Savannah." And she said, "No, Rabbi, this year." So we started out, I think, we started with either eight or ten children in a first grade, and we had quite a job. At that time B.B. Jacob had a Hebrew school on Hall and Abercorn Street, and we had quite a fight with the Orthodox synagogue. They didn't want any part of a day school, didn't even want to let us use a room in the building. We finally got 'em to where they agreed to let us use a room in the building for the first grade.

We only had one class, and we had no teachers, no Hebrew teachers, that were employed. We had an English teacher and Rabbi [Bernard] Jacobson. . . . Rabbi Jacobson, and Sam Rosenberg, and his wife, the three of 'em taught the

Hebrew studies at the school, and they were not paid for their services; they did it all gratis to help to try to get a school started and get it going. . . . The second year Jack Kiel was really the leader, and he brought Rabbi [Moshe] Possick here to be the principal and teach. **Benjamin Garfunkel, 9**

Two rooms in that building [the B.B.J. Synagogue] were classrooms. One room, the large room, was held for services. That's where the school was. You'd spend an hour, an hour and fifteen minutes. At that time the Jewish community could not afford many teachers. They had to bring a guy down from New York and pay him a salary. **Fred Rotkow, 27**

[At Mickve Israel Sunday School] we learned the Ten Commandments and we learned, we read the Bible, and of course like most children, we looked for the salacious passages. **Marion (Abrahams) Levy Mendel, 17**

Bureau of Jewish Education, 1956
Students pose for a class photo on the grounds of the J.E.A. with the legendary world globe south of DeRenne Avenue shown in the background.
JVM 003 Savannah Jewish Archives General Photograph Collection, Item 1817

I went to *cheder*, . . . we also had Sunday School on Sunday. . . . The *cheder* was held in the A.A. Synagogue on Montgomery Street. Sunday School was held at the B.B. Jacob on Sunday morning. Our teachers were all volunteers and we had a great Sunday School. . . .
When I graduated from the A.A.'s *cheder*, I went to Mr. [Isaac] Fialkow, who was located on Barnard Street between Gaston and the next street down south. And we had quite a contingent there. Everything was held upstairs in their home on the second floor and, of course, I didn't have a bicycle. So when I used to get to *cheder* at Mr. Fialkow's, I got there a little ahead of time and borrowed bicycles

like the Meddins' or the Slotins' or somebody and I went riding in the Park Extension. And God forbid if I got there a little late or the class got through earlier, I caught plenty of hell when I got back to Mr. Fialkow's for my lesson. **Samuel Radetsky, 45**

I went to Hebrew School . . . four or five days a week. I don't know that anybody remembers this, but I think he was the rabbi there - his name was Dr. [Rabbi Leonard] Palitz. I can never forget him because he was a very large man and he never induced the children to like him. All he did was walk around with his hands behind his back and his glasses lowered like that, and give you a look that scared the living daylights out of you. Those were Hebrew School days. **Bess (Eisenman) Center, 3**

We had the Hebrew School in the B. B. Jacob on the main floor. There was room for classes and we had teachers. We had a rabbi that had supervision. And we had a very nice daily attendance and then finally it developed when our social building was built. The Jewish Educational Alliance, there was some activity in that building that had to do with religious training, and then the synagogues all developed to a larger degree where each one of them had their own day school operation. **Louis Silverman, 29**

They went to Hebrew School Saturday, it was called *Shabbes* School. Everybody went to *Shabbes* School at the synagogue on Montgomery Street, and then when it moved to Drayton Street, Savannah girls and boys would teach the classes. They weren't professional teachers, but they were older. We all had a class for the ones from ten to twelve, and thirteen to fifteen, and the older children would take over. But the children were very Jewish conscious. **Lena (Feinberg)Rosenzweig, 26**

I went to Hebrew School. We didn't have a very strict requirement in those days for *Bar Mitzvah* including so many years of Hebrew School. It was standard, traditional. . . . The students were worse. We gave no cooperation. We got kicked out almost every day. **David Rosenzweig, 25**

I had one of the young rabbis teach me, but they had a Hebrew School in the *shul*; in the synagogue they had a Hebrew School. **Minnie (Bronitsky) Feinberg Robbins, 24**

[My mother-in-law] was . . . instrumental in getting the building that used to be used as the Hebrew School, on the corner of Hall and Abercorn, so much so that she even had her maid go over with her to clean the building when there was no one else available. **Charlotte (Shipper) Garfunkel, 37**

We had afternoon Hebrew School which went from the time you were seven 'til you were thirteen. . . . Our Jewish education at that point was teaching you how to read Hebrew by rote, how to *daven*, that was it. It really wasn't much of a school until just before I got *Bar Mitzvahed* and then they really structured it into a real Hebrew School. **Harris Slotin, 55**

There really weren't activities in the *shul* for children. There was Hebrew School, but Hebrew School was for boys. . . . But the girls went to Sunday School, that was on Sunday. We had lay teachers. . . . We went to assembly, we sang songs. We studied, in English only, not in Hebrew, the Jewish holidays and Jewish customs and Bible stories, that kind of thing. **Doris (Goldin) Lukin, 88**

Hebrew School, c.1969-1970
Shown at Congregation Agudath Achim's Hebrew School (clockwise left to right): Sandy (Becker) Greenberg, Susan (Ullman) Slotin, Nancy (Levine) Blumberg, Ivy (Kaminsky) Silbiger, Cantor Leon Radzik, and two unidentified individuals.
JVM 007 Congregation Agudath Achim Visual Materials Collection, Box 1,

The Hebrew School was just classes. We always had fun in the classes. . . . Julius Rubnitz . . . says to me, "Let's cut Hebrew School and go to the Bijou [movie theatre]." I said, "Okay." I got home that night, . . . my daddy said, "How was Hebrew School today?" In those days there was no confrontation between parent and child. My father looked at me and I looked at him, and I said, "I didn't go today." I knew he knew I didn't go today. To tell a lie, that was blasphemy. You wouldn't dare. So he said, "Yeah, Mr. [Rabbi Hirsch] Geffen reported you." I never cut Hebrew School again. **Leon Slotin, 47**

I never went to Hebrew School. I've never been there. While we were in New York . . . my mother hired a *melamed* to teach me. When we got back to Savannah, my grandfather Usher Levy, who was considered the *talmid chachem* in this part of the country, . . . I learned with him. I guess I was like almost everybody else; as soon as I was *Bar Mitzvahed*, I didn't pursue it, much to my regret now as I get older. **Walter Lowe, 54**

BAR MITZVAH AND BAT MITZVAH

I was *Bar Mitzvahed*, I had good training. We also took private lessons from Rabbi [Hirsch] Geffen who was the *chazan* in the *shul*, and he was from the same town my mother was from in Lithuania. . . . Rabbi Geffen said to me a week before my *Bar Mitzvah*, "Rosenzweig, you will never learn," which was a great confidence builder. Well, anyway, I got through it and had my *Bar Mitzvah* ceremony. None of the kids did as much as the present generation does with running all of the service. We did our *Haftarah* and that was it.

The celebrations were very minimal. . . . Ten kids to Jerry George's for a ten cent. Jerry George's was a soda fountain, a lovely romantic place. . . . It was on Broughton Street, near Barnard. . . . You took ten kids, they had a limit of ten cents they could spend for a drink, and then you went to a movie which probably cost another dime. And the gift, I well remember, we cherished them, were Tom Swift books, which cost twenty-five cents apiece. So at a *Bar Mitzvah*, you were with ten kids, you'd usually get the whole series of Tom Swift books. **David Rosenzweig, 25**

My *Bar Mitzvah* lessons were given to me by Cantor Schatz. He was our *chazan*, great voice. . . . My *Bar Mitzvah* was at the synagogue . . . on Montgomery Street. . . . *Bar Mitzvah* in my day was a little different than the *Bar Mitzvahs* of today in certain ways. For example, I *davened,* . . . everything, including *musaf*, the whole ball of wax.

After that was over, we all partook in refreshments. Refreshments in those days was homemade *challahs*, *kichel*, *mandel bread*, maybe a *kuchen,* . . . it's a dough bread with a lot of raisins and cinnamon in it, it was delicious. You know, all those were homemade. In addition to that, there was some moonshine. There was a little whiskey there too, and of course wine. And all this was downstairs at the A.A. on Montgomery Street. The women joined us, the men joined us, and I had quite a *Bar Mitzvah.*

I was very proud of myself, as a matter of fact. . . . Then I invited a handful of my friends and we went to the movies that afternoon. And from there we went to a drugstore on Bull Street, if I remember correctly, it was called Livingston's

Drugstore, or something like that. It was on Bull Street between Broughton and the next street over . . . right off the alley. . . . They had marble floors there, with the wrought iron chairs, and we had ice cream sodas there, and this was for my friends. . . .

Uncle Phillip [Kaplan], my Aunt Bessie [Kaplan], my parents, Abe Samuels and his wife, they all came over to the store Sunday morning and we had rye breads, we had corned beef, we had salami, we had bologna, we made sandwiches. . . . And we used to take the big wash tubs and fill them full of soft drinks, Coca-Colas, ginger ale, they even had a few bottles of beer there also. That was the *Bar Mitzvah* in those days. It wasn't a big deal on Saturday night and then again on Sunday and all that. That was a very simple deal and it was very lovely. **Samuel Radetsky, 45**

The year before your *Bar Mitzvah* you prepared for your *Bar Mitzvah* lessons. . . . The *Bar Mitzvah* was a very momentous occasion for me because at that same time my sister Rita was marrying Mike Rosenstein. They announced their engagement the same weekend of my *Bar Mitzvah*. So it was like a double good thing. . . . As you know, the *Bar Mitzvahs* in those days, you went to the Lucas or whatever theatre you chose. . . .

After that you went to Nunnally's, if you remember, ice cream shop. It was a soda shop, but you went there and you usually had about fifteen, twenty kids and everybody sat around after the movie, you had your soda and all. . . . That was a tremendous day for me. It stuck with you. **Leon Slotin, 47**

All the boys in the family attended Hebrew School and took special *Bar Mitzvah* lessons. One from a Mr. [Isaac] Fialkow and the other from Rabbi [Hirsch] Geffen who was the *cantor* at the B.B. Jacob. We attended Hebrew School for some years until *Bar Mitzvah*. . . .

The girls in those days, very few attended Hebrew School and the *Bat Mitzvah* had not been invented because that was unheard of in our time. The affairs, weddings, *Bar Mitzvahs*, and whatever were much more modest, nothing like the present scale. A small group of boys contemporary to the *Bar Mitzvah* boy went to a movie and had a ten-cent drink after that. **David Rosenzweig, 63**

Mine had a little bit more meaning to it because I started my *Bar Mitzvah* lessons in September. My birthday is March so I had lessons with Cantor [Hirsch] Geffen for the six months. There were a few words that I could never get right. Never did, until the day of my *Bar Mitzvah*. That was the first time that I did everything, I sung the whole thing, and got all the words right. I was *Bar Mitzvahed* in the old B.B.Jacob on Montgomery street. **Karl Friedman, 85**

I was *Bat Mitzvahed* at the Conservative synagogue downtown. . . . I believe this was the first year, well the fall before I was *Bat Mitzvahed* was the first year that the Conservative synagogue in Savannah had *Bat Mitzvahs*. It was very well received. There were about nine girls the very first year that became *Bat Mitzvahed* and I think I probably was about the third or the fourth. We conducted the Friday night services and talked about the *Torah* portion and had a reception afterwards. Then I believe when I was like fifteen I was confirmed, . . . also at the A.A., and there were about nine or ten people in my confirmation class. Some of the same girls that had been *Bat Mitzvahed* also became confirmed. **Phillipa "Bunny" (Sherman) Cohen, 90**

Sunday School and Hebrew School, 1934
Congregation B'nai B'rith Jacob Graduation Class (left to right): (front row) Wilbert Bonchek, Rebbitzen Jessie Max, and Rabbi Morris Max; (center row) Goldie (Klugman) Adelman, Eunice (Friedman) Sheills, Jeannette (Wexler) Shiffman, Dorothy (Nathan) Palefsky, Esther (Lieberman) Solomon, Lillian (Rosenzweig) Director, Florence (Kolman) Adler, and Samuel Berliner; (back row) Beatrice (Heyman) Goodman, Tillie (Center) Lefkowitz, Evelyn (Center) Goldberg, Rocky (Kaplan) Shindell, and Martin "Maier" Rabhan.
JVM 006 Congregation B'nai B'rith Jacob Photograph Collection, Item 0001

All the mothers sent cakes on Friday for their sons' *Bar Mitzvahs*. Some of the families would go to hear their sons say the *Haftarah* and some of them didn't.

The father just took the son to the *shul*, he said the *Haftarah*, and they set up a table with wine and cake. The most popular cake was a honey cake. . . . But the families didn't go. Right now it's like a wedding. It's out of hand, it's unbelievable. It runs into a couple of thousand dollars. It's terrible, just awful. And then they have a dance at night, and that didn't happen.

When my brother got *Bar Mitzvahed*, we didn't even go to *shul*. Mother sent the cake. And I know a lot of other Jewish mothers would bake and send it in. The boy would say the *Haftarah*, the prayer, and that was it. It sure has changed. . . . For our sons, it wasn't too elaborate, but we had a dinner at the synagogue, a nice meal at the synagogue. We had nothing at night, nothing like that. But today it's a night affair and a morning affair, you know. A lot of money goes down. Of course, the kid gets presents. . . . It loses some of its sacredness, I think. The music messes it up somehow. All that dancing music, you forget what your *Bar Mitzvah* is for. I think it's overly done. But it's none of my business. **Lena (Feinberg) Rosenzweig, 26**

It was just that you went to *shul* and you got an *aliyah*. Do you know what an *aliyah* is? You get called to the *Torah* for the first time at your *Bar Mitzvah*. Afterwards, if you want to entertain the public, and when I say the public, people who were present, you'll have a bottle of wine or a bottle of *schnapps* on the table, and some sponge cake or something like that. It was no big to-do like today. Today they make a wedding out of it. **Fred Rotkow, 27**

[My *Bar Mitzvah* party was in] this living room where we're sitting. We had to have, Mama had to have new carpets 'cause it was a big occasion. We had wall-to-wall carpets put in and it was a big party. My mother was one of five children and they came, . . . the brothers and the sisters came. Yeah, yeah, it was very nice. **Jack Golden, 74**

There were caterers, but not like they have today. So everybody made their own stuff. We'd have some family from New York and they'd always say they'd never seen so much potato salad and turkey in their lives because everybody was at my house cooking and cutting and making the party. I was *Bar Mitzvahed* in May of 1949. My birthday's the end of March but the *Bar Mitzvah* was in May, and I think part of it may have had to do with Passover. You could be *Bar Mitzvahed* any time that you want to after your thirteenth Hebrew birthday. **Anchel Samuels, 86**

My brother Karl is three years older than I and our first cousin, Buddy Portman, . . . their *Bar Mitzvah* gift was a trip to New York by boat. There used to be these ocean-going liners who left from Savannah and went up the east coast of the United States and it was pretty. . . . When I was going to be *Bar Mitzvahed*, that was going to be my gift. Man, I thought about it a lot. And then came December 7, 1941, and there were no more liners between Savannah and New York. So when I got *Bar Mitzvahed* in 1944, I didn't get my trip to New York. . . . My mother did have a hot dog roast for me, for my ten kids, my ten friends. We did go downtown on the bus, go to a movie and then to the soda shop, but she had a hot dog party for us. The gift of choice then was a fountain pen. I got a lot of fountain pens. **Erwin "Ernie" Friedman, 71**

In those days we would just invite a group of our friends and we would go to a theatre, and then afterwards we'd go to . . . an ice cream parlor, Jerry George or Nunnally's. . . . They would have ice cream or banana splits or whatever they wanted, a soda, and then that's the way we celebrated in those days as far as I know. And as far as gifts are concerned, it wasn't elaborate like it is today. You either got a book or something else, maybe a pen. **Samuel Plotkin, 8**

There was no such thing as a big *Bar Mitzvah*. You get your friends, your eight friends, six friends. [Your] family would take you to the movies. After the *Bar Mitzvah* you'd go to the movies. You went to the ice cream parlor here. You'd have your ice cream. **Harry Eichholz, 57**

Bat Mitzvah, 16 January 1988
Rachelle Klise Haysman, Bat Mitzvah student at Congregation Agudath Achim.
JVM 003 Savannah Jewish Archives General Photograph Collection, Item 1661

The big [*Bar Mitzvah*] gift was a twenty-five cent copy of Tom Swift, one of the novels that all of us read avidly in those days. You had ten boys to the thing, you got ten Tom Swift books and you were just, that was a fabulous library for a kid our age. **David Rosenweig, 63**

I got *Bar Mitzvahed* at the B.B. Jacob. . . . In those days you took ten of your friends and you took them to theatre for fifteen cents, and then you took them to Nunnally's for an ice cream for another fifteen cents. . . . Ten times thirty cents was three dollars. Big deal. Spent three dollars on the whole thing.

My Aunt Bessie [Kaplan] . . . and my Aunt Lena [Rosenzweig] and my Aunt Mrs. [Annie] Rubin and Mama, they'd got together a couple of nights before and they made salami sandwiches, corned beef, pastrami, and all that, and wrapped them up in cellophane. And they had two bottles of *schnapps*, one bottle of bourbon and one bottle of scotch. That was the whole entertainment. . . .

If you were coming down those steps, if you remember they had big steps, and they'd say, "Mr. Rosenzweig, please, have a drink and sandwich. *L'chaved* the *Bar Mitzvah* boy, in honor of him." They begged you. And we did them a favor by eating sandwiches and drinking their *schnapps*. Today it's a different story. They spend ten, fifteen, twenty thousand dollars on that sort of thing. **Nathan Karnibad, 41**

RELIGIOUS ORGANIZATIONS

ADULT ORGANIZATIONS

We did have [a] Jewish social club. Of course, Jews weren't invited to the Oglethorpe Club or any organization like that, so they formed the Harmonie Club and it was on the corner of Jones and Bull. They used to serve dinners there and have card games, dances occasionally. . . . Mostly the Reform group was in there. . . . I guess it was founded in the nineteenth century. **Samuel Hirsch, 52**

The Harmonie Club was a private Jewish organization; my father was a member, my uncle was, and it was basically, primarily one hundred percent of Reform Jewish men. . . . They had a couple of socials, I suppose, time to time. But they played poker, and there was a place for the men to go. . . . Sol Starrels . . . came here as the rabbi of the congregation. . . . [He] was here a very short time and it was getting to be New Year's Eve which fell on a Friday, and the Harmonie Club, of course, liked to have a New Year's Eve party. . . .

The subject came up of what should we do. Someone said, "Well, let's ask the rabbi." I said, I voted against asking the rabbi because the rabbi can only say no. . . . Finally they went and they asked the rabbi anyway. And the rabbi said, "No, you can't have it on *Shabbes*." So they had it anyway. . . . But this was the attitude of some of the people, members of the Harmonie Club in those days. Nothing really mattered. Religiously very little mattered. **Stephen Traub, 32**

Harmonie Club which was a Jewish club. Men used to go there, they played pinochle and poker, and the women played bridge and mahjongg there. It was just a social club, a Jewish club. . . . The Harmonie Club was at a peak when men who would now be over a hundred years old were at their peak. . . . It didn't have tennis, or swimming, or golf, or anything, therefore in the '30s when I was a teenager . . . it wasn't part of my life. . . . Just a city club. Harmonie Clubs were established all over the country. **A. J. Cohen, Jr., 6**

The Temple had the Harmonie Club, which had a building on their own. In those days whoever was a member of that were members of the Temple. You know, that's changed over the years, but you were basically a member of the Temple, and they, I believe they blackballed people. I never knew. But they voted you in. You really had to be a Reform Jew at the time to be a member of that. **Harriet (Kanter) Konter, 43**

My father was blackballed out of the Harmonie Club by Leopold Adler who ran the department store. Why? Because my father was an upstart. **Harris Slotin, 55**

[Regarding Eugenie Garfunkel and her work with the Hebrew Women's Aid Society:] She was, of course, very active in it and raised funds for it. It was a completely charitable organization. She had three or four ladies that for years worked with her very diligently; Mrs. Sam [Fannie] Blumenthal, Mrs. Harry [Rose] Blumenthal, Mrs. [Frances] Kandel. . . . I don't think there was ever a Jewish person in Savannah that had a problem financially . . . that they were not taken care of by the Hebrew Women's Aid Society, and it was done in a quiet way. They had two or three that knew, and no one else knew who was given charity or what was done.

I remember many nights ago, when I was just a young man, if she would get me on a Saturday night, I'd take her an automobile and we'd go to five or six different homes, and she'd go there and give this one ten dollars for the week, and the other one fifteen dollars for the week. She just took the money and handed it to them. There were no checks or no records or anything. **Benjamin Garfunkel, 9**

The Hebrew Women's Aid was, and still is, the only benevolent society, Jewish. . . . It was started many years ago by a lady in Savannah by the name of Mrs. S. K. [Bessie] Friedman. She was very, very active. She owned Friedman's Art Store; she was the original owner. And everything took place at Mrs. Friedman's Art Store, when it came to planning an affair, or iron out differences. . . . We are an organization of women who are dedicated to care for our own people. If we know of someone who unfortunately are in need, we take care of that, but no one knows where the care came from. That was established at the beginning and is true today. When someone comes to us, someone calls to our attentions a family in trouble, we manage to get the information, and if they are eligible they receive a cashier's check, and they do not know where the money came from. . . .

It is without doubt the most unique organization anywhere. . . . [Dues] started at two dollars and they were two dollars for I don't know how many years. I assume that was because they wanted every woman in Savannah to be a member, and they wanted to make the dues available.

We had this Hebrew Women's Aid Ball at Purim, and other raffles that were going on, that was our fund raising, plus the fact that Mrs. Sam Blumenthal, Aunt Fannie Blumenthal, used to go to different places every year and ask for something that she could raffle off. She would go into a jewelry store and ask for silver tea servers. Then she would sell tickets for a whole year, and at the Purim ball the names were drawn. She went to the Gas Company and asked for a stove, and we raffled off a stove. Then she went to the Electric Company and asked for a refrigerator, and we raffled off a refrigerator. Whatever Aunt Fannie could get her hands [on]. . . .

After we stopped having the ball, then we sent out letters and we would get as much money from the letters as we did before. And every time that our treasury is low and we have a request for something that's been investigated, we can go to certain people, no matter what time of the year it is, and get what we need. We've helped many, many families. We helped people stay in business. And I hope that it will go on as long as the world is alive. **Frances (Ehrlich) Rabhan, 21**

[My mother] took me to this meeting that Mrs. [Eugenie] Garfunkel had been president at the time for thirty-six years I think. And the same Mrs. [Fannie] Blumenthal was treasurer, and that was the age group that was there, and they asked for a treasurer's report. Now, understand that those ladies did work and still do in the secrecy of what's going on, and nobody knows what they've got. This woman, Mrs. Blumenthal, stood up . . . and she said, "Don't worry about it, everything's okay." And with that she sat down. And I just thought that was the worst thing I had ever heard in my life. "What kind of treasurer's report?" My mother said, "Don't worry about it. Everything's okay." **Harriet (Kanter) Konter, 43**

There is the Hebrew Women's Aid Society, which is a social service organization. [It] is a very charitable organization giving help to anyone in need and who try to preserve the dignity of the people who are in need of our help by even the officers not knowing to whom the help is being given. . . . As far as I know they [H.G.H. Society] were the men's organization that did the same thing that the Hebrew Women's Aid does. They took care of a lot of transients, I understand, that came through the city and they would help these people while they were here or help them with bus fare or train fare or whatever. **Charlotte (Shipper) Garfunkel, 37**

The Hebrah Gemiluth Hesed, also known as the H.G.H. Society, had a loan program in which they would lend money to its members without interest. In that respect it was one of the better known and leading organizations because it was the oldest fraternal and charitable organization in the city. . . . The Hebrew Women's Aid was equally as active and equally benevolent and beneficial in helping Jewish families. **Benjamin Silverman, 29**

Hebrah Gemiluth Hesed (H.G.H.), 1938
H.G.H. celebrated its 50th Anniversary at the J.E.A. in 1938.
JVM 003 Savannah Jewish Archives General Photograph Collection, Item 0044

Our H.G.H. Society, Hebrah Gemiluth Hesed, they are not active now. All of us went through it; Pop had been a president, Barney had been a president, I've been a president. . . . This is the society that when you needed a loan without money, you'd go to one of the members and he could recommend to the trustee committee to make that loan. You paid, it was like four hundred dollars, you paid forty dollars per month for ten months, no interest. If you took a little longer, why that was all right, too. Workmen's Circle was entirely separate. . . . Ours was non-profit and theirs was to make money. . . . Every Passover we saw that no Jewish family went without matzo and wine. The committee would do that.

We also had a transient relief committee. Pop was, 'cause he was always downtown, these traveling Jewish people . . . *meshullahs* used to come through. Pop used to give them his [donation] and then tell them to go see the rabbi and they'd work out something. . . . A lot of them came collecting who looked like a *meshullah*, and what they were were somebody that had some kids and had a daughter that wanted to get married and didn't have the money to give her a dowry, so they came through with that one and all kinds of stories, not legitimate, but Pop could soon see through it.

Through the years, when Pop passed away, they made me the caregiver or whatever you call it, to give money. . . . There was a story that Pop, when he first saw him, Robert Mitchum [actor] was one of the bums that came through with a Jewish guy. They had him in jail; they had jumped one of the trains. They caught them in the railroad tracks and put them in jail. Pop got them out. Mitchum has said that he served on the Georgia chain gang. **Benjamin Portman, 20**

During the Depression we had what you called an H.G.H. Society. Now that was strictly for philanthropic purposes. Mr. Sam Portman who had a pawnshop on Broughton and West Broad was head of it. He more or less distributed what was necessary, and especially when transients came through of Jewish faith and they needed assistance in order to either go to Florida or whatever. The merchants of Savannah, when they were approached, were always sending to Mr. Portman, and he'd put them up for the evening and take care of them. **Herbert Blumenthal, 76**

Hadassah at that time was very active and they had their yearly "Hadassah Presents" program, which was a variety show. I became very involved in that, in designing of the sets and making the sets. And that became a really fun thing to do because I got to go to all the rehearsals, flirt with all the girls in Savannah, and do the set design. **Eric Meyerhoff, 18**

I was in B'nai B'rith Women for a long time. I got up as high as vice president, but I got sick and got frightened because it was very serious. . . . I was in Hadassah, too. I worked in Hadassah. I was active in everything, the Women's Club, everything. And I also worked. So the women that say they don't have time, there's plenty of time for everything if you want to do it. **Lena (Feldman) Solomon, 82**

B'nai B'rith Women came along and that did things in the United States and I just thought that was something I wanted to be involved in. They had B'nai B'rith Men at that time also. I can remember that one year I chaired the booth at the fairgrounds, and the Cadillac affair which you paid fifty dollars and had a chance to win.

As the chairman of ways and means, I must have been out of my mind because I can remember we were in the supermarket business at that time and Larry and I would go out to the fairgrounds every night at about eleven o'clock and pick up the money and take it to the store and put it in the safe. . . .

That was probably the most organized group, . . . and they did what the United Jewish Appeal [did]. . . . We did the organization that they now do because we had a chairman of the week, we had a chairman of the day, we had a chairman of the hour, and I would say that we involved two hundred Jewish women in that week of working out at the fairgrounds. It was the place to be and the place to do and everybody worked and that was the kind of organization. **Harriet (Kanter) Konter, 43**

When Hadassah had a rummage sale . . . we would bring in our *shmattes* and sell them. And there was a day, I remember the lady, she came in with a coat and put it down. Well, it looked like a *shmatte*. I sold her coat. Ooooh, she got ready to go and her coat's not there. . . . I said, "Hold everything." Alvin Karsman had a wholesale place then up on West Broad Street. I went up there and said, "You've got to help me. You've got to give me a coat for ten dollars. I can't spend any more than that. It's not my money." So I got another coat and I brought it back to her. It was so funny. I sold the lady's coat. You can imagine what it looked like. I thought it belonged with the rummage. **Sadye (Steinberg) Rabhan, 22**

Senior Hadassah, c.1960s
Members in the organization's annual fashion show included (left to right): Elaine (Schwartzman) Radetsky, Jacqueline (Karsman) Friedman, Pauline (Chazen) Karp, Jennie (Javetz) Horovitz, Sara (Ehrenreich) Jospin, and Joan (Ehrens) Gefen.
JVM 003 Savannah Jewish Archives General Photograph Collection, Item 1769

My husband's Aunt Sadye [Garfunkel] was always interested in the Council of Jewish Women, and she was an officer in that. Of course, my Aunt Eugenie [Garfunkel] was the president as long as I've known of the Hebrew Women's Aid and the burial society, the women's burial society, *Bnos Hesed Shel Emeth*. **Charlotte (Shipper) Garfunkel, 37**

I immediately became a member of the Savannah Section of the National Council of Jewish Women. The Savannah Section was one of the very old ones. . . . I always took a very strong part. I am a past president of the Savannah Section. We disbanded in probably the '60s. There were a good many organizations and things were becoming a little overcrowded in that direction, and we weren't able to maintain the program that we had been carrying on. **Mildred (Wolf) Weichselbaum, 51**

YOUTH ORGANIZATIONS

Prior to A.Z.A. [Aleph Zadik Aleph], Young Judaea was formed in Savannah then. We had the Zangwell Club which was earlier, and I was a member of that. We even went to a convention in Montgomery, Alabama, I guess when we were about fourteen, fifteen years old. . . .We had a group that was called the Knights of Judah. . . . We finally evolved into the A.Z.A. and all of us joined up from those other clubs. The Young Judaea lost, apparently lost control in Savannah and B'nai B'rith seemed to be attracting more kids. . . .

Zangwell, I don't know if you remember the miracle of Zangwell? It was a big man with the Jewish, you know, the worldly Jewish community. . . . We were supposed to be like a literary club. We would have debating teams, speeches, but basically we were more to the basketball and softball, but we did have some people that engaged in debates and made speeches and stuff. . . . This would have been probably in the '30s. **Marvin Arkin, 76**

After the Young Judaea Club when I was seven, and that club was called the Flowers of Zion, our crowd decided that we would just have a bridge club on Sunday afternoon. And I think there were about eight or nine of us who would go from one house to the next person's house and we did that for a year or two. **Doris (Goldin) Lukin, 88**

[Young Judaea] was a national organization. Something on the order of A.Z.A., but the A.Z.A. hadn't started then. . . . They had the groups say from ten to twelve, and then from twelve on, and after eighteen there wasn't too much. That's when we got into the literary societies, and we would do that kind of work at that time. **Sanford Wexler, 48**

A.Z.A and B.B.G. [B'nai B'rith Girls] were big activities for us. Our lives centered around those two clubs, the girls' B.B.G. and the boys' A.Z.A., and that's where our social life was. We, that's where we met the girls, A.Z.A. and B.B.G. meetings on Sunday. That's where we debated and we had A.Z.A. ball teams, basketall teams. And Sanford Wexler, he was a wonderful, he was the A.Z.A. advisor and the A.Z.A. debating coach. I remember I used to love to debate. We would debate against A.Z.A. in Atlanta, Charleston; we had a wonderful time. . . . He had a great influence on a lot of young Jewish boys. . . . He shaped a lot of youth, Savannah Jewish youth. He shaped their characters. He did a lot for them. **Alan Gottlieb, 40**

Aleph Zadik Aleph (A.Z.A.), 1974

Attending an A.Z.A. Sweetheart Dance are Fran (Kooden) Herrell, Cynthia Berman, Gay (Kaminsky) Udinsky, Cindy (Kaplan) Goldstein, Terry Danzig, Susan (Odrezin) Eichholz Timna, Jodi (Lasky) Sadler, Susan (Kelly) Biedinger, Deborah (Adler) Welis, Lynn Levine, Rachel (Cooper) Perling, Jan (Freedman) Katz, Rachel Kronowitz, Cindy (Cooper) Bauman, and Joseph Cooper.

JVM 003 Savannah Jewish Archives General Photograph Collection, Item 1343

Our A.Z.A. days were, this was a great organization! We had, in Savannah, we had some great advisors like Abram Kantsiper, Judge [Emanuel] Lewis, Abe Rosenthal, Jerry Lewis, . . .Ted Lewis, . . . Ben Silverman. . . . But in those days also we had big conventions once a year, too. We had a convention in Savannah, and I was put in charge of the program. I went out and I got ads and we made a lot of money on that book. Our convention was most successful. . . . [It was held] in the Savannah Hotel, . . . located on Bull and Congress Street.

We had a lot of other people; at the conventions, you know, one of us would register and about seven guys would sleep in the room. . . . Take the mattress off and people would sleep on the box springs, on the mattress, in the bathtub, whatever. We had dances. We had luncheons. We had basketball games, contests with various basketball teams from this town and that town. It was just a super, super convention. . . . As a result of this convention, the money we made on the program book, we bought the J.E.A. a complete set of lobby furniture. . . .

Now, whenever we had our banquets, whenever we had anything going in the way of food or luncheons or whatever, Matilda Meddin was like our A.Z.A. mother, and she and I would go out and do our shopping and we'd buy what we'd have to buy. What we didn't have to buy, like we'd go to Movsovitz and

Musky would give us whatever we needed in the way of vegetables, fruit, and other things. . . . At the time, . . . the Meddins . . . had a LaSalle. And I was riding around with her in the LaSalle. Oh, did that feel great! . . . It was like a Cadillac. . . .

There was more togetherness in everything in those days. Because today it seems like everybody is so busy. Too busy to do this and too busy to do that, but in those days everybody got into the act. **Samuel Radetsky, 45**

During our teen ages the most popular thing we had was the A.Z.A. You know that's under the auspices of B'nai B'rith. It was a junior group, it started off at say age fifteen to twenty, twenty-one. We had a tremendous chapter. . . . The chapter that I was involved was called Chapter 206. . . . We had over one hundred sixty members. . . .

We felt that the chapter was too big for some members so they split up and the next thing you know we had two A.Z.A. chapters. One was called 206 which was the original chapter, and the other was called the David Finn Chapter. He had earlier passed away and they named it after David Finn. **Herbert Blumenthal, 76**

Most Jewish boys were in A.Z.A. during my growing up days. There was a rather large crowd. I can't remember how many, maybe fifty or sixty, and I think twenty or twenty-five of us broke off and formed another chapter which is called the David Finn Chapter, and I think that's the name it goes by today. . . . [David Finn] was a local person well-liked in the community that was killed in an automobile accident. **Herman Cranman, 36**

I remember when I belonged to the A.Z.A., the club you know, and they have an affair in Charleston, and they were going to put you up in Charleston, and we were going to play on the basketball and soccer, volleyball or whatever, and it cost one dollar transportation to go there and back. Give them one dollar, they'd take you and then you'd get there and have a place to sleep, place to eat and dance and all that. **Nathan Karnibad, 41**

We were called to go to a retreat at Jacksonville and both boys and girls met with a rabbi at Jacksonville, and he wanted us to forget Ballyhoos and Jubilees [social clubs] and to form a new organization which is now called "SEFTY," Southeast Federation of Temple Youth. . . . That was the first meeting of Southeast Federation of Temple Youth, and I think I was secretary. . . . It was to be different because now you would have a religious thrust. **Danyse (Greenwald) Edel, 35**

We had a club called the Zangwell Club. That was the name of the club. We used to meet on Sunday and talk about current events. **Nathan Karnibad, 41**

Zangwell, . . . he was a prominent Jewish person up in New York City at that time. Nathan Schultz Club. Nathan Schultz, . . . we used to debate against them. And I debated, as a Young Judaean I debated in Atlanta one time and in Macon one time and in Savannah one time. . . . We debated about . . . how could Israel support a small country, support all the Jewish people? . . . This was back in '28, '29, '30, '31. . . . We also debated whether it should become an agricultural country or a manufacturing county. **Sanford Wexler, 48**

Junior Hadassah, c.1940s
Attending a formal affair at the Hotel Savannah (left to right): (front row) Phyllis (Dana) Shoob, Mary Hannan, and Mickey (Kapner) Siegel Levy; (back row) Matilda "Minda" (Rubnitz) Brownstein, Bertha (Plotkin) Freedman, Miriam (Plotkin) Stein, and Pauline (Manning) Rosenfeld.
JVM 003 Savannah Jewish Archives General Photograph Collection, Item 2115

CHAPTER 5: JEWISH EDUCATIONAL ALLIANCE

ORGANIZATION

If I remember correctly, . . . Rabbi Solomon who was the rabbi for the Mickve Israel, he was mainly responsible for the establishment of the Jewish Alliance or the J.E.A. It was supposedly to take care of the older people who'd come in who didn't know too much about English, so that they could [have] some place together and establish themselves, meet and talk and shower. Lots of people had no bathtubs or bathrooms or showers. . . . That's why it was established. . . . Mr. [Jacob] Gazan at that time . . . was a very prominent Jewish lawyer. . . . Between the two of them they raised enough money, mostly from the Mickve Israel. **Sanford Wexler, 48**

The Jewish Educational Alliance . . . was a place where the refugees who came over here could learn English, and it was a teaching situation. And since the Jewish boys and girls were spending so much time in these community centers, it naturally evolved that they would become athletes in handball and boxing and basketball, and some of your greatest boxers, fighters, and basketball players were Jewish. **Robert Gordon, 11**

The history of the Alliance was . . . to educate and Americanize the immigrants, basically. **David Rosenzweig, 25**

As a teenager, I knew that we were going to have a Jewish Educational Alliance. They bought a house on the corner of Harris and Barnard Street. The first J.E.A. was a private home, and a few years later they built a nice building across the street from it [Barnard Street]. . . . At the time that I got married . . . the J.E.A. was on Barnard Street. It had already moved from that tall stoop house on Harris and it was already on Barnard. . . . I pass it now and I look and see what the Alliance looks like. It's like a dream. I can't believe it. The first Alliance comes to mind and I look at what I see. **Lena (Feinberg) Rosenzweig, 26**

At one time, during the war years [WWI], the Alliance closed. . . . Daddy really was instrumental in getting that place opened again. . . . When they built the new building, they let Mama lay the cornerstone. I got a picture of Mama. We laugh about it, 'cause there's Mama with her stole. **Ida (Slotin) Wilensky, 34**

Jacob Gazan, J.E.A. Leader, n.d.
After helping establish the J.E.A., Jacob Gazan served as president of the organization several times (1918-1919, 1925-1929, 1932-1935).
JVM 003 Savannah Jewish Archives General Photograph Collection, Item 1675

I don't . . . as a child ever remember going into the J.E.A. It was just a different ball game at the time in Savannah. There was a strict line between Reform and the Orthodox. Basically, between the German and the Eastern Jew. . . . I'm talking prior to . . . World War II. . . . My two uncles [Herman and Sigo Myers, the mayor and his brother] had put up the money for the J.E.A., but I know my parents weren't members. **Julius Edel, 35**

We've turned this facility from an educational, social building into a fitness center. . . . I'm not saying entirely. We used to have great cultural art series. We had regular weekly classes that did not offend any of the synagogues. . . . We studiously avoided . . . religious content because that is the business of the *shul*. However, when we did have an occasional speaker, and they were all local, they were all very good. . . . What happened was . . . there was a void left there and the synagogues ran in to fill that void. Now they are the ones, and maybe rightly so, that are offering all these classes. **Walter Lowe, 54**

LEADERS AND STAFF

William Pinsker was brought here to become the second director and he was truly responsible for the influence of the J.E.A. upon boys. . . . When he left, we then had Rabbi Jerome Labovitz for a while. When he was able to return to the rabbinate, we needed an executive director, but we couldn't pay very much, so I proposed the name of Matilda Shapiro. . . . I prevailed upon her to come back to Savannah and she took the job at eight dollars a month. It was every day but Saturday, and included Sunday. . . . As Vice President, I had to make certain that she got home safely every night, . . . so every night I'd be there to take her home and we eventually married . . . in 1933. **H. Sol Clark, 5**

I remember that when fall came, I went to school and I liked to play ball, and I told my mother that . . . I had heard about the Jewish Educational Alliance and I wanted to go there. . . . She had to stay in the store, so she just sent me over there and told them to enroll us as members, and she'd send the money as soon as she could. And I remember very vividly Rabbi Labovitz, who was at that time the head of the J.E.A., took one look at me and said, "Forget about that, just go ahead and play ball." That affected me very much. It wasn't like that in New York. **Norton Melaver, 15**

[I] remember so many things that went on there; the clubs, the athletics, the people who ran the J.E.A. The executive director was Rabbi Jerome Labovitz. After Rabbi Labovitz, the athletic director was Mr. Jerome Eisenberg who was the math teacher *par excellence* at Savannah High School, and he coached basketball at the Alliance. He was a part-time employee but he always seemed to be there for us. Sonia Geffen [Elkin] was the only person in the office besides Rabbi Labovitz, and Alan Rivers was the janitor.

It's amazing - I don't know what the Jewish population was then as compared to now, but there were no computers, there was next to no sophisticated equipment, and yet they managed to be in contact with everybody in the community. In retrospect, they just did an amazing job with that little bit of help. **Walter Lowe, 54**

Jerry Eisenberg was the director of athletics there. I remember Rabbi [Labovitz], he had been a practicing rabbi and he left that and became head of the J.E.A. . . . He actually, he ran the J.E.A. . . . Jack Chilnick was the activities director when I was there. **Erwin "Ernie" Friedman, 71**

[During World War II], I took over most of the athletic department at the Alliance. . . . Later on they asked me to take over the A.Z.A., and I became . . . advisor to the A.Z.A. And I coached the basketball team and the debating team. . . . And I was president of that Junior Board of Directors for a time. **Sanford Wexler, 48**

Staff, May 1987
Staff has always played an important role in the success of the J.E.A. Photographed during the 75th anniversary celebration, staff included (left to right): (seated) Charles Grossman, Linda Smith, Stanley Ramati, Beverly (Kelner) Greenspan, Ava Meadows, and Mary Roberson; (standing) Clarence Robinson, Sr., Clarence Robinson, Jr., Michael McGettigan, Leon Silver, Charles Moss, Tony Flowers, and Joe Stripling.
JVM 003 Savannah Jewish Archives General Photograph Collection, Item 1521

When I first became involved in the Jewish community, we were a very, very tight-knit Jewish community, and almost everybody who worked in programming or in the offices in the J.E.A. were volunteers. . . . Gradually, as our society had changed, we have come to understand that paid personnel . . . do just as conscientious a job, and they are more professionally able to do the work that's asked of them.

I've seen this change, and with this change has come, I believe, a change from a very tight-knit family, Jewish community situation, to one that is more mobile, as our whole society is. And people still, in my opinion, think of the Jewish Educational Alliance and the Savannah Jewish Federation as the home address for the Jewish community, but it just resides there sometimes as a reminder, and is not the place around which their whole life revolves as it used to. It used to be, the Jewish Educational Alliance was our home, actually. When we were not at our home, we were here at the Jewish Educational Alliance. That's the only place we knew to be. That was especially at the J.E.A. on Charlton and Barnard streets before we moved out to the location on Abercorn. **Norton Melaver, 15**

SENSE OF COMMUNITY AND OVERALL INFLUENCE

Now, I must tell you probably the greatest influence in my life . . . was the Jewish Educational Alliance. . . . It was a unifying influence of the Jewish community; that and Hitler created a complete Jewish community where we thought in terms of trying to help other Jews. . . . The Jewish Educational Alliance had been originally opened as a community center. All during my boyhood years I had been told that the reason for the creation of the Jewish Educational Alliance was the fact that Rabbi George Solomon of Temple Mickve Israel . . . had been in Juvenile Court during a hearing in which a young Jewish girl was involved. I never knew who it was. But he undertook, with the aid of others of course, but he provided the leadership, and in the end the creation of the Jewish Educational Alliance and the building was built on the corner facing the square on Charlton and Barnard Street. . . .

I cannot emphasize too much the influence that the J.E.A. played in my life and the lives of all my generation, boys and girls. What happened was during World War I, the Alliance, because of lack of funds, had to close up and then became a public school for a short period of time, until the Jewish community . . . all joined together and raised the funds under the leadership of Morris Slotin, Louie Weitz, Rabbi Solomon, Jake Gazan, and were able to reopen the J.E.A. During my boyhood years, . . . that building was really home to all of the boys and girls of my generation. There were the boys' clubs, the girls' clubs, the Men's Club, the Women's Club; there was the H.G.H. Society, there was the Workmen's Circle, all had meetings there. **H. Sol Clark, 5**

The Jewish Educational Alliance . . . was actually our second home. My sister Ceil [Barker] says she don't know why we kept our second bathroom over at the Jewish Alliance. But we all grew up right there at Charlton Street which was wonderful because we were right across from the Alliance. . . . I went to kindergarten there at the Alliance. . . . We really grew up in the Alliance. All of our activities were around the Alliance. I went to dramatic club at the Alliance, dancing at the Alliance. We had gym at the Alliance. **Ethyl (Richman) Rosenzweig, 25**

Unfortunately, my Dad died when I was twelve. . . . That's when I started actively going to the Alliance, . . . participating in activities and club work. The Alliance was a second home to us. . . . It has been a great thing for Savannah. **Benjamin Silverman, 29**

My memories of Savannah, really, other than my family, would have to be what centered around the Jewish Alliance. Because friendships were made, lasting friendships, that endured for fifty, sixty, seventy years until this very day, were begun at the old Alliance. That, because of the lack of mobility . . . and the lack of television, . . . that was the meeting place. That was our recreation, entertainment, and education. Funny the things you remember, that Marvin Arkin and I shared locker number eight at the old J.E.A. I'm seventy-nine now, and I guess that's when I was eleven or twelve years old, so it goes back a pretty good ways. The Alliance was, as I say, central to most all of the Jewish kids in those days. **Walter Lowe, 54**

The Alliance has been more than just a second home. I mean, it's been . . . physical, psychological, emotional. . . . As far as I'm concerned, Savannah, the Alliance, and the Jewish community . . . there's nothing like it in the world. **Meyer "Johnny" Becker, 70**

My generation, as well as the generation before that and continuing on for a while after my generation, we lived at the Alliance. That was what you did. You went to school, then you went to Hebrew School, and when you weren't doing either of those two things, you were in the J.E.A. You were doing whatever there was to be done. . . . We played basketball, we played ping pong, we played handball. We hung around a lot. We went to A.Z.A. meetings.

I was very active in Cub Scouting and that's where the Cub Scouts met. I was very active in Boy Scouting. That's where the Boy Scouts met. Of course, the J.E.A. sponsored the second oldest troop in Savannah, . . . the Jewish troop. Its number was Troop #2. I don't think anybody ever knew what happened to Troop #1, so really, for many years, that troop was the oldest extant troop in this area. Everything that meant anything, all the little boys' clubs that we had, were athletic clubs. **Erwin "Ernie" Friedman, 71**

The Jewish Educational Alliance, then located at 328 Barnard, was the glue that held this local Jewish community together. It was our every day activity except for *Shabbes* when it was closed on Saturday, but every other day there were activities for all of us at any age. We had clubs. We had gym classes. We played chess and checkers. We hung out and talked to everybody. . . . I don't know what our parents paid for memberships in those days, but it was very little, and it afforded us a wealth of activities and friendships and a feeling of closeness that we carry with us to our present ages. It was just a remarkable, fabulous institution in what we thought of as a fairly large building, until we were able to move to the new building out on Abercorn Street and see what a center could really offer in the way of swimming pools and handball courts and whatever. The J.E.A. loomed very large in our lives and our maturing and developing as active, contributing members of the local Jewish community. **David Rosenzweig, 63**

Jewish Educational Alliance Fifty-Year Members, 1962
Left to right: (front row) Norman Mirsky, Fred Ehrenreich, Morris Horovitz, Rose (Slifkin) Blumenthal, Fannie (Rolette) Blumenthal, Flo (Slifkin) Gordon, and Fannye (Jacobson) Raskin; (center row) Ida (Levy) Barnett, Mary (Lipsitz) Levy, Lena (Slotin) Ehrenreich, Mary (Lind) Karp, Fred Rotkow, Henry Shonfield, and Hyman Perlman; (back row) Morris "Mesch" Rosen, Max Lipsey, Joseph Mirsky, Max Gordon, and Robert Raskin.
JVM 003 Savannah Jewish Archives General Photograph Collection, Item 1087

Of course, most of the social activity went on at the J.E.A., at the old building on Barnard Street. But it was a real treat after being . . . in the country for the whole week, to come in to town, to Savannah, and go to the J.E.A. and meet the kids. And there were dances and everything. **Albert Ullman, 33**

I was brought up in Jacksonville, but we never had that unity in Jacksonville like you have here. The Alliance was really the heart, the hub of the Jewish people. . . . The young people used to come here, everybody came, even the ones that couldn't pay dues, they were allowed. . . . That is one of the reasons I can't understand that a lot of people don't support the Alliance. . . . They say they got no more children. . . . I don't know how they can forget it, I really don't, 'cause this is something very unusual. **Reuben Schneider, 28**

My partner, Bob [Gunn], . . . directed me to the J.E.A., which at that time was a new building on Abercorn, had just opened in 1956. I was immediately accepted by the Jewish community here. Many people invited me over to their house for dinner and *Shabbat* and so forth. It was a very comforting feeling for a young man to come into a strange city and be accepted by the Jewish community. **Eric Meyerhoff, 18**

I don't think there's a better place to indulge yourself, enjoy yourself, than coming to the J.E.A. I come here every day and the companionship, the camaraderie, to be found nowhere in the United States. I've been to J.E.A.s in Dallas, Atlanta, but you don't have that friendship you have here in Savannah every day. Every time I come here I'll be bound to meet somebody I don't know and everybody is so very friendly.

The Jewish people here, the people of Savannah, Georgia, are just great. I would like to see nothing but great things happening to Savannah, Georgia, and the surrounding community. It's just a pleasure for my family who have been brought up here and my wife and I to live here now. **Charles Becker, 64**

I think as we age we need socialization, and the J.E.A. is just a wonderful institution. It offers so many things for so many age groups. When you walk in the front door, it gives you a feeling of being a part of something. . . .

I was in the grocery store one day and a non-Jewish friend came up to me and said she really wanted to leave Savannah. She just wanted to move. I said, "My goodness, you wouldn't want to do that, I mean, you're already in your seventies, why would you want to just pick up now and move to a new place?" She had a husband, but her children were not here. She said, "Well, Bunny, it's just not the same thing." I said, "What do you mean?" She said, "Well, you have the J.E.A., you have a building to go to."

I really had never thought about that but it is the truth. I mean, if you want to be involved and you want to feel that you are a part of something, you just walk in the front door of the J.E.A. and you should get that feeling. **Phillipa "Bunny" (Sherman) Cohen, 90**

ABERCORN STREET BUILDING

Cornerstone Laying Ceremony, 31 October 1954
With the exception of William Wexler, all of the then living Alliance past
presidents attended the laying of the cornerstone for the new J.E.A. on
Abercorn Street. Pictured left to right: (front row) Emanuel Lewis, Samuel
Hornstein, Jacob Gazan, Morris Bernstein, Isaac Meddin, and current
president Raymond Rosen; (back row) executive director Irwin Giffen, Max
Hornstein, H. Sol Clark, Harry Friedman, Morton Levy, David Rosenzweig,
Benjamin Silverman, Bernard Eichholz, and Philip Bodziner.
JVM 003 Savannah Jewish Archives General Photograph Collection, Item 0391

The decision [to relocate the J.E.A.] was made by, I imagine, the entire board,
that this would not be a process whereby one or two people on the board would
take over and decide what we were going to have. . . . I remember that they had
meeting after meeting, and everybody in the community was involved, expressing
their opinion as to what we should have in this brand new building. I believe this
building was built in 1955. I think we moved in 1955. . . . I was involved, my
mother was involved, everybody was involved. My mother said, "I don't know
what these people want, what they think they want. They want everything, . . . we

don't have enough money to give them everything. And when we have these meetings, it's probably a good idea to ask everybody, but you get a wish list that is, that's a mile long, and it's just going to be impossible to do what everybody wants to have." Somehow I think it worked out and it worked out well. We've enjoyed these facilities for over forty years now. **Norton Melaver, 15**

I was on the committee that bought that land, . . . for the new J.E.A. In fact, Abercorn Street wasn't paved at that time, when we bought that land. And we wanted to buy the strip on . . . DeRenne Avenue, where the shopping center is [but] we didn't have the money. We could have bought it for $20,000, and we didn't have the money to buy it. **Sanford Wexler, 48**

ACTIVITIES AND CLUBS

A lot of our social life, I would say the majority of it, centered around the J.E.A., which was on Barnard at that time. There were clubs, activities, and I would say probably ninety-five percent of the "in" Jewish people. They just congregated there. . . . It was mostly the children. . . . We had Kadema Club, we had a number of organizations, and basketball games, and all sorts of social activities, and our lives literally revolved around the J.E.A. **Selma (Greenberg) Dunn, 7**

I used to go to the Jewish Alliance . . . primarily to take a shower. We were poor, we had just a round tub, galvanized tub, which I got into and poured hot water for a shower. . . . The Jewish Alliance . . . had regular shower stalls . . . and I and Irvin Center, may he rest in peace, used to take showers there every Friday afternoon when the janitor was out. We'd sneak up there and we'd take showers and have a good time.

The Alliance was really a wonderful thing for me. I always felt fond of the Jewish Alliance. It did more for my bringing up than the synagogue or anything else. We had a club called the Zangwell Club. . . . We used to meet on Sunday and talk about current events, and then we played basketball on Sunday afternoon and at night. And we had a gym class with Jerry Eisenberg, . . . he was quite a guy. . . . He was very instrumental in helping boys get scholarships to college. **Nathan Karnibad, 41**

The J.E.A. had all kinds of activities, and I don't know how many people have been around that building, but the main floor, the lower level, had a kindergarten in it, and then behind that was a . . . so-called health club. And then on the next level, when you went upstairs, was like a reading room on one side . . . and a kind of sitting room on the other side, behind the office, and then they had some rooms on that level for meetings and get-togethers. And then the next level was the basketball, the auditorium . . . and the social, or ballroom, were all one big room with a stage in it. . . .That was the place we had our dances. Everything that you did socially as a Jewish group, was done at the J.E.A. **Harriet (Kanter) Konter, 43**

When the J.E.A. got back, we covered a whole panorama of cultural activities. For instance, we had dramatics, . . . we had a great debating society, . . . we had essay contests. . . . We had skit nights, which was a great thing we ought to bring back. Every organization, the Men's Club, the A.Z.A., the Women's Club, every organization that had a meeting in the Alliance would have to put on a skit and everybody would come. . . . The worst punishment you could get was to be suspended. . . . You'd play a prank, or something would back-foil, or you were heard cursing or something. . . . The day you tell a kid he can't come to the Alliance for two weeks. . . . Our lives were built around the Alliance. **Harris Slotin, 55**

The J.E.A. was everything, not only to my life but all the young Jewish boys. . . . A lot of us went there to shower, I mean daily. . . . Many people went there every day to shower. They used to sell us the towels, five cents, . . . we turned them back in every day; so any time you took a shower it cost you a nickel. . . . Everybody went to the New Year's Eve dance, the Thanksgiving Eve dance, and the Purim Ball. The Purim Ball used to be a sell-out crowd. Jacobson's Orchestra, Sammy Goodman's Five, . . . the local bands were great.

Then after they closed that building, I was chairman of the first dance held here at the J.E.A. [on Abercorn Street]. We brought in Tommy Tucker and his orchestra from New York. I figured it'd cost us five-hundred dollars, and it was standing room only. In fact, it was such a big crowd, the Fire Marshal sent somebody in to look it over, and called me over, and he said, "You know, you can't have this many people in here." At the time my brother, Elbert, was captain of the Fire Department and he happened to be at the dance, and he took the guy outside and talked to him a few minutes and [he] let us continue. **Harry Eichholz, 57**

Everything revolved around the Alliance. . . . It was on Barnard Street. And there, we used to walk there. Not everybody had cars in those days. So, it was no problem. It wasn't that far. . . . We had tea dances on Sunday afternoon, which was very nice. **Samuel Radetsky, 45**

In my younger days we square danced, and we used to square dance at the J.E.A., and we had more Jewish square dancers in town than ever were. . . . The J.E.A. had their own club and their own caller. We had every age group square dancing. **Harriet (Kanter) Konter, 43**

All congregations went to the J.E.A. But we [our congregation] had a sister-hood, a brotherhood, and we had our individual functions, just like they do today. But when it came to Purim, then everything went to the J.E.A. We had the services at the synagogue, but then after that, any sort of celebration like the Purim Ball we used to have every year. **Frances (Ehrlich) Rabhan, 21**

[The old J.E.A. gym on Barnard Street] was a square hall; . . . it was exactly square. . . . Basketball was played there, and when it didn't interfere with basketball, softball was played. . . . A lot of spectators sat in bleachers on the stage. They had a stage for productions and entertainment, vaudeville . . . all in one room. . . . Some of the functions were weddings, *Bar Mitzvahs*, dances where the Hebrew Women's Aid would have a Purim Ball. If there was anything Jewish, it was at the J.E.A. **Robert Gordon, 11**

Adult Activities

The Woman's Club [of the J.E.A.] used to have a . . . supper once a year. You know, for one dollar and your dues you got supper. Well, we had to have something that was inexpensive, so we used to get ground meat, that was three pounds for a quarter. And we were going to make meat sauce, you could stretch that. . . . One woman came in and said it wasn't boiling, so she turned the light up, and one turned it down, and one said it had too much salt . . . throw in a few crackers. . . . Then somebody turned it up so high that it scorched. Well, it was terrible.

I said, "What are we going to do now?" So they said bread pulls out the scorch. So we threw in a loaf of bread, it was a big pot. That didn't help it. Silverware. So we put in six knives, six spoons, and six forks, honest to God, and we let it all boil.

The first one to come through the line, you know some people don't wait 'til they sit down to taste it, . . . I thought, "Oh, my goodness, here comes the first complaint," 'cause we never did get the scorch out. She said, "You'd better tell me how you made this." So I said, "I'll be glad to. You saute onions, celery, and you add the meat, and then you put in six spoons, six knives, and six forks, and a loaf of bread." And she turned around to the woman in back of her and said, "Some people will never give you a recipe." **Sadye (Steinberg) Rabhan, 22**

[New Year's Eve] there was always an affair. The Women's Club would put on the affair in the Alliance. I was always amazed, when I think of it now, what a chance we took. . . . We'd have tables all over that place and the dancing floor in the middle, and people would smoke. And how we never had a fire in that place, it's amazing when you think about it. If we'd had a fire there, it would have been a disaster, because you only had two steep fire escapes on each side and then the floor. It would have been a disaster. And we had a curtain, like a ceiling, . . . above it. And God knows if that would have caught fire and fallen down, it could have been tremendous. Luckily it never happened. . . .

The Women's Club would [cater] it. . . . Every New Year's Eve we could depend on that. I think it was five or ten dollars a couple, or twenty-five dollars a couple. Dinner at twelve o'clock, and the band. You got to bring your own whiskey or your own beer. At that time we were all beer drinkers, and so we used to get a couple cases of beer and put it in a tub and put it underneath the table and have beer. **Sanford Wexler, 48**

Way back in November 1954, the Women's Club of the Jewish Educational Alliance had their first "That's Entertainment." . . . It was strictly entertainment. Local people and everyone was volunteer. . . . No one got paid a dime . . . except the pianist. **Allan Cotler, 97**

J.E.A. Variety Show, November 1962
Performers ready for their skit include (left to right): (front row) Ethel (Cohen) Palefsky Meddin and Louis Cranman; (back row) Bernie Lennox and Daniel Schlucker.
JVM 003 Savannah Jewish Archives General Photograph Collection, Item 1070

The [women] had their own Women's Club. . . . They had a yearly show called "That's Entertainment" at the Alliance. . . . Rosalie Cotler . . . got people to come and rehearse and she taught us different dancing routines. **Julius Rudikoff, 46**

The Women's Club was very important at that time and I can remember that . . . we did the last spaghetti supper in the old building before we moved to the new building. . . . We were pretty youngly married but we were proud of that and the Women's Club was big and we had those Women's Club variety shows. **Harriet (Kanter) Konter, 43**

I became active in the . . . Alliance. Then when I became president of the Men's Club, . . . we were . . . trying to raise money all the time. . . . One year the Globetrotters were on the world tour, touring the United States. So I brought up at the meeting, I said, "You know, we ought to bring the Globetrotters in here.". . . [They said], "Oh, there ain't no way. We can't take the responsibility. We can't, they ain't going to draw nothing." I said, "The heck they won't." To make a long story short, . . . we brought them in and they were at the auditorium. We turned away—I won't exaggerate—we turned away a couple of hundred people. **Reuben Schneider, 28**

The only things that I remember [about the J.E.A.] Men's Club was during the summer months when we'd have a camp at the Alliance, and some indigent people [who] had children couldn't afford to pay. . . . The Men's Club used to give money for that. We had a young people basketball team. When they had these tournaments in different places like Charleston or Jacksonville or different places, the kids couldn't afford to go, so the Men's Club used to raise money for that. Over the years we bought curtains for the stage, we bought curtains for those old windows in the old building, . . . we bought refrigerators. We did a lot of things like that. **Julius Rudikoff, 46**

At the Jewish Alliance we had a lecture series and brought substantial and well known literate lecturers, . . . almost every big name in the Jewish literary field came. **David Rosenzweig, 25**

My parents used to go to all those things . . . because they were interested in lectures. . . . They went to everything that was at the Alliance. **Ethyl (Richman) Rosenzweig, 25**

Herman Myers [first Jewish mayor of Savannah] had a brother named Sigo Myers, who dedicated a lot of his time and money in memory of his brother, Herman Myers, toward the Alliance. Jacob Gazan and some of the others from the Mickve Israel were very active in it. As a matter of fact, we had in those days the Herman Myers Literary Society, which I have the honor of being a past president. It was a debating society, and we debated locally. **Benjamin Silverman, 29**

YOUTH ACTIVITIES

Early on I had discovered the J.E.A., the Jewish Educational Alliance, and began very rapidly to become involved here. . . . About the same time that I turned twelve, thirteen, I really became active in all kinds of organizations. . . . The A.Z.A. was very, very big. A major, major opportunity to meet people and to be a part of the community. **Robert Friedman, 38**

We all used to go down to the J.E.A., down on . . . Barnard and Charlton [streets]. . . . We belonged to the Girl Scouts, Troop #4 of the Girl Scouts, and Naomi Mazo was our leader. And I used to love her stories; I used to be mesmerized by her stories. . . . We had a Young Judaea chapter. And we had dances. . . . People were selected to go off to the camps and to learn, you know, everything about Zionism, and to come back and teach us all. And from that we went into Junior Hadassah, and I was president of the chapter here. And of course when you got married you went into Senior Hadassah. The Alliance downtown was . . . the melting pot. **Bertha (Plotkin) Freedman, 8**

Honor Boys' Efficiency Contest, c.1923-1924
Left to right: (front row) David Danish, Edwin Mazo, Bernie Slotin, Jacob Rubin, and Jerome Lewis; (center row) Samuel Goodman, Morris Homansky, Morris "Pony" Wagman, Samuel Lang, and Nathan Estroff; (back row) Joseph Mirsky, H. Sol Clark, Saul Blumenthal, Jack M. Levy, and Alex Heyman.
JVM 003 Savannah Jewish Archives General Photograph Collection, Item 0009

That [J.E.A.] was like a second home to me. I spent a lot of time there. . . . We'd get out of school and get through with *cheder*, and all the activities were there. They had literary clubs, and we had debating clubs, and a lot of that going on, and it was the hangout. . . . This is where we went when we got through with school. . . . You'd come there, and as I said, it was my second home. I would spend a lot of time at the center. It was a wonderful place to go to. **Samuel Plotkin, 8**

At the Alliance, we call it the Alliance, it's the J.E.A., we had social clubs at various ages. We had Herman Myers Literary Society, we had the Zangwell Club; these are boys' clubs that I'm mentioning now. We had the B'nai B'rith Girls, the A.Z.A. for the boys. We even had one independent basketball team called the Knights of Judah.

The Zangwell Club was a club that when I was around twelve years old I was in that club. The Herman Myers Club was a club that you joined when you were older. These were affiliated with the Young Judaean Organization which was national in scope. **Robert Gordon, 11**

David [my husband] was in clubs at the Alliance; he was in everything—the debating club, the Xanadu Club, the Herzl Club, and I was in the Grace Agula Club. . . . We were very active in that and our whole social life revolved around that. And those were the same girls that I have been friendly with all my life. **Ethyl (Richman) Rosenzweig, 25**

I went to kindergarten in the J.E.A., and also I took dancing lessons from Mrs. Pinsker, who was the director's wife. . . . We had a dramatic group and a choral group with Miss Joy Mendes. . . . We were *Zionist* from the time we were six years old because we had Young Judaea Club there and all sorts of clubs and all sorts of dramatic groups. Even as a teenager, we went to dances there. **Beatrice (Heyman) Goodman, 39**

We had all kind of conventions and things and gatherings there. We put on all kind of minstrels and all kinds of dance routines. I was always in everything up there. I sang my lousy voice, but I sang and I danced. Everybody got on the stage and did all kind of things. . . . We had wonderful times at the Jewish Alliance. That was a place where everybody went. **Evelyn (Ward) Karsman, 53**

I used to go to the downtown J.E.A. on Charlton Street for dramatics and other organization meetings and things. When the new building was built, we had our B.B.G. meetings at the new building . . . which was the new J.E.A. on Abercorn Street. My sister was driving so she would pick up all of my girl-friends and she would take us to the meetings. Meetings being Young Judaea meetings and B.B.G. meetings. We were very active in B.B.G. **Phillipa "Bunny" (Sherman) Cohen, 90**

You know, even when my children were growing up, the J.E.A. was a great part of their lives, 'cause their Hebrew School was in there and everything. Any kind of program was in the J.E.A. Everything. The boys belonged to clubs, . . . they did everything there. When they went off to college they really didn't come back to the J.E.A., but then they didn't come back to Savannah either too much. Not until they were [had a] family. **Beatrice (Heyman) Goodman, 39**

I had a Brownie troop at the Jewish Alliance. I was working, but I had a troop every Friday. I had the largest Brownie troop in the city of Savannah. We had almost twenty-eight girls, which was against the law because they did not allow that many girls. But there were so many Christian kids that lived around that area, and they wanted to join. **Evelyn (Ward) Karsman, 53**

I started off being a member of one of the first Brownie troops and I didn't even have a Brownie uniform. **Phillipa "Bunny" (Sherman) Cohen, 90**

Brownie Troop, c.1945
The J.E.A. Brownie Troop during the mid-1940s was led by Evelyn (Ward) Karsman, Elsie Singer, and Mildred (Goodman) Rosen.
JVM 003 Savannah Jewish Archives General Photograph Collection, Item 0080

I went to the Jewish Alliance. I went to gym there. That's an old building that now belongs to the Savannah College of Art and Design. Salvation Army had it for quite a few years. We had two Jewish Boy Scout troops at that time. I belonged to both of them. Of course, one broke up eventually and I was in Troop #2 and Ben Friedman was the scoutmaster. . . . The other was [Horace] Friedman, Troop #22. . . . We used to drill in the square at night and enjoyed it. **Samuel Hirsch, 52**

I remember I was a Boy Scout. We had to go raise the flag at the Gould Foundation [Home], which was on 54th Street. We caught the street car and got off at 46th and Abercorn and walked to 54th Street. It was all wilderness then. . . . I don't remember if it was Thanksgiving or Christmas, we had to go raise the flag for them, the Boy Scouts, Troop #2. . . . Troop #2 was the best troop in the city. **Martin "Maier" Rabhan, 75**

When I was about three years old, like in September of '25, I went to the J.E.A. to kindergarten. . . . I distinctly remember we had the kindergarten down in the basement of the old Alliance on Barnard Street. Also I remember they had a tiny toilet in there for kids. . . . It always impressed me. That was my beginning connection with the Alliance, and I guess I've been connected ever since for the last seventy-five years or so. **Marvin Arkin, 76**

My first formal schooling was at the kindergarten at the J.E.A. on Barnard Street. It was on the ground level of that building, a very nice, bright, airy, big room. Sauchie Blumenthal was my teacher along with Hannah Rotkow. There was a little bathroom that we had there that was ours with small fixtures appropriate for children that age.

One of the things that I remember best was when Sauchie had a glass prism, that when the sun was the right spot, she was able to hold that prism in the window and the reflection from the sun would make the rainbow on the floor, and we just used to love that. Sauchie also played the piano and we would sing, and that was a very, very good experience. **Doris (Goldin) Lukin, 88**

SPORTS

We played half rubber in the park in front of the J.E.A. building, and we played handball in the basement of the old J.E.A. building, as well as we played softball upstairs in the gym, which was on the second floor. **Irvin "Sonny" Rubnitz, 49**

I never took a bath at home! I took it at the J.E.A. We'd go to the gym to play basketball, . . . and when it was time to go you had to take a shower to put your clothes on. So we'd always kid, "I haven't taken a bath in weeks!" **Fred Rotkow, 27**

The most rewarding thing that I got from the Alliance was being asked to coach young people. This meant as much, or more, to me than anything that I ever got out of the Alliance. . . . A few years ago I was inducted into the Greater Savannah Athletic Hall of Fame, being recognized for twenty-five years of coaching at the J.E.A. It is something that I was honored for doing something that I love, because I enjoyed so very much and probably would still be coaching if I hadn't taken time out to be on the Board of Directors of the J.E.A., and subsequently was honored by being the President of the J.E.A. But I've never forgotten those years, and fortunately for me, some of the young men that I coached have never forgotten it either. **Robert Gordon, 11**

The Alliance of today is certainly different than it was in the 1930s and 1940s. . . . While the J.E.A. today serves essentially as a health club and Jewish cultural center, back then members were also involved in a wide range of competitive sports with perhaps basketball being the most prominent. But we had also championship caliber handball players and excellent boxers.

Starting in 1939, along with my brother Irvin, I played [basketball] for the Alliance. We were very competitive and had a winning record every year. We had an excellent coach, Jerry Eisenberg, who was the Athletic Director at the J.E.A., and who died an untimely death at age forty-four in 1944. Jerry was also the Athletic Director and Assistant Principal at Savannah High School, and he worked closely with Coach John Varnedoe in the early '30s to produce state championship basketball teams at Savannah High.

In those days I worked for Union Bag, so I also played for them. In fact, there were times when I played one half for one team and then ran to another gym to play the second half for the other, going two blocks from the Y.M.C.A. to the J.E.A.

I went to work at Union Bag and began to box as an amateur. And although I worked at Union Bag and boxed for them, I did train at the Alliance, along with several other Jewish boxers: Joe Dinerman, a welterweight, who also worked at Union Bag; and Jay Shoob, a bantam weight. We had a great coach at the Alliance, Dick Leonard, whose real name was Harry Marcus.

I got a manager, Meyer Sable, and began to fight in the southeastern part of the United States. By December of 1941, I had had fourteen professional fights and won thirteen. . . . Perhaps one of my proudest moments was in early 1942 when the Navy allowed me time off to come to Savannah to box for the Navy Relief Fund. Gene Tunney, the former heavyweight champion of the world, refereed that fight which was before a tremendous hometown crowd. **Leo Center, 4**

I was a little fat boy around nine or ten years old, and my mother brought me up to the Alliance, which, at that time, was on Barnard Street. And the gym was composed of just a square area where basketball and even softball was played. . . . The athletic director at that time was Jerome C. Eisenberg, and he had been there since the early '20s. And it was there that I got indoctrinated, more or less, in basketball and athletics of the Alliance. It was very limited then, but I finally got to the point where they didn't laugh at me. . . . Downstairs at the J.E.A. was a conditioning room. It . . . had weights that you could lift, it had boxing bags, had a handball court, and the J.E.A. produced many championship teams. **Robert Gordon, 11**

Softball Team, c.1921-1922
Posing in front of the old J.E.A. building on Barnard Street, the intermediate softball team members were (left to right): (front row) Maxwell "Mike" Brooks, Lipman "Lippy" Wise (batboy), and Hyman Meddin; (center row) Abram "Sleepy" Wagman, Benjamin Sheftall, and Samuel Goodman; (back row) H. Sol Clark (manager), Louis "Libe" Gittelsohn, Joseph Mirsky, Mortimer "Bud" Fischer, and Irving Gottlieb.
JVM 003 Savannah Jewish Archives General Photograph Collection, Item 0021

On Barnard and Charlton Street was the old J.E.A. . . . Jerry Eisenberg was the coach and he was in charge of the gym class and the athletics at J.E.A. He was a marvelous person. . . . We went to gym like three days a week, Monday, Wednesday, and Friday. We played all sports in the gym on the second floor at the J.E.A., on Barnard and Charlton Street.

We played a most unusual game—indoor softball; . . . the outfield was the stage. Two guys would stand on the stage and that was the outfield. We became very good at playing indoor softball. Nobody could beat us. . . . No athletic team in town could beat the Jewish team on the indoor course, because that was our home grounds and we just knew how to play, play the balls off the walls and so forth. . . . The only thing we thought we were missing in the J.E.A. was a swimming pool. . . .

[The J.E.A.] was the focal point of our lives. . . . After school we'd go to the J.E.A. and we would play ball, play softball, basketball until eleven o'clock at night, then go on our bicycle and ride home through the streets of Savannah. **Alan Gottlieb, 40**

Jerry Eisenberg, who was the Athletic Director of Savannah High School, also was the athletic director of the Alliance and he conducted gym classes. . . . If you ever displayed any display of temper on the basketball court or the softball or gave out an expletive or something that was out of order, he would point . . . to the door. He didn't have to say anything. He would point to the door and you knew you were through. **Leon Slotin, 47**

After Mr. Eisenberg died, we created a club called the Jerome C. Eisenberg Athletic Club, . . . and we all became members of that. . . . There was one man who had a really great influence in my life in the Alliance. His name was Sanford Rubin, . . . his nickname was "Cowboy." . . . He was kind of a wild guy, but he was the director or counselor . . . for the Jerry C. Eisenberg Athletic Club that all of us were in.

Our principal activity was playing basketball. For whatever reason, he liked me. I became his protégé and I worshipped that man. Nothing that he could say or do wasn't right, no matter what it was. He inspired me to do a lot of things. He had so much confidence in my athletic ability that he inspired me to try to be the best I could. Particularly in basketball, basketball became my favorite sport. . . . I played it in high school and I played it in college. He was always a hero to me. We need our heroes in life and I guess outside of my parents who were always heroes to me, . . . in the athletic area, Sanford was there. **Erwin "Ernie" Friedman, 71**

The guiding light to me, in Savannah, was Jerry Eisenberg. Everybody loved him. He was responsible for, I would say, most of the . . . successful athletic endeavors in Savannah, as far as the Jewish boys were concerned. And girls, 'cause there were girls' activities in the '20s also, and that's important to know that. It was not as widespread . . . as the boys', but the girls were involved and they had basketball teams and . . . they participated in track events, too. **Robert Gordon, 11**

We had [a] basketball team. As a matter of fact, in those days Savannah had, we had one of the best basketball teams in the city. . . . Teams from out of town used to come and play, from the Jewish center in Jacksonville, and other places. The Alliance team used to travel to these towns also and play them. . . .

But all the activities, as far as athletics, were in the building at the Alliance. We played softball upstairs, we didn't have any place outside to play. Basketball was in the building, and a handball court, and it was very active. I mean, if you came there in the evenings you could hardly ever get a chance to get into the handball court. **Samuel Plotkin, 8**

The J.E.A. was your life. They had basketball teams; that was the biggest thing. You didn't miss that. You know, the J.E.A. played citywide and that was a very exciting time. Everybody had a party afterwards. So we did a lot of that. **Harriet (Kanter) Konter, 43**

We won most of our games on the senior basketball team, and the intermediate team. When I played, . . . for about three, four, or five years, we never were defeated. We won every game we played. . . . I managed to play with the varsity a few years, too. . . . Well, we played Georgia Southern at that time. Of course, it was Georgia Normal Teachers' College. . . . We'd go up to Statesboro and play them. We had some wonderful experiences doing that.

The fact is, in one game, I lived up in Statesboro when we played them, at the end of the half we were ahead twenty-three to nine. Of course, that was big scores in those days, not like it is now, you know. The coach said, "I didn't want to tell you before," this was Mr. Eisenberg, when he said, "Fellows, this is my birthday. I'd like to win this game." Well, we had a lead, twenty-three to nine at the half. About three minutes at the start of the half, it was tie score. We all thought we were going to die. But we managed to beat them up there, and that was quite an experience to beat them up there. **Sanford Wexler, 48**

While we played basketball at the J.E.A., we were pretty near the . . . only good team I'd say. We only played colleges in those days. We played Clemson, we played Citadel, we played Georgia Tech, we played Wofford, we played Newberry, we played College of Charleston. . . . When we played the old gym was packed, standing room only. . . . Basketball at the old J.E.A. was letter perfect. I mean, you had to get there early to get a seat. Especially, our big game was Christmas. . . . That was a big, big deal. Big drawing card. **Harry Eichholz, 57**

One year there was the Boston Celtics, New York Celtics, I think it was at that time. They were on a bond-selling tour. . . . They were great basketball players. We played them. . . . We had a lot of good players and we could play long. I played until I was about thirty or thirty-five. . . . Harry Eichholz was exceptional. Leo Center was an exceptional player. And before my time, I heard that Benny Sheftall was quite a player. **Sanford Wexler, 48**

Johnny Becker came here after the war, opened an army-navy store, and became . . . one of the only left-handed violinists that I met, although he wouldn't admit to playing the violin. But he loved racquet ball, and he became nationally known in racquet ball. He was the perennial champion in Savannah, and he went to national tournaments where he was very, very successful. Became champion one time, one or two times, I'm not sure. He's constantly remembered, fortunately, in the Alliance. He was inducted into the Greater Savannah Hall of Fame. **Robert Gordon, 11**

When I came here I became active with the Alliance and they had me come down and they had what they call a four-wall handball club. . . . Racquet ball came after. Racquet ball is the same game as handball except you're using a racquet instead of gloves. In fact, there were some people playing years ago, didn't wear gloves. I remember one in particular was Paul Robinson's father [Samuel Robinson]. I played with him at the Alliance. He never wore gloves. His brother, . . . Abro, he played handball. He was a pretty good player. The best one at that time was Walter Lowenkopf. **Julius Rudikoff, 46**

Handball Players, 4 March 1957
The Championship Flight J.E.A. Handball Tourney members included (left to right): Meyer "Johnny" Becker, Reuben Grunin, Maurice Alpert, and Walter Lowenkopf.
JVM 003 Savannah Jewish Archives General Photograph Collection, Item 2224

I lived at the Jewish Alliance on Barnard Street. . . . Of course, in those days you walked there. Parents didn't push you there. They didn't give a damn what you did. I mean, you just get out of the house. I used to go there and play ball. I played a lot of . . . handball in there. **Murray Bono, 68**

There were also gymnasium activities. We had afternoon softball, basketball; I think there was handball there, too, if I'm not mistaken. But every afternoon, kids, teenagers were there playing in the gymnasium or downstairs in the locker room, and the handball court, or whatever they were doing, but we always had activities going on. That was in the downtown Barnard Street building. **Herman Cranman, 36**

The J.E.A.'s boxing team really got started about . . .'38, '37. . . . It gave rise to some national prominence in the amateur circles, . . . and Leo Center became the tenth ranking light heavyweight. The J.E.A. team would box the Holy Name Society which was a precursor to the C.Y.P.A., the Catholic Young People's Association. Those things would be a tremendous rivalry, but out of this grew some form of respect. . . .

Of course, you had the Golden Gloves Tournament which was sponsored by the Men's Club of the J.E.A. One year they went to New York, to the finals, to the national finals of the Golden Gloves. We placed about five of the eight people in the national finals. **Harris Slotin, 55**

We did have a boxing team. Yes, we boxed. I was the manager one year and we boxed the Catholic Young People's Association in the city auditorium. That was downtown at that time. We had two or three thousand people at that time. Joe Dinerman was on the boxing team. Leo Center was on the boxing team. Maurice Alpert was on the boxing team. David Rubnitz was on there, . . . Coleman Mopper. **Sanford Wexler, 48**

Our great, great [boxing] hero here was Joe Dinerman. He was a little bit older than Leo Center, and Joe would consistently fight . . . Billy Dyer of the C.Y.P.A. [Catholic Young People's Association], and you'd pack 5,000 people into the auditorium to watch this match. Joe would always win. That instilled a great sense of pride. **Harris Slotin, 55**

CHAPTER 6: THEIR EARLY YEARS

CHILDHOOD

I was born at the old Oglethorpe Sanitarium. . . . It was torn down probably about fifteen or twenty years ago. But it was built by a group of doctors and operated 'til after World War II and a little bit thereafter, but it was outdated. I remember it being a wooden structure, which I always thought was a terrible fire hazard. **Julius Edel, 35**

I was born in China; came to New York when I was about four and grew up, for the most part, in a little town called Bethpage. . . . I remember being on what was known as "relief" in those days. Today you call it welfare. This meant, you know, that you were really poor, . . . you had nothing to eat. You didn't have money to buy coal to put in your furnace. I remember sifting the ashes out of the coals so we could use the coals again the next day.

Wearing my father's underwear which was very embarrassing to me in high school because when we all got undressed to play ball, I had it twisted around and folded under so it would fit. Anybody who could wear underwear that would fit perfectly was a legend. Anyway, they were wonderful times. The people were close. **Meyer "Johnny" Becker, 70**

I was born in Savannah, Georgia, at the . . . Oglethorpe Sanitarium. . . . It was a two-story regular house that they made into a hospital. Had some real top doctors involved in that. In fact, there was Dr. [William B.] Crawford, Dr. [A. J.] Waring, Dr. [Henry] Levington, . . . and Dr. Kandel, Harry Kandel. He was one of the main drivers of that particular institution. **Herbert Blumenthal, 76**

I remember the little things when I was a little boy. . . . For instance, the chewing gum, you couldn't buy in little pieces. It was a nickel a box made in Nashville and it had a sarsaparilla flavor. It was very hard. And he used to cut off a little piece at a time for me. And our servant used to chew it up for me, because I couldn't chew it, it was so hard. When she chewed it up good, then I'd take over. **Aaron Guthman, 12**

At that time we boiled clothes . . . in a big metal boiler, probably two and a half to three feet in diameter. It was solid iron. . . . The nurse, maid, or whatever she was . . . had a big stick that they pushed the clothes around [with]. . . . Some stuff they'd put in the water, like a bleach or something . . . to keep them white.

This little sister, who at that time was two years old, came behind her and pulled on her skirt. She thought it was a dog, 'cause we had all kinds of dogs there. She took that stick and swung around and hit her. When she did, the child was holding on to the skirt and fell in the tub. Well, the whole town was praying for us. The child lasted about a week. . . . She's now buried in Laurel Grove Cemetery, and I've gone there several times. **Benjamin Portman, 20**

I guess it was a life of simpler times and the children all played in the park together, mixed, not segregated. All of them, of course, had servants, and the children of the servants were known, when they played together. **Mildred (Wolf) Weichelsbaum, 51**

Childhood, n.d.
An unknown child with her favorite toys.
JVM 005 Congregation Mickve Israel Photograph Collection, Item 0006

Kids of my socio-economic background in those days had nurses. Mine [was] called "Nursie," her real name was Margaret McCord. . . . Nursie was my whole life in those days. Of course, when I started the first grade I was a young man, . . . I shouldn't have had to have a nurse walking with me. So my mother tells the story that I would set off every morning with Nursie about five steps behind. But like a trained dog, she tells me, I would stop at the streets so Nursie could cross the streets with me. **Alan Gaynor, 62**

We lived on Perry Street. . . . They usually had the gangs there, but they weren't all over. I think they were just in certain areas. 'Course we had a maid. . . . When she came to work, I'd go outside to play, and the first thing I was fighting with one of the fellows, and she come out and watch. If I was gettin' the best of him, she'd let me fight. Otherwise, she'd pull me in the house. **Beryl Bernstein, 67**

You have your cousins and your family and your neighborhood friends, 'cause nobody could drive all over town. It was a small town and whoever you had in the neighborhood, that's who you became buddies with. **Rupert Heller, 80**

Dad's favorite hobby was fishing, and my long-looked-forward-to ambition when I was too young to go fishing with him, was that one day I'd be old enough. He did take me fishing—the first trip was on a rather large boat. . . . I guess I was probably, I don't know, nine, ten years old at the time, and Coca-Cola was a treat back then. There was a whole bucketful of Cokes and I drank so much that I don't think I slept much that night. **Karl Friedman, 85**

We thought we had a great life. We didn't have air conditioning, and we didn't have central heat, and we had one bathroom with four or five kids in it, but we lived a good life, and our parents always made us think we were as good or better than everybody else. We didn't have any dumb children in school, Jewish children. And there was a reason for that. Because our parents said education is what you need and you will study. You've got this opportunity and we would be embarrassed to not be in the better class. **Harriet (Kanter) Konter, 43**

[We] walked across Victory Drive [to go to school]. Of course, there wasn't as much traffic in 1928. That's when I started school at age six. . . . I'd walk past Annette's Dairy and take a good look in there. And then on the way home from school, if I hadn't bought lunch that day, I could take a nickel and go in there and get something, an ice cream bar or something like that. The owner's last name was Bull. . . .

It was a family dairy, and they did all the processing right there. They got the raw milk and produced it. Of course, the milk you bought those days was almost half milk, half cream. There was no . . . homogenized. They delivered milk to the door. . . . They had these little horse-drawn wagons with chilled milk in crates and . . . you could hear them clopping down the street at five-thirty, six o'clock in the morning. They'd stop and come up to the back door always, and put down a quart or two of milk, whatever, and pick up the . . . coupons. . . . You bought your coupons and left the tickets out for the milkman. That's the way it was handled back in those days. **Stephen Traub, 32**

[We would] pass, I think it was, Mr. Gittelsohn's Delicatessen, put our hand in the barrels, the pickle barrels, . . . take out a pickle, buy cheese crackers, walk down Broughton Street. **Ida (Slotin) Wilensky, 34**

You had dinner in the middle of the day, and you had supper at night, because everybody came home at two o'clock when the maids were there. . . . Your parents came home from the store, and you had a big meal. And then at nighttime we had what we call *milchiks*, . . . sour cream and that type of thing. Not like we live today. And Sunday dinner in the middle of the day was a big deal. **Harriet (Kanter) Konter, 43**

[In] those days we had dinner in the middle of the day. Dinner was bigger in the middle of the day, and the evenings you might eat a bowl of cereal or whatever, an egg. . . . The businessmen used to come home for lunch.

My father, with his dad, . . . [other men and] family would all come and would eat at Mama's house on 36th Street, then they would play cards. All of us were hopeful that the card game would run over our time when it was ready to go to Hebrew School, because the Hebrew School was at the B. B. Jacob Synagogue on Montgomery downtown, which happened to be very close across the lane from Slotin & Company. So what we would do is, we'd pile in the car and they'd let us off at Hebrew School and go on back to work. **Leon Slotin, 47**

School was over at two o'clock and . . . Daddy would pick us up or else I would walk home, but dinner was at two o'clock in the afternoon. . . . The family sat down together at two o'clock for dinner. . . . [For our evening meal] we had supper. We usually had salad and grits, or we'd have some kind of a seafood salad. **Adele (Meddin) Schneider, 61**

I grew up near a library. There was no television. Radio was a poor imitation of what we have today. The reception wasn't good. The programming was limited. And so I spent a lot of time at the library which was on 36th and Bull Street, and we read and read all the time. I well remember my folks telling me, "Turn out that light!" And we tried to read under the cover with a flashlight, so I think that is where I developed my reading love. **David Rosenzweig, 25**

As a child we used to go to the Hodgson Hall. . . . It was the library which now is the [Georgia] Historical [Society] library on the corner of Gaston and Whitaker. We used to go there to get out our books. We used to go there all the time, and we walked everywhere we had to go. My parents did not have an automobile and we walked. We used to go on hikes with the girls, . . . with my friends on Sundays. We would hike from the J.E.A. . . . to Thunderbolt, take lunch with us. We did that all the time. **Ethyl (Richman) Rosenzweig, 25**

Rosen Children, c.1907
Pictured left to right are siblings Raymond, Ruth, and Morris Rosen.
JVM 003 Savannah Jewish Archives General Photograph Collection, Item 2237

I used to sit in my bedroom and look out the window facing Washington Square and watch the bonfires [on New Year's Eve]. The young people who lived in that area would collect up wood and boxes and everything else, whatever they could get their hands on that was made of wood during the year and store it. If you had something that was made of wood you had to hide it, unless you wanted it to be burned in the bonfire. And on Christmas Eve and on New Year's Eve, they would have a big bonfire in Washington Square, and a lot of people would come in from all around to watch it.

The fire station was around the corner on Broughton Street, and they would always send a couple of firemen over there to supervise and keep an eye on it to be sure that it didn't get out of hand. And that was quite an event. **Benjamin Silverman, 29**

I remember Paulsen was a dirt street. I can remember when it was paved. . . . They were digging ditches and I was riding a bicycle up and down the ditches, and the bicycle busted in half and the handlebars went into my face and I busted a tooth. I've never had such pain. **Julius Edel, 35**

Forsyth Park . . . was my playground. . . . I recall birthday parties which we celebrated in Forsyth Park. . . . There was always a goat cart to give the kids rides.

There was a little . . . black boy, probably not much older than we were, who would hold on to the goat and walk it around with us in the little cart. **Alan Gaynor, 62**

We used to play out in the park, . . . Franklin Park. . . . They'd bring the cars that were open on both sides . . . and they'd park the car there and sometimes . . . we'd get on there and play with them inside. I remember Mrs. [Yetta] Arkin calling me one time, said, "Get off there!" She gave me hell for getting on. **Beryl Bernstein, 67**

I have a scar on my finger to prove that a firecracker went off when [the principal of 35th Street School] happened to catch me, and I was holding the firecracker so he wouldn't know. It exploded! **Herbert Blumenthal, 76**

We used to go, most of the time, to the park on Bull Street by the old Savannah Theatre. One of the activities that I remember there . . . was making Indian headdresses out of magnolia leaves. We would collect the leaves, and we would also collect the wooden match sticks from the short wooden matches that people used when they smoked. We would pin the leaves together and make all sorts of things that we would put on our heads, and run around and chase each other. . . .

We also used to go to Colonial Park which is on Abercorn and Oglethorpe Avenue because there was a playground on the southern end of that park. We used to go to that playground. **Doris (Goldin) Lukin, 88**

We had what was called ice boxes. . . . The ice man would come by . . . with a wagon full of ice, three-hundred pound blocks. And you'd buy a quarter's worth of ice which he would chip off, and it would fill the top of the box and would keep the box cool just like a refrigerator. . . . The kids would crowd around and they would . . . eat the chippings. . . . The ice would melt and would drain so you'd have to keep a pan under the ice box, and it would have to be emptied regularly or it would run over, which was one of the things we kids used to do. **Benjamin Silverman, 29**

I must have been seven, maybe eight. My closest [friend was] Eddie Humphrey who lived just to the south of us on the corner of Bolton and Whitaker in a humongous big boarding house. His father was a Central of Georgia Railroad engineer. The greatest thrill of my life was on Saturdays when Mr. Humphrey would take Eddie and me and maybe other folks, young kids in the neighborhood, down to the Central of Georgia Railroad yards where we would stand and watch the locomotives turning around on the turntable. **Alan Gaynor, 62**

As a boy . . . we used to all collect together on 36th Street and we were sort of mischievous. At that time I remember West Broad Street was part of the highway going from Florida to up North, and the orange trucks used to come down 37th Street and turn into West Broad. . . . They were laden with oranges and watermelons, whatever the season was at that time. . . . The trucks couldn't pick up speed, so we'd run behind the truck and one little fellow, or it could be the littlest, we'd run up on the truck . . . and we'd start pitching the oranges off to the fellows that run in back. **Arthur "Bubba" Horovitz, 77**

There used to be an athletic social club in Savannah called the Tigers. . . . I was a member of that. That was an athletic club where we participated in football and all the athletic sports for three or four years. We belonged to both the Temple Mickve Israel and the B. B. Jacob. I was *Bar Mitzvahed* at the B. B. Jacob, but I went to Sunday School at the Temple. Our activities were both within the Jewish community and in the gentile community. Some people that I am still quite friendly with today were both phases of the community. **Martin Karp, 42**

When we were in our teens . . . all of us girls . . . used to get a nickel for spending money. When we were getting a little older, we used to go to the store and buy five or ten cigarettes and hide in our bedroom and smoke the hell out of them. Big deal! **Celia (Scheer) Hirsch, 1**

I don't remember any *Bar Mitzvah* parties. I don't remember being included in that because I really didn't know a lot of Jewish kids other than the ones at Temple Mickve Israel, and in those days the Reform children did not go through *Bar Mitzvah* training. That was not very typical in those days. So our parties were sorority parties, and we went to Ebba's Dancing School for our beginning training, and there were tea dances. We entertained among ourselves. . . .

I went to high school parties at Savannah High and Benedictine dances, and felt included in the general community parties. . . . I also remember that the times were such that you could go to Johnny Harris at age fifteen or sixteen and order a drink. It might be served in a coffee cup so that if someone was checking they couldn't tell that you were having a drink, but it was pretty loose and open. That's how Savannah got to be known as the party city, I believe. **Barbara (Smith) Levy, 19**

Any kid that came there couldn't come there and dive off the dock and do anything else unless we taught them how to swim. We showed them how to swim. If they said they knew, we took people like Pete Grossman who was a cocky little kid and he said he could swim, . . .we had all of us that could swim out there, they couldn't possibly drown, and just threw them overboard. When they came up, that's when we'd grab them and put them back in the boat. "Want to go again? What happened, Pete?" He said, "I didn't get my stroke up. You know when you do that it pulls you up." I said, "You want to try it again?" He said, "No, I'm not going to try it no more." So then we took them back to shore, where the water was shallow and showed him how to float and how to do things. In fact, once a year we'd have a whole entourage of fifteen or twenty kids . . . swam all the way across. . . . We used to do it at Isle of Hope, too. **Benjamin Portman, 20**

[My husband, Matt Levy,] always wanted to be a lawyer. He used to play hooky from school and go to the courthouse. . . . As a youngster, [he] skipped classes to go to . . . Judge Meldrim's court, and to sit there and listen to cases. **Pearl (Spivak) Levy, 44**

All the Jewish people had their stores open on Saturday . . . and all the kids that were teenagers helped in the store, no matter if it was a grocery store or a clothing store, whatever it was. So Sunday we'd get together, sometimes at our house. Mom bought us a piano. . . . We'd meet either at our house or at Lena Rosenzweig's. She was Feinberg then at that time.

So if you want to know where anybody was over the weekend, you called either our house or her house because that's where they had a piano, too, and that's where we congregated. . . . There was room to dance, we'd sing and dance, and then they started walking each one home, and drop 'em off as they went along. The last person was usually a fellow. It was really very nice at that time. **Ida (Bronitsky) Stein, 56**

When we were in the sixth grade one of the things we had to learn to do for our history lesson, we had to start at Forsyth Park and walk down Bull Street to the river. We had to learn the squares and whose monuments were on the squares, and that was a deplorable history lesson because it was always in the winter time when we had to take the walk. **Adele (Meddin) Schneider, 61**

Along the way I got interested in flying. I made my first flight when I was sixteen and I wanted to take flying lessons then. After a year . . . of persuading my parents, they finally gave in. When I was seventeen, I started to fly.

The license available to a young pilot at that time [was] a pilot license which simply allowed you to fly solo. That was after eight hours of instructions. Then I went on to get a private license which allowed me to carry a passenger, not for hire, but I could take somebody up with me. **Karl Friedman, 85**

Children didn't drive cars, and in those days it was quite safe to walk, and we walked to Leopold's Ice Cream on Gwinnett and Habersham. That was quite an outing. So life was simple. **Selma (Greenberg) Dunn, 7**

Now you know the house that they call Scarbrough House. In my day there was actually the West Broad Street School for Negroes [there]. . . . That school had

[a] Georgia, Georgia gray brick [wall that] encircled this play yard. . . . I think it was about two feet wide and six feet tall. That didn't stifle us; all the kids used to play in there when they closed the school. . . .

Across the street from us at that time was the Bluestein's little confectionary shop. We used to go there and buy sour pickles and candy and all kinds of stuff. **Benjamin Portman, 20**

Cousins, c.1920
On the left is Evelyn Robinson and on the right is Evelyn (Nathan) Bethlahmy.
JVM 003 Savannah Jewish Archives General Photograph Collection, Item 2227

We had a holiday and David Rosenzweig and Herman Blumenthal and I were sitting out during recess, and we got into a discussion about how to turn on a fire alarm.

Herman said you had to break the glass and then turn it on. I said, "No, you just have to open it like this and turn it on." And I opened it and the glass fell down and broke, and there was a fireman sitting across the street. He put us all under arrest. Took us home and told our mothers that we turned in a false alarm, which we never did. **Sidney Raskin, 23**

In summertime, sitting on the curb on 49th Street, and these black peddlers, both women and men. The women would have the stuff balanced on top of their head, the men would have a pushcart, selling vegetables. **Philip Solomons, Sr., 30**

EARLY JOBS

Coming up during the Depression you didn't really have much money to play around with, and each summer I had a drink stand right in front of that little drug store [near City Market]. . . . Coca-Cola wasn't a big deal then. The big one at that time was Ne-Hi, because it was the biggest! That's where I really got most of my spending money. **Philip Solomons, Sr., 30**

I got a job [at] Marilyn's Slipper Shop. At that time Marilyn's Slipper Shop was quite big, one of the biggest in the South. I worked with them, but the hours were killing. Dressed windows twice a week, Tuesday and Thursday night. Then the pay was good, though. If I'm not mistaken, I think I made twenty dollars a week. That was pretty good then in those days.

Then we were dressing the windows one night. Mr. Joe Lesser, Lesser's Men Shop, passed by, and he saw me come outside and look at the windows. . . . And he said, "I'm going to open up. . . . How would you like the job?" And that sounded big to me because the hours I was putting in daily at Marilyn's Slipper Shop was unbearable. . . . I went to see him on Sunday, . . . and he offered me, if I'm not mistaken, . . . about twenty-five dollars a week, plus either one or two percent of whatever I sold. **Harry Eichholz, 57**

I used to go around and sell matches, the big boxes of matches. They were a nickel a box. I sold them three for a dime. . . . Then I started selling salt, boxes of salt, going from house to house around my father's store. . . . I was nine years old, ten years old.

And then I went to work for Julius Asher on Saturday at Yachum & Yachum. . . . That was two brothers on West Broad Street. . . . They were two boys that served in the service, and their motto was, "Uncle Sammy's boys served in war and serving in peace.". . . Hymie Perlman and Morris Perlman [were their names]. But they were referred to as Yachum & Yachum because they yakked all the time.

To understand them you really had to listen very closely. They couldn't write, couldn't read. . . . But they were able to sign their name on checks, and that was the important thing. They started out with one store, then the store next to them went broke. They cut a hole in that wall and expanded. They had the whole block. . . . I went to work for them when I was ten years old, after *shul* on Saturday. I was working for Julius Asher. At that time we had a whole group of Jewish boys working there on Saturday. **Samuel Radetsky, 45**

[My aunts] were real characters, . . . all of them very, very, very hardworking people. . . . My Aunt Annie Melaver . . . and my mother opened a grocery store because my grandfather was so inept [in business]. . . . My mother at that time was thirteen and my Aunt Annie was twelve, and they went into business! **Walter Lowe, 54**

As I mentioned before, my family were quite poor. I had to go to work. I left school in eighth grade. I went to work. I went to work on several different jobs. One job in particular was on West Broad Street when I was maybe fifteen, sixteen, and I worked there for six dollars and fifty cents a week. At that time West Broad Street stayed open until seven-thirty daily, nighttime, and also on Saturday night, twelve o'clock. We figured it out, Sidney Raskin and I figured it out one time, how much that was a week and it boiled down to being about eight cents an hour. . . . I gave my family half. **Harry Eichholz, 57**

During high school I worked at the Grocerteria, which was a large public market on Barnard Street, Barnard and Congress. I was paid one dollar a day, plus my meals. I also raised chickens in the backyard and I sold the eggs. I was able to save enough money to go to the World's Fair in Chicago in 1933 off of egg money. There were three of us that went, Martin Kirschbaum, Jr., Samuel Herman, and myself. **Martin Leffler, 14**

I got a job delivering circulars to the merchants after school. When they had sales they used to put a bunch of papers they'd deliver to the black neighborhoods. . . . Joe Levin gave me a bunch of them and he said, "Ralph, you be the chairman of this thing. You watch them." So the next thing I see he had two other black boys, one of them took a bunch of these folders and dumped them in the sewer. I ran over and had a fist fight with him, "Don't do that." So when we got back to Joe's, I said, "Joe, don't give him a nickel. He dumped all of them in there." I had another fist fight. . . .

Finally I get a job, at Sam Blumenthal's five and dime store on Broughton and West Broad, from eight in the morning 'til twelve o'clock at night. He paid us a dollar. . . . I got the dollar and ran home; I ran from Broughton and West Broad to Jefferson in ten minutes. Jefferson and Bolton, ten minutes flat. One day Mr. Blumenthal pays me ninety-five cents. I said, "Mr. Blumenthal, how come?" He said, "You goddam tinhorn, you came five minutes late from supper. I docked you a nickel. So you questioned me. You're fired!" So, what the hell am I to do? I ran home. I got my ninety-five cents and Papa [was] waiting for me. I told him what happened. He says to me, "That *momzer*. That's just like him."

Anyways, next Saturday I get a job in a grocery store, Bennie Warshaw's grocery store. I went in there and he says, "I'm going to show you how to sell chickens." So he sold two chickens. He says, "Watch me, I'm going out in the yard." And he took a cleaver and he chopped their heads. Next thing, another guy came in and bought two chickens, and he said, "watch him." We went outside and he took their heads in his hands, and did this. One chicken fell down on this side and the other, and goddam, he's got the heads in his hands. So I went home for lunch. "Papa, if that's the way they kill these chickens, I can't do it no more." So guess where I end up and get another job? Yachum & Yachum. Oh, boy! . . . [I was] thirteen or fourteen years old. **Ralph Tenenbaum, 58**

A Special Treat, 1928
Louise "Sister" (Gordon) Rudofsky Zachs and her brother Robert Gordon.
JVM 003 Savannah Jewish Archives General Photograph Collection, Item 2286

I went to work for them [Yachum & Yachum] when I was ten years old after *shul* on Saturday. I was working for Julius Asher. At that time we had a whole group of Jewish boys working there on Saturday; Marvin Arkin, Harvey Gordon, myself. Every now and then we also had Jake Plotkin who was the regular there; Gus Lipsitz . . . was also an extra help. . . . Dollar a day. . . . If he could use me on Friday afternoon, he'd call me in. I'd make another fifty cents. We had P.M.s [prize monies for discontinued styles] in those days. . . . It's a shoe that was already out of style. If we sold it we'd get an extra fifteen cents. **Samuel Radetsky, 45**

Around June . . . [in] the big Park Extension, about two blocks away, they had baseball games there. So, on the corner of Bolton and . . . Barnard there was a fellow by the name of Zeke Meyers and a Coca-Cola stand. We got a job from him selling Coca-Cola during the ballgame. I made a quarter. Meyer made thirty cents. Albert made fifty cents. That's what we did.

During the game, the people used to stand up. So one day we decided to build benches. We built about four benches and rented them at ten cents to sit there. So the following year we built more. First thing you know we made sixty-eight dollars that year, which is a lot of money that season. The following year we did the same thing.

The third year we come up there, we got competition. . . . Gentile boys took our spots. So we walked over, we said, "We've had these for three years. Why don't you go on the other side?" "No, you Jew babies, we're going to stay right here." Again there was one little fellow, two bigger ones. And in a fist fight, I took the little one and beat the living hell out of him. They went on the other side. From then on we became very good friends. We made money. **Ralph Tenenbaum, 58**

When I graduated school, I went to work for my father-in-law because all the boys were called into the service. I was like eighteen years old, just out of school. All my father-in-law could do was right in Savannah. Therefore, I had to do everything, all the ordering, marking, figuring out the prices, did everything.

At the time . . . the shipyard was going strong. The workers would come in when they got their checks to shop at Joe Levin's and they would buy their little pair of socks or whatever. And we would cash the checks, and then we would get low on money and I would get the checks ready and take them to the bank, which was about four blocks away. I carried, by myself in a little paper bag, thousands of dollars, and never worried about it. Never. I had to go a couple of times a day to do that on a payday. **Audrey (Galkin) Levin, 89**

I worked at the *Savannah Evening Press* during the summers and when I first graduated from college, and I had two big stories. . . . One was, I was in the first car to cross the old Talmadge Bridge in 1954. . . . The other big story I had . . . was . . . 1967. . . . Mills B. Lane had called a press conference and . . . that was the day that he announced he was donating the land for Armstrong College to move from downtown Savannah out to the south side. **Jane (Guthman) Kahn, 93**

EDUCATION

Public Schools

We're sitting in the house [312 East 48th Street] that I spent most of my life in. We moved here in 1938 [or] '37. . . . I went to Savannah schools that are within a half a block. Charles Ellis [Elementary School] is at the corner where I went from kindergarten through sixth grade. A block in the other direction is

Savannah High School. Except for . . . one year at Richard Arnold Junior High School, and then Washington Avenue Junior High came into existence. **Jack Golden, 74**

We all went to Barnard Street School . . . [which] had an outhouse in the yard. . . . One of the teachers was a Mrs. Oliver and she . . . compared me with Emanuel, my brother. . . . It was up to the seventh grade at that time. **Anne (Lewis) Buchsbaum, 2**

I went to Montgomery Street School which was located on Montgomery . . . where the present Chatham County Courthouse is. We had six grades. The bathrooms were in the yard. . . . I remember our janitor's name was Amos Eubanks. And the school was strictly a reading, writing, 'rithmetic. I mean basics. There were a number . . . of Jewish children that went to that school because that was where most of the Jews [lived]. **Selma (Greenberg) Dunn, 7**

Montgomery Street School, c.1923
The Chatham County Courthouse is now on the site of the old Montgomery Street Elementary School. The known Jewish children in this photograph are Nina (Kanter) Greenholtz, William Cohen, and Ann (Berliner) Rudnick.
JVM 003 Savannah Jewish Archives General Photograph Collection, Item 0053

Our school was Montgomery Street School, which is about situated across from the old *shul*, the old synagogue. The square there was called Liberty Street Square, and of course the whole building there now is the county jail. But this is where the school was.

There was a Catholic school. It was run by Catholics and was part of the school system. I will never forget that. The principal of that school was Mr.

[Arthur J.] O'Hara, Father O'Hara was his name. He had a big, wide belt that he carried on a strap. In those days it was more popular to whip a kid than to try to talk him out of it. My hand was always tender because of that. **Benjamin Portman, 20**

I first started off at Barnard Street School. It was a school there on . . . Barnard and Taylor. My brother, they had a grocery store right there . . . in front of the school. At recess . . . I'd come over there and pick up a tray with all kind of sandwiches, cookies, cakes, candies, and bring it across the street, and I'd sell all that to the pupils. And when they rang the bell, he'd come over there and get the money and get what was left and take it back across the street. **Sam Steinberg, 31**

I started off the first day of first grade at Barnard Street School until my grandfather realized that they had privies in the backyard. He would not put up with his darling grandson going to a school that had privies in the backyard.

So he contacted his son-in-law, Edmund H. Abrahams, who was either president or on the Board of Education in those days, and I was immediately transferred to Henry Street School which did have bathrooms in the backyard, but they were, as I recall, flush toilets. Barnard Street, as I recall, was dry-pit latrines. All the rich kids in downtown Savannah in those days who lived on the east side went to Massie School. Us poor kids went to Henry and Barnard. **Alan Gaynor, 62**

My brother Alvin [and I], . . . we both went to Charles Ellis Grammar School. We both went to Richard Arnold Junior High which is on Bull and 35th. **Herman Cranman, 36**

I went to Charles Ellis, . . . a wonderful neighborhood school. Every morning I walked to school except when it was raining. Then my mother would take me to school. Along the way we would pick up other classmates. **Phillipa "Bunny" (Sherman) Cohen, 90**

The old Savannah High [was] on Bull. . . . I went through that school until my senior year when they finished building the Savannah High on Washington Avenue. I was in the first class to graduate from that old Savannah High. . . . Governor Ed Rivers came down to give us our address at graduation. It was very exciting. . . . We had graduation in January as well as in June. There were eighty-five in the class. **Adele (Meddin) Schneider, 61**

By the time I graduated from Junior High School in 1937, the old Savannah High School building on Washington Avenue had been built . . . by the W.P.A. during the Depression. The first students occupied that building in

September of 1937, I among them. I graduated from that school in 1940. **Doris (Goldin) Lukin, 88**

Savannah High School, Spring 1939
Girlfriends pose in front of the school (left to right): (front row) Miriam (Schmalheiser) Nathan; (back row) Florence (Karpf) Alterbaum, Louise "Sister" (Gordon) Rudofsky Zacks, and Ruth (Wolson) Einhorn.
JVM 003 Savannah Jewish Archives General Photograph Collection, Item 2003

I went to 38th Street School. It's on Montgomery and West Broad. I luckily was elected May Queen at the May Festival . . . where they dance around the flagpole. I remember my mother taking me to the full dressmaker and having my thing [gown] made, and their taking my picture and a real big fuss was made. It was impressive. **Annette (Berman) Gray, 87**

Walter's [my son] love was really basketball, but he also played football. They were down on the field and [Savannah] High School was playing somebody, and he was on the football field, and somebody turned around to Riette [Pollack] and said, "Riette, which one is your brother?" She said, "The one with the clean uniform." He never even had a chance to play football. **Sadye (Steinberg) Rabhan, 22**

PRIVATE SCHOOLS

[Nina Pape] was really quite the grande dame and she represented the sterner, authoritarian lady. . . . At the time that I knew her she was already in a wheelchair and she would make frequent visits to us, especially at assemblies, . . . once a week. She'd be wheeled into the room. She always had a black ribbon around her neck, which was part of her older fashion, and she would say to us, "Good morning, ladies,". . . and we would always say, "Good morning, Miss Pape," in unison. . . . Also I can firmly remember her telling us that "chewing gum should only be chewed in the presence of a lady's boudoir." Those were her stern admonitions. **Barbara (Smith) Levy, 19**

Pape School, Class of 1941-1942
The Jewish students in this class are left to right (front row) #1 Jane
(Guthman) Kahn and (second row) #3 Mary Jane (Mayer) Stinson.
JVM 003 Savannah Jewish Archives General Photograph Collection, Item 1366

Oh! I didn't tell you that I went to Pape School, first, second, third, and
fourth grades, because they took boys for four grades. It was down here on Bolton
and Abercorn Street; . . . there were four or five boys. We went there for four
years. **A. J. Cohen, Jr., 6**

I started off at Pape School and went through the seventh grade there. I was
anxious to change over to a public school because most of my really good friends
did not attend private school, and finally I was able to make the change. My
parents wanted me to continue with Pape School because they wanted me to go
to a good college, and they thought that I would be better prepared. But one
summer they were in Europe and I was staying with my grandmother, and it was
time to register for public school, and I begged to be allowed to go to public
school. And she said, "All right, you can register and go to public school, but
when your parents come back, if they want you to go to Pape School, that's in
their hands. I can't do anything about it." So I registered and went to 35th Street
Junior High School, and when they came back they decided I could continue
there, so that's what I did. **Marion (Abrahams) Levy Mendel, 17**

My mother and my father had both attended Pape. My mother had graduated
there before she went off to college. So it wasn't so strange that I went there. . . .

I started in the first grade unlike many of my classmates who had begun in kindergarten. I remained at Pape until I graduated in 1952.

It was a different kind of schooling. The school was housed in an old building which was on Bolton Street and Abercorn, that was the lower school. The upper school was a two or three story building on Drayton Street facing Forsyth Park. . . . I learned a lot in that school, and yet there were a lot of things we didn't have because it was a private school. It was small. It was intimate. Class sizes were very small, yet our workload was heavy. We felt we were getting a lot of education. Our teachers were well educated in their fields. . . .

The other Jewish girl in my class was Anne Solomon, who is now Anne Clavel. Anne was brilliant, and even when she tried to fail she couldn't. She won the National French Awards, and oh, she was a terrific scholar! But you see, when we graduated, there were only nine in our class, and nobody could be in the upper ten percent. I found that rather amusing.

And our graduation was not cap and gown; we were clothed in the beautiful white long dresses. I remember having a hoop skirt, carrying red roses, and the dress being so tight that I had to stand up in the car and be taken by my father to the class. I was so afraid that I was going to burst my seams when we had to sing. **Barbara (Smith) Levy, 19**

During those days we had the choo-choo train to Tybee. And the windows were all open. Miss Pape who ran the school, a long stalk of celery who was a spinster with a black net around her neck, she was a long John with a whistle around her neck, and would blow the whistle.

We would all get on the train with our lunch and go down to the beach, and I forgot how we changed. But some place we changed to go swimming and she would blow the whistle and you would have to get out of the water and get back on the train. **A. J. Cohen, Jr., 6**

[Pape School students] used to have picnics at the beach once a year, at the Fresh Air Home. We weren't allowed to go in the water, but we did get to go to the beach. **Barbara (Smith) Levy, 19**

My oldest child is Carol, and she is a social worker. She got her start in Jewish community work when she was still at Savannah Country Day School. She did her senior project . . . at the J.E.A. . . . Carol elected to produce *Fiddler on the Roof* for seventh and eighth grade students. . . . She did the whole thing. She produced the show. . . . Carol still remembers the people that were in *Fiddler on the Roof* and their parents talk about it still to this day. **Jane (Guthman) Kahn, 93**

Savannah Country Day School, 3 February 1974
Fiddler on the Roof was produced at the J.E.A. by Carol Kahn. Pictured (left to right): Rebecca (Cohen) Jacobson, Earl Berman, Lisa (Markowitz) Kitchens, Rachel Kronowitz, Patricia (Galin) Guggenheim, Amy Gellins, Eric Platock, Janet "Tova" Melaver, and James Teller.
JMS 062 Guthman-Kahn Family Papers

I attended Savannah High School for two years, I think, . . . [then] transferred to Benedictine. . . . Historically, the school had always had a Jewish student in almost every class that graduated. When they had religious classes, we had study period, and it was very comfortable, in my opinion. . . . My reason [for going to Benedictine] was a number of things. I was not a very good student. . . . I was borderline passing and I thought I'd do better without distractions. . . . I also thought maybe that it was a little easier, because the classes were smaller. **Herman Cranman, 36**

I went to Benedictine, and there were probably fifteen or twenty Jewish boys in there at that time, and we were taught by a Benedictine priest, and it was a very, very fine school. . . . I played basketball at Benedictine, and so did David Center. As a matter of fact, the first team consisted of two Jewish boys and three Protestants. The Catholics always said a prayer before the beginning of a game, and the first team used to step aside because none of us were Catholics. **Albert Mazo, 50**

COLLEGE

Of course, my folks' ambition was to give all of us educations, and all four boys were college graduates. My sister went to college for two years, and she had to quit so the boys could go to college. It was considered important for the boys to go to college because they had to make a living. **Albert Mazo, 50**

I was in the first class at Armstrong Junior College. . . . I think there were something like seventy-five or eighty students in the class when it first opened. **Herbert Traub, Jr., 79**

I went to Armstrong College. . . . I went for two years and graduated. I was in the first graduating class of Armstrong. . . . It was a junior college. **Nathan Karnibad, 41**

My folks couldn't send both my brother and I to college at the same time. During my brother's senior year at the University, I went to Armstrong. It was a savior, really. Armstrong never has gotten the credit in this community that it's due. And having gone from Armstrong to Georgia Tech, I don't know whether I would have made it at Georgia Tech without that good basic that I got at Armstrong. I mean, going straight from high school to Georgia Tech, that would have been tough. **Philip Solomons, Sr., 30**

I went to Savannah High School, the original one downtown on Bull Street, now used by the Board of Education. I graduated in 1935, just in time to attend Armstrong Junior College, which had just opened in the beautiful Armstrong home. So I was a member of the charter graduating class in 1937. Then off to the University of Georgia in Athens for my last two years. **Elizabeth "Libby" (Levy) Price, 69**

When you got out of college in our day . . . you came home and went into your father's business. . . . It was predestined. You didn't have any choices. Today there are a lot of choices out there. Family businesses in Savannah are gone. Those days are gone. And that's what it was. So that, I would say, was a dramatic change. I think World War II changed a lot of the direction of where guys wanted to go after they came back from the war. They had the G.I. Bill and could go on to college. That changed it. **Leon Slotin, 47**

University of Georgia, Fall 1942
Savannah girls in this photograph of the Delta Phi Epsilon Sorority at
University of Georgia include (left to right): (front row) #2 Frances
(Solomon) Gretenstein, #3 Doris (Goldin) Lukin, #4 Florence (Karpf)
Alterbaum, and #5 Dorothy (Alkon) Maslanko; (second row) #4 Esther
(Berger) Rabhan and #5 Thelma (Reed) Rosen.
JVM 003 Savannah Jewish Archives General Photograph Collection, Item 0074

EARLY HOMES

EARLY NEIGHBORHOODS

They [Jewish immigrants] lived all over. They lived on Bryan Street and
Yamacraw and a little place called Frog Town as some people called it; . . . it
would be over . . . where I-16 comes in there with the Union Station. It was back
over in that section. **Sanford Wexler, 48**

A lot of Jewish people had [lived in Yamacraw]. . . . The Cranmans lived in,
they used to call it Frog Town by the school. **Samuel Hirsch, 52**

Yamacraw [was] where we lived, in the Jewish section, which was on Bryan Street, . . . in that section, where most of the old-timers used to live. Of course, high class people for that time lived on West 36th Street. That was the goal of every Jewish family: "Let's move to 36th Street." **Benjamin Portman, 20**

They were living in Yamacraw. . . . They had a little store there, grocery stores. . . . A few of them that lived in the Old Fort District, that is on East Broad Street where the Pirate's House is, called the Old Fort District. A lot of the Jewish people lived there. . . . Some lived on East Broughton Street right off of Price and the Old Fort District, which was Bryan Street. And a lot of them lived in Yamacraw. And then a lot of them that prospered moved up to 36th, 37th Street. **Reuben Schneider, 28**

Living in the Old Fort was a sort of an interesting experience. We got along pretty good with our Irish neighbors, but there was also always some squabble between the kids. . . . I have often said when I walked a block to go to Washington Square, I didn't know whether I was going to be picked to get on the softball team, or whether I was going to have to fight my way back out of the square. **Benjamin Silverman, 29**

LIVING DOWNTOWN

When I was five or six years on, I was very friendly in the neighborhood. There again, except for Hebrew School which came later, there was no afternoon. There was no dancing, no karate, no television. We stayed in the neighborhood.

We played from the time we got out of school until dark, 'til after dark, and apparently with some safety because the family never worried about us. My family came home from the grocery store downtown. They came home from the store after dark and I would be sitting on the porch waiting on the stone steps. **David Rosenzweig, 25**

We lived upstairs at my father's store on 244 West Broad Street. The entrance was in the lane, however it was very beautifully arranged. We had . . . a gorgeous apartment; the living room, dining room, and . . . a large bathroom. And it was a big place because it was the size of the store downstairs. **Evelyn (Center) Goldberg, 10**

I remember vividly from 1912 on. I was six years old. I was born on 415 [West] Broughton Street, where the Courthouse is now. . . . That block, the 400 block, there were stores on both sides of the block, and with the exception of one person they were all Jews. They ran the stores and everybody lived over the stores. The houses were over the stores and the businesses were downstairs. There was only one gentile on the block.

I have a lot of memories of it because in the summer we'd stay up real late. There was no air conditioning in those days and the only relief we had was a fan. A lot of people couldn't afford the electricity all night, so the kids stayed up real late. I remember every night, of course, we'd play games. The boys would play "Hannah Hannah Haro" and the girls would play all kinds of games.

At nine o'clock every night, a Greek man would come by with a little wagon, a whistling wagon, and he would sell popcorn. We'd all wait for the little man to come by and get the popcorn. **Lena (Feinberg) Rosenzweig, 26**

We lived in many places. . . . For a while my mother and my father, for reasons of poverty, I guess, at that time lived with my aunt and uncle, Joseph Rubenstein. And he lived on Bryan Street around that square where . . . the First African Baptist Church [is]. And we lived on the corner there. . . . We lived across the street from the Kirschner family, and they were bitter enemies because of business. . . .

On the corner of Bryan and Jefferson the Rubnitz family had a second-hand store. . . . Jake Rubin's family had a store in the following block. . . . A lot of Jewish people lived on Bryan Street behind Broughton Street. . . . At one time while I was still living there, Morris Horovitz had the place on the corner of Montgomery and Bryan. **Evelyn (Ward) Karsman, 53**

We lived at first on West Bolton Street. . . . [When] I was about three years old . . . we moved to Broughton Street. My father had [a] store on the 400 block of Broughton Street between Montgomery and West Broad. We lived over the store there. . . . We remained there until 1928. We moved from there to 120 East Duffy, between Abercorn and Drayton. **Marvin Arkin, 76**

Gaston Street was like city limits. People went to the bay for recreation, to the river. It was beautiful, just as it is today. Of course, another memory I have from when I lived on Broughton Street at five years old, I would hear the black people singing. They had a church on West Broad Street, West Broad and Bolton. They had on white robes and they would march down West Broad Street singing on Sunday morning, to be baptized. And they walked from Bolton Street all the way down to the bay to where the river was, and that's where they were baptized. **Lena (Feinberg) Rosenzweig, 26**

A very interesting thing that occurred when we lived at 34 East Broad Street was the fact that there was a baptism almost every Sunday morning at the foot of

East Broad Street and the Savannah River. And they would have a parade and the people who were going to be baptized were dressed in white, and they were transported in a buggy and a horse with a fringe on top of the buggy, like you see in the movies, the old-time buggies that sometime you see in the present day westerns.

They would pass by and they would be singing and sometimes there'd be a band. They'd march down to the river and they'd have the baptism, and we would often go there and watch. And then they would transport them back to the church or wherever they took them to dry off and redress. **Benjamin Silverman, 29**

I lived on Broughton Street as a young girl. . . . The Savilowskys had a shoe store between Montgomery and Jefferson, it was called the Hole in the Wall. I believe that was the name of it. We lived up over that shoe store. **Evelyn (Ward) Karsman, 53**

Yamacraw's Best, n.d.
Local baseball players on Bay Street with City Hall's gold dome in the background.
JVM 003 Savannah Jewish Archives General Photograph Collection, Item 0058

I was born on Harris and East Broad Street in 1914. My family was quite poor, very poor people. And after I got to be about eight years old, we moved to Park Avenue and Abercorn. **Harry Eichholz, 57**

In those days . . . we didn't have gas [natural gas] furnished to us as we have now. Gas was manufactured in a plant on Bay and East Broad Street, and we had then what we called gas meters. . . . When your gas ran out, you'd drop a quarter in the meter and you'd get a quarter's worth of gas. . . .

When we lived at 34 East Broad Street, we had no electricity. We used kerosene lamps, and my mother had a wooden stove and oven on which she cooked and baked delicious meals and managed fine. And when they finally installed electricity it was a drop cord with a bulb attached to it, and a socket in the bulb in the middle of the room, so that when you came into the room and it was dark, you had to feel around for the cord, and you usually hit it and tried to catch it when it swung back. And that was the type that people endured those days and didn't have any better and didn't know any better. **Benjamin Silverman, 29**

We lived over the store on Bryan and Jefferson Street, right on the corner. The store was downstairs and the house was upstairs. . . . I had five sisters, all older than me. We had three bedrooms, we had a dining room and a kitchen. That was quite a house. We had one bathroom! **Irvin "Sonny" Rubnitz, 49**

Our life was really around the Jewish community. The J.E.A. was downtown, the B. B. Jacob Synagogue was downtown as we grew up, and . . . what developed into the A.A., was a little tiny synagogue on Montgomery Street where the B. B. Jacob was, down the street about two blocks. . . .

So the majority of the people belonged to the B. B. Jacob Synagogue, and our age group and everybody that came before us and after us spent their lives, basically, at the J.E.A., which was on Charlton Street. Down the street from that, you could walk down to Solomon's Drugstore and that was a big deal, 'cause you know you could get a Coca-Cola at that time for a nickel. Put a little cherry in it and that made it really uptown. **Harriet (Kanter) Konter, 43**

I was born on Oglethorpe [Avenue] . . . between Barnard and Habersham. But most of my early life was spent on York Street between . . . Barnard and Jefferson. There were a row of yellow houses there; they still exist. . . . It was sort of a townhouse. It was a two-story house. The Slotins lived there also. We were probably the only Jewish people living on that street. **Albert Mazo, 50**

When we came to Savannah [when I was eight years old], we lived in a Jewish boarding house; . . . it was on the northwest corner of Oglethorpe and Barnard. It was a big old-time rambling house. . . . I remember, across the street from the boarding house, J. C. Lewis' original automobile distributorship was on that corner. We were just two blocks from the Jewish Alliance at that time. We finally got a house on Waldburg Street. Later on, for some reason, there was a synagogue built across the square, and I think it was origins of Agudath Achim. I'm not certain, but I think it was. And we used to go to services there and I was *Bar Mitzvahed* there. **Samuel Hirsch, 52**

There were certain pockets that were known to be rough areas. . . . [Where] Montgomery Street School used to be, well it's not even there now, but you know, the square ran through by the old *shuls*. So if somebody let you off on Oglethorpe [Avenue] and you had to go through that square to get to Hebrew School, sometimes you had to fight your way through it. **Harris Slotin, 55**

I was born in an apartment on Barnard Street, near Gwinnett. I think it was 1101 Barnard. I was right around the corner from both my grandmothers. My Grandmother [Cecelia] Abrahams lived on the corner of Gwinnett and Barnard, and my Grandmother [Fannie] Guckenheimer lived . . . at 811 Whitaker Street. We were well centered there and I was the recipient of a lot of attention and love. **Marion (Abrahams) Levy Mendel, 17**

Dr. Weichselbaum, Sr., married Carrie Kayton whose father [Lewis Kayton] had come from New York, and I think she was born in the house, . . . the red brick house on the corner of Hall and Drayton. At that time there was a fence around the park [Forsyth Park], and the cows grazed there. So that was quite a mansion to go up on that particular corner at that time. **Mildred (Wolf) Weichselbaum, 51**

At the time I was born [1924] we lived on West Bolton Street, . . . 310 West Bolton Street. . . . My first memory was an apartment on East Duffy Street which was close to Paulsen. . . . There were two Jewish families that I recall there, the Bellah family lived upstairs, and the Meyers family lived next door. **Herman Cranman, 36**

My grandparents . . . bought a house in 1919 at 308 West Bolton Street. . . . In this area of Bolton Street and Gwinnett Street there were a lot of Jewish people living. In the apartment next door to where my grandparents [lived], the Buchsbaums had it. . . . Mary and Morris Levy, who had the men's store on Broughton Street, lived there. Mary Levy's parents lived there. The Levin family lived on Gwinnett and Jefferson streets. I think, after the first World War, Arnold Tenenbaum's grandfather lived on the corner of Jefferson and Bolton streets. **Martin Karp, 42**

My first six years we lived at 21 East Gordon, across from the Temple. I was born in a hospital, but my parents lived there. My first year of school was at Massie, and then at the end of my sixth year we moved to Gwinnett Street and we were there 'til I was fifteen. Then we moved to 46th Street. **Adele (Meddin) Schneider, 61**

On 35th and Montgomery, it's the only place I ever lived until I got married. It's the only house in that area that's been torn down. It was a dirt street. . . . We used to play stickball. . . . It was all mostly Jewish and it was wonderful. **Betty (Blumenthal) Cantor, 66**

I was raised . . . on 321 West 35th Street, that's on Montgomery and 35th Street. At that time we didn't have any paved streets. . . . We associated with a lot of Jewish families in that block. There was Mr. Kaplan. [He] had a grocery store, Phillip Kaplan was his name, on the corner of Jefferson and 35th Street. Then there was the Itzkovitz family. There was a Rosenthal family. Quite a few [Jewish] families in that area. **Herbert Blumenthal, 76**

We moved to . . . 412 . . . West 36th. That was three doors from West Broad Street or Martin Luther King as we know it today. It was a big Jewish section on 36th Street. Starting at West Broad, on the north side of 36th Street, was . . . the Blairs, and then the Greens, then us, Dr. [Louis] Freedman's family, the Palefskys, and the Clarks.

On the other side of the street there was a mixture. You started off from West Broad, we had Jake Fine. . . . Then the last one on the other side of the block was the Smithbergs. In growing up, we had a nice group of Jewish people plus . . . the gentiles were very friendly at that time. We grew up with a nice bunch of people. I think that our childhood was as good as you want to have. **Arthur "Bubba" Horovitz, 77**

When my parents were first married, before either Karl or I were born, they lived in what is now called the Gingerbread House, which was then an apartment house on Bull and 36th Street. . . . 36th Street, of course, was a Jewish neighborhood at that time. My grandparents lived on the corner of 36th and Montgomery Street, and quite a number of Jewish families lived on 36th Street. . . .

As was then common and had been common before in the history of the eastern European Jewish community in Savannah, they kind of moved in the ghetto approach. When my father was young, his family lived on what was called Margaret Street, what is now York Street, and that's where the Jews congregated at that time. **Erwin "Ernie" Friedman, 71**

We lived on 36th Street, and among the families that lived on 36th Street at that time: next door to us was a Falk family; and then going on down the block there were the Mazo family; the Friedmans on the corner of Montgomery and 36th; Sol Clark's family had a boarding house; . . . next to them were Palefskys; there was a Dr. Freedman; my Aunt Lena Ehrenreich; the Blums; Carly Green's family lived there; and the Blairs were on the corner; and then going across West

Broad Street, which we now call Martin Luther King Boulevard, was David Segall's family; across from him was Mrs. [Frances] Kandel; my Aunt Ida Berman; and next to them the Nathans; and then coming back down the street were the Fines. **Leon Slotin, 47**

My first remembrance was the home . . . on York Street. . . . I remember that the Telfair Academy was right across the street. And I remember it was row houses. I think there were either four or five of them. . . . I think we lived there when the end of the war [World War I] was announced. . . . I do remember my mother telling me that before they moved to York Street, they lived on Perry, East Perry. I think that's the only time they ever lived on the east side. . . .

Then I remember we did move to 36th Street. . . . I think Whitaker to past West Broad Street were Jewish people and the Catholic people. . . . We lived [in] the second house from Whitaker on the north side of the street. . . . We were also a block from the public library. . . . We would go to that public library every Saturday. . . . That public library was like our home. **Ida (Slotin) Wilensky, 34**

I may mention that on 36th Sreet we had a three-bedroom; it was a two-story house. There was three bedrooms, one bath, and a half-bath downstairs. In this house it was my grandfather and grandmother, my mother and father, we three boys, my Uncle Mike [Brooks], my Uncle Harry [Brooks] and his wife Annie. All lived in one house, with no arguments. Well, a little spat here and there, but it was a natural thing that everybody lived together. **Arthur "Bubba" Horovitz, 77**

It was an interesting neighborhood. . . . There were a number of gentile families also lived on that street. And the library which has been refurbished today in general, that was a main thing. The little park there on the side, and everybody went to the library. And the Gingerbread House, that was Mr. [Adolph] Asendorf owned that house, on the corner of Bull and 36th; they call it the Gingerbread House now. **Leon Slotin, 47**

My life really started on West 38th Street, to be exact 308 West 38th Street. That's where most of the Jewish community lived. They lived from 39th . . . back to about 34th Street. . . . They lived from . . . Bull Street to West Broad, which is now Martin Luther King Boulevard. **Harriet (Kanter) Konter, 43**

My grandfather, . . . David A. Byck, Sr., lived on 38th and Barnard on the southeast corner. . . . My mother's parents lived on 36th between Bull and Whitaker. So my father and mother grew up just two blocks apart. They were almost childhood sweethearts. **David A. Byck, III, 72**

We were already out of my childhood when everybody lived on the west side. By then people were going to the east side. As I grew up as a teenager it was not uncommon for us to walk from 38th Street to what we called the "Big Park," that is now the Forsyth Park, and play tennis or do something, and turn around and walk back. We just walked everywhere. **Harriet (Kanter) Konter, 43**

In World War II, I was married and lived at the famous Tomochichi Apartments which was on Habersham and 40th Street. . . . There were eight apartments, and there was so much fun that went on in those apartments. . . . There were seven Jewish families that lived in the Tomochichi and one gentile family. That's where both of my children were born and I thought I was in heaven living on 40th Street. . . . I probably paid twenty-one or twenty-five dollars a month rent. . . . That was a great place to live because everybody had a friend and everybody had something to eat and everybody shared. It was wonderful! **Evelyn (Ward) Karsman, 53**

MOVING SOUTH

We lived on 55th off Waters Avenue in an apartment. . . . The whole area was called, there was 53rd, 54th, and 55th, it was called Edgemere. They were duplex apartments, they were built during the war and we rented a place there. **Julius Rudikoff, 46**

Until the end of World War I, most of the Jewish population was downtown. . . . There wasn't an east side and west side, particular. It wasn't sides at all, really. Of course, a lot of the B. B. Jacob people moved to the southern part of town, around Victory Drive and Ardsley Park area. **Samuel Hirsch, 52**

The city itself has changed. . . . [It] ended almost at Oglethorpe Avenue. . . . 37th Street, . . . lots of Jewish people lived there, and they lived in nice big houses. . . . That was the beginning of the turning of the tide when they moved out there. And then after that you could go as far as Victory Drive. If you got that far, that was a big accomplishment. . . .

Washington Avenue became a lovely street. . . . Loads of Jewish people moved out to Habersham Woods. Then all of a sudden we started going to . . . Isle of Hope and these other areas where Jewish people never went [before]. They're just spread all over. The Landings and Dutch Island, I mean, there's Jews all over Savannah now. **Evelyn (Ward) Karsman, 53**

After Henry Street, when I was five years old, we moved to the Ardsley Park area. Ardsley Park was the first subdivision that used automobiles. It was only about ten minutes from downtown. There were many Jewish people that lived in the Ardsley Park area. . . . I lived on 46th Street. . . . I believe the real Ardsley Park only goes up to 51st Street. But it was bordered by Bull and to Waters Avenue. We had sidewalks and gutters and you had a mixture of ethnic groups as well as a mixture of homes. You had Arts and Crafts homes. You had two-story homes. You had bungalow homes. **Phillipa "Bunny" (Sherman) Cohen, 90**

Henry Street Apartment, 1942
Sisters Phillipa "Bunny" (Sherman) Cohen and Carol (Sherman) Allen enjoy playing in the sprinkler with friends.
JVM 003 Savannah Jewish Archives General Photograph Collection, Item 2175

I was born in this house [134 East 45th Street], I've lived here all of my life, never lived anywhere else. My mother and dad built the house in 1915, 1916, when they were married. . . . My brother, Steve Traub, was raised here, as certainly I was. We spent our formative years here. **Herbert Traub, Jr., 79**

When I came on the picture, we were living on Anderson Street . . . between Barnard and Whitaker. It was 116 West Anderson Street. . . . There were three houses exactly alike, which are still there. . . . Underneath us lived my aunt Lottie Kapner and [uncle] George Kapner. And next door lived Sheila Gottlieb [Miller]. . . . On the other side, . . . upstairs, were Belle and Sidney Lasky, who was my dad's brother, Sidney was. And, so I was raised right there on Anderson Street until I was eleven years old. Then we purchased a house at the end, in the sticks, which at that time was DeRenne Avenue, . . . on Columbus Drive or 59th Street. **Maxine "Midge" (Lasky) Schildkraut, 81**

Our first home [after marrying] was in Sylvan Terrace and there were lots of Jewish families there and lots of children. You could just walk out the door and there were children. It was a very convenient area to live because there again it was very close to the [new] J.E.A. **Phillipa "Bunny" (Sherman) Cohen, 90**

BOY SCOUTS AND GIRL SCOUTS

Somehow or other we were excited about joining the Girl Scouts of America. There were about four or five of us that always cliqued together at recess and whenever we had time, and so we decided we were going to join it.

[Juliette Gordon Low who inducted us] was a lady whose home we used to go to for meetings and the activity, and she was the one that started this whole thing in Savannah. . . . I had a tacky uniform; it was a skirt and a jacket with buttons down the front. . . . Ours was the first Jewish group in Savannah. **Minnie (Bronitsky) Feinberg Robbins, 24**

The Boy Scouts, that played a real important part in my childhood. I was very involved in scouting from about thirteen to nineteen. . . . The first troop I ever went to was Troop #6, which was one of the church troops. And then a group of us, mostly kids from the same neighborhood and school, formed our own scout troop, . . . Troop #60. And it was at the peak about thirty boys and it was really one of the better troops in the city.

In 1937, I was fortunate enough to be able to go to the National Jamboree in Washington. And the reason that stands out is that in 1937 the Jamboree was canceled because of polio. Today that really brings back the terror of that disease. Anyway, they did call it off, but it was re-instituted and I went up there in 1938 and had the opportunity to meet Franklin Delano Roosevelt. . . . I believe there were twenty-five thousand scouts there. . . .

I continued in scouting until I really went off to college. I've been involved in scouting since then but more on a financial basis. . . . Jack Coleman really is the only one that I know of and have sort of kept up with [from the troop]. Also, he was, he and I were the only Jewish boys in the troop. . . . I didn't want to leave out the scouts though, because they meant so much to me during my formative years. **Philip Solomons, Sr., 30**

When I turned twelve years old, I joined the Boy Scouts, and I don't know whether we had a Jewish troop or whether we didn't. But the troop I joined was Troop #6, and it was [at] the Hull Memorial Presbyterian Church on the corner of 37th and Bull next to the library. . . .

A man named Lon Keisker said, " I want my garage to be a Boy Scout troop." So we started Troop #6 in Lon Keisker's garage back there. I can't remember who all was in it: I know Philip Solomons was in it, Jack Coleman was in it. **A. J. Cohen, Jr., 6**

I was about twelve years old, it was time for me, I guess, to join the scouting program, and Henry [Levy] had joined a Scout troop, Troop #11, and it was sponsored by Christ Church. This was kind of unusual because there was a Jewish troop here that was . . . more or less sponsored by the J.E.A. **Julius Edel, 35**

During my high school years, my activities were an active member in A.Z.A. and the Boy Scouts. Boy Scouts really got to me. I was very active. I stayed in probably longer than most other scouts do. I was an Eagle Scout, had several leaves on the Eagle badge from continually getting merit badges.

During the summer, my junior year in high school, I was seventeen at the time, I was the waterfront director at the local Boy Scout Camp Strachan, and then the following year I graduated high school and I was a lifeguard at Tybee. Somewhere along the way I got interested in the Red Cross life saving courses and that's where my interest in water safety arose. **Karl Friedman, 85**

Boy Scout Camp, 1943
These campers, some with colorful nicknames, are left to right (front row) Roger "Roddy" Meddin, Erwin "Ernie" Friedman, and Aaron Buchsbaum; (back row) Joseph "Jody" Zerman, Milton "Boogie" Blair, and William "Ish" Alpern.
JVM 003 Savannah Jewish Archives General Photograph Collection, Item 2307

PLAYTIME AND GAMES

After school we played in the playground and I was my father's son. I was a big tomboy. I climbed fences. I loved sliding down the sliding board. At that time little girls did not wear jeans or shorts, and my mother used to make my under-wear. She used to use a bolt of cloth, I think, every two months, keeping me provided with underpants. Anyway, it was fun. It was a fun childhood. **Beatrice (Heyman) Goodman, 39**

We used to go to the "Big Park," which was Forsyth Park, and I think a Miss Kelly [Cecile Arenson] was in charge of all the sports for the young people. We played dodge ball and whatever. **Adele (Meddin) Schneider, 61**

We used to go to the park and square dance in the park or play kickball in the park. In the afternoons when we came home, we always had time to play paper dolls or read comic books. **Phillipa "Bunny" (Sherman) Cohen, 90**

Boy on a Bicycle, n.d.
Unidentified tintype of a young boy on his bicycle.
JVM 005 Congregation Mickve Israel
Photograph Collection, Item 0017

We knew . . . every little place, every little place, every wrinkle, I'd say, every little, tiny place that you could hide in. We used to play all the games down there. We made games, you know, including when we went to the West Broad Street School, we'd play "King of the Mountain" that most of the kids played then. We'd climb up on top, . . . rough playing but nobody got hurt. **Benjamin Portman, 20**

We played games, kicked a stick, "Buck, Buck, how many fingers up?" You don't know that one? That one was played quite a bit. . . . "Buck, Buck, how many fingers up?" is, you get a bunch of fellas and the first one holds on to anything that happened to be there, and the next one puts his hand between the leg of that one and they make a line, and then you run and jump as far as you can up the line on the backs of the fellas, and you say, "Buck, Buck, how many fingers up?" Crazy game, . . . but it was really a lot of fun. **Arthur "Bubba" Horovitz, 77**

We played something called "kick the stick." We'd stay on the street corner late at night until the . . . city lights went out. Then we gradually learned to drive an automobile around sixteen years old. We use to drive around. . . .

One thing we did, on a weekday night sometime, when Daddy Grace had a church on the other side of Martin Luther King Boulevard, which was then West Broad Street; . . . the boys and girls used to go down there and sit and watch the proceedings of the church. **Sidney Raskin, 23**

Fun Time in Pulaski Square, August 1947
Pictured left to right at the J.E.A. summer day camp are Norman Dolgoff, Mickey Greenfield, unidentified, Sammy Feinberg, Jack Louza, Jerry Rosenthal, and Robert Roth.
JVM 003 Savannah Jewish Archives General Photograph Collection, Item 0150

[After school] three or four kids got together. If they had a bat and ball, they'd play ball. Very often we didn't have a bat and we didn't have a ball. We didn't have anything. If you had a penny in your pocket, you did well. Do you know what a penny is? Have you ever seen a penny? They were not easy to get. The average kid didn't get pennies. We didn't get anything. You could buy ice cream on the street corner for a penny. **Fred Rotkow, 27**

We had one of the squares where we lived and we played. . . . We played baseball in the square and . . . wherever there were some sidewalks. . . . We would play hopscotch, and we'd jump rope, and we played jacks, and all that sort of thing which you don't see around any more. **Ida (Bronitsky) Stein, 56**

Herbert and Bert [Kayton Rosenheim] were very fond of each other. They used to play ball, or throw a ball to each other, in the cemetery [Colonial Park]. There was nobody there that was going to interfere. **John Kayton, 65**

In 1927, I think it was, I was the city champ on an item called "horse-shoe.". . . . As time went on, I started playing basketball, and I really excelled. . . . My first week in junior high . . . they made me captain of the team. **Harry Eichholz, 57**

I remember learning how to ride a two-wheel bicycle in Forsyth Park. . . . Dodge ball is one I remember in that tiny little backyard at Henry Street School. **Alan Gaynor, 62**

There was an open field . . . behind the Pirate's House and the old gas tank. . . . We used to use that as a ball park. We would play softball and half-rubber in that field and the neighbors didn't seem to care. Every now and then we'd break a window but we'd manage to get it fixed. **Benjamin Silverman, 29**

One activity was we played half-rubber in the park in front of the J.E.A. building. [Half-rubber was a regional game, similar to baseball, played with a rubber ball cut in half.] **Irvin "Sonny" Rubnitz, 49**

I loved to build model airplanes. Make these little crystal radios, . . . the biggest thrill was picking up Cincinnati or one of those stations. And I got in stamp collecting. . . . There wasn't any money to put in stamps or any hobby. I used to bike down to the bank buildings and go into . . . the big trash bins in the back, because that's where you could get some foreign stamps. . . . Somebody who knew me, and knew my parents, said I was down there digging in the trash, in the garbage baskets. So my parents said, "No more." **Philip Solomons, Sr., 30**

We used to make rubber guns. A rubber gun was a piece of wood cut out like a pistol and it had a clothespin on the end of it. . . . You stretched a rubber band which was an old tire cut into ribbons . . . over the front and connect it into the clothespin. We used to have fights with this. We used to fight between the houses [at Tybee]. Not that we were mad at each other, but it was a fun thing to do.

I remember one day the fathers came home from work and they got into the action. It was such great fun at the time. . . . [Maybe] you got hit with a rubber band, got stung a little bit. . . . That was the type of fun that we had. **Arthur "Bubba" Horovitz, 77**

Nobody had any money. It was Depression times. So we made pluffer guns. . . . We used to carve a handle and an eight inch, ten inch rod from the handle . . . that went through an elder bush, big round stalk, and all we had to do was wiggle out pulp inside the stalk and fit the gun, the pluffer, to the stalk like a piston.

And then we stuffed the chinaberry down in it, . . . it was a little berry that was hard and green, stuff one in there to form a pressure. Then you'd put another one in there and you'd push it against your stomach and by air pressure, like a BB gun, it shot the other berry out. Very painful if it hit you. . . . Lotta injuries, the kids were pretty wild. We went into the woods a lot and did a lot of BB gun shooting. **Rupert Heller, 80**

Summer Time, n.d.
Youngsters enjoy diving in for a cooling dip at Camp Osceola.
JVM 061 Golden Family Photographs, Folder 1, Item 2

The kids used to roller skate on the street and on the sidewalks down there [on] Bryan Street, and it was quite an experience. **Irvin "Sonny" Rubnitz, 49**

The streetcar was something then. I also, fortunately, I loved tennis and golf, and the street car went out to Bacon Park. So I could go out to Bacon Park and play golf. . . . Ten cents to play, or something like that. And bike over to the tennis courts at Daffin Park. Daffin Park was real popular then. I mean, that's where we went swimming, played tennis. Growing up at that time, to me it was a wonderful time. **Philip Solomons, Sr., 30**

CHAPTER 7: ENTERTAINMENT

MUSIC AND DANCING

I remember going to concerts, a lot of concerts. During the winter months they would bring down so many big artists, and my father loved good music, . . . [and] I had a love of it. I love opera. I love classical music in general. In fact, I love all music. But we went to concerts and we saw the biggest stars and it was just heavenly. I just sat enraptured. . . . I can't describe the way I felt. I was just a young teen-ager.

When I went to see these artists, I just wanted to be on that stage and I wanted to do something with my life. It was just a transformation. . . . Grace Moore and Lawrence Tibbett, Lily Pons, Andre Kostelanetz with his orchestra, . . . Nina Martini, all of these old, old people. It was so wonderful. And orchestras, the finest orchestras from all over the world. **Gertrude (Scheer) Barr, 1**

[A tea dance] was an afternoon dance at the school that they played records, famous band records, and they had a little phonograph, Victrola. I don't know what people would call it today. And they would play music through a speaker and the kids would dance. . . . Nothing was served, maybe a Coke or something. But they called it tea dance because it was an afternoon dance. **Herman Cranman, 36**

There were many Jewish players in [the Savannah] Orchestra. There was Murray Bono, there was my father [Harry Ginsberg]. There was David Odrezin who was a soloist sometimes; he's now deceased. There was Aaron Malitz and his wife, Edgar Morrison, and many others.

But there was a big corps of Jewish players who were music lovers from a long time ago. My sister and I played with the orchestra for about a year or two. We took lessons from Rudolph Jacobson who was a concert master of the symphony. We were not the greatest players but it really made our dad happy to have us play with the orchestra. **Suzanne (Ginsberg) Kantziper, 84**

I took violin lessons from Rudolph Jacobson. . . . When I came out of the Army, Jacobson says, "You want to, how about joining our little concert orchestra?"

I says, "Fine, I don't play very well any more.". . . Aunt Fannie [Eisenberg] says, "Look, when they play fast music, what you do, you play every other note." She says, "Somebody is gonna play the other note. So as long as you play every other note, you'll get along fine." So Aunt Fannie, look, she's a professional musician, she should know. . . . So that's how I played; I played every other note.

They organized a symphony orchestra; I joined that. David Odrezin was a very hot violinist. They didn't like me when I played every other note there. I played in there for about two years and that was it. **Murray Bono, 68**

Savannah Concert Orchestra, 1948-1949
Many local Jewish musicians performed with the Savannah Concert Orchestra including: Aaron Malitz, Joseph Geffen, Rudolph Jacobson, Marjorie (Cooper) Gordon, Murray Bono, David Odrezin, and Harry Ginsberg.
JVM 003 Savannah Jewish Archives General Photograph Collection, Item 0767

LIVE THEATRE

[Savannah Little Theatre] was at Remler's Corner. It was a nightclub on Victory Drive and Skidaway Road, and we had theatre in the round, which was a very intimate theatre. Later . . . they went out to the old Savannah Golf Club . . . and then later managed to buy the old Savannah Theatre. **Stephen Traub, 32**

Mother had originally, as I said, been a part of Town Theatre, and then during my elementary school years belonged to the Children's Theatre and was active with that group. I can remember hearing tales about different performances in those days. And then they began the Little Theatre. In 1950 the Little Theatre was organized. I understand that they practiced in Ruth Goodman's dance studio across from the Guards' Armory and then they performed at Remler's Club Royale. That was on Victory Drive. It's now Remler's Corner. . . . For about two years they had their performances there. Then they would only get to go into Remler's for two weeks before the show; . . . they couldn't use it because [the owners] used it as a nightclub the other nights and they didn't want to give up the space. They just had a little bit of time to get their shows together. Mother was active in many of the shows then. Daddy didn't play as active a role in the shows as my mom did.

And then they [the Little Theatre] moved. In 1952 they moved into the gas house down in Trustees' Garden. The gas company gave them a large building and they were there successfully for ten years. I think that was the great growth of the theatre in those days. . . .

They also enjoyed performances at Barbee's Pavilion which was at Isle of Hope and that was good for summer theatre. They had a lot of dances, maybe a lot of musical comedies things there. They had some great things to tell about that.

They later moved to Savannah Golf Club, in 1962. And then there was the terrible fire and the golf club burned down; they lost all their props and everything. It took them a little while to reorganize before they were able to buy the Savannah Theatre, which they opened in June of '81. **Barbara (Smith) Levy, 19**

Theatre Performances, c.1950s
Pictured in this Congregation Mickve Israel skit left to right are Alvin Schwab, Max Guthman, and Kayton Smith, Sr.
JVM 003 Savannah Jewish Archives General Photograph Collection, Item 1412

When Hadassah would have "Hadassah Presents" here, I used to get invited to take part. . . . We did a lot of those plays. They would give me songs and things to sing. I was Calypso Lipshitz, you know, the typical Caribbean outfit. . . . And sometimes I would try to throw in a little *Yiddish*. . . . I didn't really know *Yiddish* that well. . . .

Rosalie Tenenbaum was attending one of our rehearsals and I gave them a little bit of my *Yiddish* in one of my ditties, and she said, "Stop, stop the rehearsal!" I said, "What is it? What is it?" She said, "Stephen . . . what are you saying up there?" I said, "This is bayou *Yiddish*." She said, "No, this is *Yiddish* by you." It brought down the house, and of course we, I couldn't use it. She wouldn't let me use it. She was the watchdog for Hadassah. She was wonderful. **Stephen Traub, 32**

MOVIES

My grandfather, Abe Guckenheimer was . . . in the movie theatre business, and he had several very profitable movie theatres on West Broad Street. The Star was one of them. This is before my time. Arcadia Theatre [on Broughton Street] was one of them. My mother used to talk about how she got to go to the early movies for free. **Jane (Guthman) Kahn, 93**

We went to the movies downtown, and it was fifteen cents at the Lucas. And that's what we did every Saturday afternoon and every Sunday. . . . We would meet down at the Lucas. . . . We would pick up something [to eat] at McCrory's. . . . And then we went and enjoyed the afternoon. When summertime came we used to go down and have lunch at Livingston's before we went to the movies. **Adele (Meddin) Schneider, 61**

Broughton Street held everything. They had the movies, all the movies were down there; Odeon Theatre and the Lucas Theatre and the Bijou Theatre. I remember as a youngster going to the Savannah Theatre, and the Savannah Theatre . . . always had a stage show. To me that was the tops. That was the tops. They had these little chorus girls dancing away and they had the comedians and then they would show you a cartoon. You'd have serial and you'd have main feature, usually a cowboy picture.

Sometimes my brother Izzy and I used to go, but most of the time I used to go with Mozelle [Jefferson] and I'd sit upstairs with her, 'cause she wasn't allowed downstairs. [Mozelle was African-American.] I said, "One of these days somebody's going to beat my brains in." I used to run home with her, just run, 'cause I was so afraid they were going to attack me because I sat upstairs. **Gertrude (Scheer) Barr, 1**

The movie theatres, well, they were all on Broughton Street. They had the Folly Theatre, the Arcadia [both owned by a Jewish man, Abe Guckenheimer], the Bijou, the Odeon Theatre, and the Lucas Theatre, and that was all the theatres. The Weis Theatre and all that, that came many, many years later. But those were the ones on Broughton Street.

The only one that was on Abercorn was the Lucas, and the others were just west of Abercorn, between Abercorn and Drayton. The Bijou and the Odeon were on the north side of Broughton, and the Arcadia and the Folly were on the south side of Broughton Street. . . . In those days we'd get out of theatre at night, late at night, you never had any fear of walking down Broughton Street, going home. Everything was lit up, I mean, and it was wide open and you never heard of any problems or trouble, you know, anybody getting hurt. **Samuel Plotkin, 8**

[We] went to the movies at least once a week, because on Friday nights . . . we went to the Lucas, and we wore a coat and tie after six to get in. . . . Then we had the Odeon. We had the Bijou. At the Bijou they used to have eight acts and eight beautiful girls. . . . And then after that they would show movies. And, of course, we had the Odeon which was on the corner of Broughton and Abercorn. And the Arcadia across the street, and the Folly, and then the Avon where City Lights Theatre is now. **Sidney Raskin, 23**

It was a very, very loose atmosphere down there [on Broughton Street in the 1920s]. A lot of young people, a lot of activity. . . . All the theatres were down there except the drive-ins which came up later. But the Odeon and the Arcadia and the Lucas and the Bijou. [The] Bijou had live entertainment.

Usually the traveling shows would come to the old Savannah Theatre, . . . but in the early days it was a movie house. Mr. [Frederick] Weis had that. Of course, we used to save our lunch money at school and on Friday go to the movie there and throw spitballs from the balcony. You know, I had a little fun. But those were very laid back, easy days. **Stephen Traub, 32**

Watching Movies, August 1947
The cinema was the most popular entertainment of the period. These J.E.A. campers are enjoying a movie.
JVM 003 Savannah Jewish Archives General Photograph Collection, Item 0131

[Sam Blumenthal's store] had a candy department, 'cause Hannah [Brown] and I would go to the movies every Saturday and we would stop there first and she'd get a bag of candy; didn't cost us anything. It was great. It was great! **Ida (Slotin) Wilensky, 34**

I remember my brother Isadore, Izzy. . . . Being poor we had just [enough], it cost a nickel or a dime to go into a movie at that time. We would buy these long licorice sticks, long things. He'd take one end and I'd take the other. That was our big outing. **Gertrude (Scheer) Barr, 1**

I guess we were seven, possibly eight, we'd be given ten, fifteen, twenty cents. We were supposed to take . . . the trolley car downtown to go to a movie. Trolley cars were then a nickel each way. But walking Barnard Street was kind of danger-ous because what is now called the Alida Harper Fowlkes' House, back then it was . . . the Champion-McAlpin House. [It] was what today we'd think of as a Charles Addams' cartoon.

The magnolia trees in front weren't quite as big as they are today, but they were pretty big, and a witch, that was the rumor, a witch lived in that house. So we would walk Barnard Street, but we'd always run like hell across that square so we didn't have to stop in front of the Champion-McAlpin House. We also had the extra dime to buy things at the movies. **Alan Gaynor, 62**

Everything took place downtown. You didn't even think to go shopping or doing anything Southside. There was nothing out there until I became . . . fifteen, sixteen years old, . . . [when] we got a theatre on Bull Street that was called the Victory Theatre. It was on Bull and about 40th Street. And Johnny Rousakis, the ex-mayor, his daddy ran a store, I guess a soda shop, . . . called "Paul's."

And you could go to the movies for about a quarter, and then you went to Paul's and got a drink and something with it for about another quarter. And your date walked you there, so he had a big investment of fifty cents in you. . . . That's the first time the south side had anything that was commercial. **Harriet (Kanter) Konter, 43**

Where the Savannah Theatre is they had movies back then, and they used to have serials, and that's where we went on Saturday afternoon. . . . We would walk there. . . . At times . . . they had vaudeville shows. **Helen (Levington) Spiers, 73**

NIGHTCLUBS AND RESTAURANTS

I got a job with a firm called McKesson & Robbins in Jacksonville. They were a drug firm, but they had a beverage, a whiskey division. . . . So in 1938 . . .

I came to Savannah. . . . Chatham County went wet. Prohibition was over. . . .
McKesson & Robbins opened a warehouse here on Indian Street. . . . So they put
me up at . . . the old DeSoto Hotel for three months. . . . Of course, Indian Street
was quite known, quite a popular street in those days. . . . So, also on the street
was the sporting houses. . . .

That was quite an experience at the DeSoto. I had a ball! They had the Sapphire Room. . . . Johnny Mercer used to come there all the time. . . . I used to
spend all my evenings down there. I was single, you know. All the girls from the
country and everybody used to come there, but we really had a ball there.

After the three months was up, that was all they paid, I didn't want to stay at
the hotel. I could get a place cheaper than that. So there was a little house right on
the corner, called the Leslie House. . . . They took in . . . boarders, . . . so I stayed
there. **Reuben Schneider, 28**

One of the nicest places was the Sapphire Room at the DeSoto Hotel. Prior
to being called the Sapphire Room it was called the Tavern, and my parents used
to go there very frequently during the '30s and '40s. Whenever . . . you wanted to
have a nice party, you went to the Sapphire Room. . . .We used to go there very
often for social activity. **Martin Karp, 42**

Halloween Dance, 1942
Enjoying a masked dance at the old J.E.A. on Barnard Street are Rosalie
(Daub) Chernoff, unidentified, Matilda "Minda" (Rubnitz) Brownstein, Joe
Quinto, and unidentified.
JVM 003 Savannah Jewish Archives General Photograph Collection, Item 2192

[Johnny Harris] was a wonderful place! We used to go there in the wintertime. . . . For twenty-five cents you'd buy a lamb sandwich. It was more than you could eat. . . . There were curtains at the booths, yeah. And then they did away with them. I don't know why. I'll leave . . . [that to] your imagination! . . . I presume that was why they did away with them. I'm not sure now. But they had them for a while, but they didn't last very long.

They had the jukebox, and when we'd get through playing basketball or something we would go by there, or we'd go by the place called Leopold's over on Habersham and Gwinnett. And they had the finest ice cream and everything. . . . They made their own ice cream. It was the most popular place in town by everybody. **Sanford Wexler, 48**

When Johnny Harris . . . had a little place there, barbeque was fifteen cents a sandwich, french fries were a nickel. I remember that. . . . Then they had a place, . . . Remler's . . . on Victory Drive. . . . That was very popular, you know. **Reuben Schneider, 28**

Johnny Harris seemed to be the big one, and then Traub's "Our House" on Victory Drive was one of the popular ones. 'Course the Rex. 'Course we didn't go too often. . . .The Rex, I think, was on 39th and East Broad before they went out of business. **Beryl Bernstein, 67**

ISLE OF HOPE, THUNDERBOLT AND COFFEE BLUFF

We would go to [Isle of Hope to] take the air, get cooled for the afternoon. Our nurses would take us, as children, out to feed the turtles and come back in the afternoon. Maybe they'd take a picnic with us. Of course, this is [in the] days before air conditioning, so anything to get a little cooler [would] be a way to amuse the kids. **Barbara (Smith) Levy, 19**

The most fun trolley was the one that went out to Isle of Hope, 'cause it was open on the sides. It was the Isle of Hope trolley, came up Habersham Street and then it cut at an angle at what is now 50th Street, . . . and it was all woods from there on out until it got to Isle of Hope. And it wasn't much of a settlement there either, in those days. But riding that open trolley was fun, because we would get on it and it would begin to sway, and we would help it, because it did sway a lot. And it was open, open air. It was nice. It was fun. **Stephen Traub, 32**

When Sundays came around, that's one day that the family all ate together. They did do that. The big thing was to put all the family in a car and take a ride to

Isle of Hope and buy us all ice cream. That was a big treat, you know, for us. **Celia (Scheer) Hirsch, 1**

If you wanted to go to Isle of Hope, the only way that we could get there was on a streetcar, and if you had a car I guess you could get off there, but we [went] on the streetcar. And there they had a merry-go-round. And in those days . . . Barbee's was out there. They had a terrapin farm. So Sunday was a very busy place out there. **Samuel Plotkin, 8**

Isle of Hope. Now we used to go out there quite a bit. Now Barbee's used to have some of the big bands come. Red Nichols and his Five Pennies were there, and I think even Guy Lombardo came there one time. Barbee had a pavilion there, a dance pavilion, and he used to have these performers come there. . . .

It was a very popular place, and the streetcar used to run out there. Now they had to turn the streetcar around, and I remember we used to help turn it around. They had a turn table that the streetcar turned around and came downtown. The streetcar was a nickel, to ride out there. But Barbee's was a very popular place. . . . We used to take the kids out there on a Sunday. **Reuben Schneider, 28**

The Barbee family had a pavilion out there and they raised terrapins, small species of turtle. They shipped those terrapins all over the world. And that also was a wonderful place on Sunday afternoon. . . . There were dances there sometimes on Saturday night. Of course, the Jewish kids would go as a group, but it wasn't just the Jewish kids having the dance. **Albert Ullman, 33**

Well, it [Barbee's] wasn't too much to see. [Of] course they had those, what do you call them, those terrapins and all. You could go out and see them and they put up a soup, turtle soup. And I had a cousin in New York, he said they used to buy it up in New York, it was so well known. Absolutely a delicacy, . . . it came from Barbee's. You wouldn't believe it. **Beryl Bernstein, 67**

Another thing that was a treat for me was going down to Isle of Hope to Barbee's Pavilion. We'd look down and see the terrapins that they raised, and there was also a merry-go-round there that one was able to ride. **Doris (Goldin) Lukin, 88**

Thunderbolt, Isle of Hope, lot of Jewish people would go there Sunday afternoons. We'd catch the streetcar, which was open. . . . You could catch it at Leopold Brothers which was on Habersham and Gwinnett, and you could ride, that was Sunday afternoon, you could ride to Barbee's Pavilion. . . . They had hot dogs, a nickel, watch the boats go by. . . . A lot of people rowed boats, canoes and stuff like that. **Harry Eichholz, 57**

We also would go to Thunderbolt when we knew the fish boats, the shrimp boats, were coming in, and we would buy fish right on the dock there at Thunderbolt. **Doris (Goldin) Lukin, 88**

On Sunday, you took a ride out to Thunderbolt. That was great! . . . Going out to Thunderbolt was an experience. The other thing that was a great experience was going to Barbee's Pavilion. . . . They raised terrapins out there, and that was another important place to go. **A. J. Cohen, Jr., 6**

We used to get a horse and wagon, and fill it full of straw and go out to Coffee Bluff, out Bull Street, for a picnic there. There was a peanut farmer nearby. And there was a spring with fresh water, and you saw turtles floating around in it.

They had the pipe with artesian water. I went over to get a cup of water one time and it tasted like eggs, and I said, "We didn't bring any egg salad with our lunch today." And I tasted it and it tasted like rotten eggs to me. Finally, it took me a while. . . . I don't remember when I found out that that was the taste, that that was the kind of water. It was artesian water. **Ida (Bronitsky) Stein, 56**

TYBEE ISLAND (SAVANNAH BEACH)

I remember the train. Daddy used to come on the train every day. We'd go to the beach in the morning and we'd come home . . . have lunch. . . . In the afternoon we'd get dressed, walk to the station, get an ice cream. There was an ice cream parlor in front of it. Then we'd . . . ride back with Daddy. Mama loved the train 'cause he always came on time. When the road came, she never knew when he was coming. . . . Our house was like a club house. Any night you came there, there was a bridge game, a poker game, and a gin game. **Ida (Slotin) Wilensky, 34**

It was kind of nice to ride the train down to Tybee, and it is a damn shame [the train is gone]. And I understand that railroad track is still there and they're making it a bicycle track or walking track. But that raised track of where the track was is still there. And Tybee was an important place to go to. I mean you were in hog heaven. **A. J. Cohen, Jr., 6**

They only had a train that went to Tybee and that's where the train station was, on President Street. We'd walk over there and we'd get the train. . . . We'd try to miss the conductor to keep from paying the thirty-five cents, we'd go in the restroom. . . . It worked for a while 'til they caught on to it. . . . So we'd go out and we'd go to Tybee and go to the dawn dances, and we'd dance all night with the girls, and if somebody'd invite us to spend the night, we'd spend it. If they didn't, a lot of us would sleep under the pier. You know, some of us, it didn't make a difference to us. Some people invited us to spend the night. Then we'd leave Sunday night. **Reuben Schneider, 28**

Train to Tybee Island, 13 July 1919
Elsie (Galkin) Smerling Ocuin and Nettie (Galkin) Jacobowitz getting on the train for the trip from Savannah out to Tybee Island and the beach.
JVM 003 Savannah Jewish Archives General Photograph Collection, Item 2248

[The train] stopped about three stops on Tybee Island: Lovell Station, Fort Screven, and I think one more stop. . . . Those trains would be hot and no screens, and you'd go to the windows to cool off, and the most black soot would come blowing in on me. But it was fun! **Samuel Hirsch, 52**

We used to go to Tybee on Sunday morning . . . by train. . . . The train was at the foot of President and, I think, Reynolds Street there. It took about half an hour, no, about three quarters of an hour to get there. I don't remember what the fare was. . . . There they had the beautiful Pavilion that burnt down. . . . They had a place to change your clothes, you know, a locker room. And above the locker room they had a great big Pavilion with tables and chairs and all where you could sit and have your lunch comfortably. It was a massive place. But it was so nice.

And the main dance Pavilion was out on the water. Built pretty much like the one is today. . . . And all the old bands, older bands became popular after a while. Many of them started here in Savannah on a Saturday night. . . . They would come in and play on the Pavilion, and, you could come on a Saturday night. [People] that didn't have to work were there and danced, and [they] had all the refreshment stands with Cokes and hot dogs. . . . Tybee was really lovely at that time. **Ida (Bronitsky) Stein, 56**

For recreation, we would go to Tybee with our parents on the train when I was a child, there being no road as yet. It was an old coal-burning engine, windows opened. Air conditioning had not been invented yet, cinders flying in, but we loved it.

Upon arriving at the beach, we would rush to one of the pavilions—there were three—to get a table and chairs upon which to put our home-packed lunch baskets for lunchtime. From childhood to young adulthood we would lie out on the beach in the sun and literally cook. No one knew it wasn't good for you. We would use suntan oil or baby oil on our skin. The darker you could tan, the happier you were. First you turned red, then your skin peeled. What a mess! **Elizabeth "Libby" (Levy) Price, 69**

We used to go to the beach, I remember, when we were all smaller. Mama used to cook, get up early in the morning and cook a big, big meal, and had to pack it in baskets. And we used to go, before we had a car, we used to go by train to the beach. That was the thing to do every Sunday.

Then the minute we'd get off the train, . . . the children . . . used to have to run to find a place to put the food where we could sit and eat. I remember that vividly. That's what we used to do, and everybody used to go swimming. **Celia (Scheer) Hirsch, 1**

I also remember the picnics. We always had picnics at Tybee. . . . Women got dressed up. They didn't wear slacks and things. They were dressed with stockings and their regular dressy outfits to go on picnics. And I don't know how they did it after having to prepare all that food. **Bertha (Plotkin) Freedman, 8**

Mama would have the baskets . . . like the fruit baskets that the grocery stores get the things in. Anyway, Mama would cook a chicken, a couple of chickens, whatever it was, on Saturday night, so that we could go to Tybee on Sunday. And she would have, we loved red rice. Red rice by my Mama was ketchup and rice. Mama would put it in big jars. . . . And we would all run up to the Pavilion to get a table, a picnic table, on top of the bathing house. **Evelyn (Center) Goldberg, 10**

There was always chicken, chopped liver, and potato salad and vegetables. She [Mother] had it all packed up in a basket and we'd get on the streetcar and go to the Tybee Station, and then we'd catch the train. I don't know how they did it, with the kids and the food. And yet it was done, and we loved it. We had to catch the train coming back, and from the train we had to go on the streetcar to get to our destination.

Of course, our second move from Broughton Street was right across from the station. As years went by, it was quite convenient. . . . It was beautiful. At night there were dances with the orchestra. As I got to be a teenager and dated, we always stayed for the dances at Tybee. You had to come back on the last train. You caught the last train at eleven. Whatever that last train was, you had to catch it because nobody had cars then. **Lena (Feinberg) Rosenzweig, 26**

Tybee Island Souvenir, n.d.
Visitors could take home mementos to remember the good times! These two young men have not been identified.
JVM 061 Golden Family Photographs, Folder 1, Item 4

I remember plain as day when Williams, before they opened the restaurant [Williams Seafood]. I remember the stand. We used to stop there. They had a stand outside Mrs. [Leila] Williams'. A little top to it and a little wooden stand, and she sold deviled crabs and boiled shrimp from that little stand, and people would stop there and buy. And that's where the Williams got started, there until they opened their restaurant there. **Reuben Schneider, 28**

A big adventure in those years was a trip to Tybee. . . . My mother would get up early in the morning and prepare a lunch—fried chicken and butterbeans and potato salad and lemonade—and cart all of us and this lunch through this tortuous kind of trip to go to Tybee, go upstairs at the Tybrisa Pavilion and stake out a table, put your things down. . . . And we'd go in the ocean, rent a bathing suit at the Tybrisa Pavilion, and then after a swim get back into clothes and go upstairs and have a wonderful lunch at the Tybrisa Pavilion. **David Rosenzweig, 63**

When you got there, you could rent a table and spread out all your foodstuffs and water and whatever you had brought with you. That cost a quarter for the day. . . . We'd travel down in our bathing suits and then when it was time you got out of the water, we would go into the bathhouse. I think that cost a dime also. **Doris (Goldin) Lukin, 88**

My folks bought a house in 1944 for $4500. . . . I loved to fish. My mother would give me twenty-five cents and I would go get some bait. Walk down a mile, mile and a half and fish, catch fish and then I would walk back.

On 17th Street at the beach, which I'd walk by, were all the Jewish women. . . . I can't remember the names but these were all grandmothers, and they would be waiting on me to look at my fish and they would buy them for like thirty cents, twenty cents. They would say, "Oh, this one's too small." And I'd say, "Well, you can't have the big ones without the small ones." So I would sell my fish to the Jewish women. **Lewis Kooden, 91**

By the time I was a teenager and we spent time at the beach, there was skating on the Pavilion and maybe some dances, but no big name bands came. Tybee did have a bowling alley, and it had a Ferris wheel and a bingo place where you could play bingo, so there was lots of fun things to do there. **Suzanne (Ginsberg) Kantziper, 84**

In those days . . . up to 1922, the only way to get to Tybee was by train. I remember those trains. All the men wore flat boater straw hats and . . . these rolled suits, . . . seersucker. Everybody was dressed alike it seemed. Everybody would go to the beach with a coat and tie on and a hat. . . . A lot of them would take their coats and ties off for a walk on the beach.

Of course, the bathing suits, the women's bathing suits, they wore hats with them and long sleeves, and they had like a skirt that had pants going down to about the ankles, and the men's suits were long, droopy trunks, and they wore tops with them. **Samuel Hirsch, 52**

They had that light that used to shine [at the Tybrisa Pavilion], and they would have these dances with Blue Steele. I don't know if people would remember Blue Steele. They had wonderful dances on Saturday night that were great. They always had a big crowd of people, and it was really nice. Dorsey was there, too, Tommy Dorsey. And I remember on Sundays everybody went to Tybee on the train.

Oh, yes, and everybody packed a lunch to take to Tybee, consisting, of course, of boiled eggs and sandwiches and things like that. You had a little shoe box with your lunch, and you went on the train, and of course the cinders and things would get in your eyes from all the smoke and everything.

But anyway, we'd ride to Tybee and the kids would run and get a rocking chair for Momma. Miss Lillian Bragg, who was a physical ed[ucation] teacher in

Savannah, wrote a cute commentary, "Run and Get a Rocking Chair for Momma." All the kids would run ahead with the shoe boxes in their hands with the lunches, and we'd all run to the Pavilion and get a table and chairs or benches or whatever, and everyone would sit around and eat their lunch. Then after that they'd get in their suits. The dressing rooms were downstairs below the Pavilion. I've got a picture somewhere I could show you.

The parents would go too. Everybody knew everybody. It was just like "Old Home Week." There wasn't a stranger about because everybody that was there was everybody that you knew. And then after a while you got tired, and you got packed up and you came back on the train, and all of the kids were asleep. Everybody was so sleepy and tired. And then you had to ride the streetcar back. **Bess (Eisenman) Center, 3**

Residences on Tybee Island, c.1922
Pearl (Robinson) Stemer walks on the beach, with private homes in the background.
JVM 003 Savannah Jewish Archives General Photograph Collection, Item 2230

In those days the Jewish families tried to go to Tybee for the summer and there was a large Jewish neighborhood down there. Many of them began there because their doctors would recommend Tybee for the children and, of course, Jewish families always wanted to take care of their children. **H. Sol Clark, 5**

Our family stayed down at the beach. Mr. Sam Blumenthal, *alav ha-sholom*, had five or six cottages on the Back River, and all the Jewish people used to go there and rent a cottage. . . .

Pop was the number one *Zionist*. My middle name is Herzl after a very prominent *Zionist* that helped establish the State [Israel]. . . . At Tybee everything was *Yiddish*. We had a big *Zionist* flag up there . . . [and] everybody observed . . . Fridays and Saturdays and stuff like that. . . . Everybody would come there on Friday and spend Saturday and go swimming or whatever you wanted to do. But the Rabhans . . . formed a little congregation, a little *minyan*, in the house where they lived. **Benjamin Portman, 20**

We built this place here at Tybee and I started coming down here every sum-mer. I've been coming down to Tybee for the last sixty-odd years now. . . . Once we built the cottage, the road was, had been built for several years. I think it was '25, 1925 [when the road was built]. **Marion (Abrahams) Levy Mendel, 17**

The Garfunkels would hold services. [Also] the Rabhans. . . . I used to hear Benny, rest his soul, blowing that *shofar* at the beach. . . . They came to town for Rosh Hashanah and Yom Kippur and big holidays, but they'd have *Shabbes* ser-vices there in the houses because they'd get a *minyan*. . . . If they had *yahrtzeit*, instead of coming all the way in town, they'd get everybody and have a *minyan* there. **Reuben Schneider, 28**

I used to go to Tybee to the cottage, remember? It cost, I think, two-hundred and fifty dollars for the whole summer to stay there, June, July and August. . . . I used to go down there and . . . I didn't have a bathing suit, used to borrow a bathing suit from my cousin, Norman Kaplan.

In those days they used to wear one-piece bathing suits with ovals on each side, a little block like that, on each side. And these bathing suits were light-weight wool, hot, not like today with dacron and cotton, the fabric. And in the back it had holes in it so you could see part of my *tuchus* when I got out on the beach. So when I got out on the beach some of the young gals laughed at me. **Nathan Karnibad, 41**

It was a wonderful life at the beach when I was married. . . . I stayed with my mother-in-law and she left her cook in town to cook for the men, and I brought mine out to sleep, she slept out there. We would take the children to the beach and then like twelve o'clock [the maid would] come pick up the children and she would bathe them and she would feed them. And then we'd come and we'd all have lunch together, and then the kids, she'd already have the children down to nap. Then we'd go to play mah-jongg or bridge or whatever we played, and then we took them to the boardwalk. . . . So that was the kind of lifestyle. **Harriet (Kanter) Konter, 43**

Tybee has been my life. I've lived at Tybee all of my life except for when I went away in World War II. . . . I've loved every moment of it. We . . . had a house down on 17th Street, a big house, . . . it was a hang-out place. Everybody came. And then during World War II, Daddy bought the house which Ida [Wilensky] lives in now down on 10th Street. I was overseas and he wrote me that Daddy bought a house on 10th Street. I said, "10th Street, what's happening? No Jews live on 10th Street. Everybody at Tybee lives on the south end.". . . Of course, when I came home and saw the beauty of the home. **Leon Slotin, 47**

We used to, even before the Abrahams cottage was built on 8th Street, I think about 1938, Grandfather [Abe Guckenheimer], who was the world's worst driver —I think Dad must have driven the car—we would drive down to the beach on Sundays. I vividly remember, although I didn't know it was Williams', the little shack, stand on the side of the Tybee Road where these people sold live crab, boiled crab, fresh shrimp, and boiled shrimp, and that later became Williams Seafood Restaurant. **Alan Gaynor, 62**

[My grandparents] built a house [at Tybee] in the early part of the twentieth century, when the only way you could get to Tybee was by train. They had a house on 18th Street between Butler Avenue and the beach that my grandmother built. She was a good designer because it was a house that had a 360 degree porch, the only one like it at the time. . . .

My grandmother loved to crab, but of course she wouldn't eat the crabs. [They weren't kosher.] They just loved this beach. Even after they no longer owned the house, they used to come down for summers. They rented cottages owned by Mr. [Sam] Blumenthal on the Back River at Tybee. And, you know, we all came down, all of their children and their grandchildren, in and out of those houses all the time. **Erwin "Ernie" Friedman, 71**

Tybee Island, 25 August 1929
Seen in this beach scene are Jacqueline (Jacobowitz) Wetherhorn and her mother, Nettie (Galkin) Jacobowitz.
JVM 003 Savannah Jewish Archives General Photograph Collection, Item 2251

Getting back to the things that I remember most in my life was living . . . during the summer, [in] the Back River at Tybee Island, . . . what we call the Back River because it came around from the Atlantic into a sort of estuary there. Then it worked out where a lot of homes were built, but they weren't what you call real established, strong homes. They were like cottages where we had kerosene stoves. . . . To use the facilities, we had to go outside.

At that time we had a nice Jewish crowd, we called it the "Little Tel Aviv." There was Sam Portman, Joe Levin, the Friedmans from the butcher shop. So we had a nice little community. I was about twelve or thirteen. **Herbert Blumenthal, 76**

We all had some type of broken-down houses at the beach. The first little place we had was a Blumenthal cottage on the river. . . . It cost us fifty dollars. When it rained you had to have an umbrella to go to the bathroom. That's the kind of places we could afford. . . . Being poor then, it was not, you didn't even know you were poor. **Lena (Feldman) Solomon, 82**

We used to rent a house there and my parents owned property on the beachfront. . . . There were a lot of Jewish people that lived at the beach, and we'd walk up and down the beach and stop and talk to people. **Phillipa "Bunny" (Sherman) Cohen, 90**

Every Wednesday afternoon every store in the city of Savannah closed up. And that was the day you went to Tybee. And that was a big deal because all the Jewish kids went there on Wednesday afternoon and Sunday.

Now, if somebody was lucky, they could rent something for a month at the beach, but very few people owned anything. They did after a while, but when I came along, you had to go to Tybee on Wednesday afternoon because your friends were going to be right there on 18th Street sitting on that boardwalk waiting for you to come. And then you went every Sunday. The parents took you, and after a while they acquired little places down there and rented, and I can remember as a kid that my parents stayed on the Back River. **Harriet (Kanter) Konter, 43**

We didn't stay there. We spent the day there. My mother would cook up a lot of food like fried chicken and things like that. And with a basket we would walk to East Broad Street where we picked up the train, and the train took us to Tybee. From there we went to the Tybrisa. At that time it was right over the bathhouse. They had all these tables up there and benches.

And you'd leave your lunches, leave your clothes too sometimes, and those were the days when people were pretty honest. Whatever you left, when you got back there, is what you found. So we used to go bathing, [lie] on the beach, and then go back upstairs and have lunch. Go back on the beach and spend a little time there, and then you'd get dressed and take the train back to Savannah. . . .

Later on we used to rent [a] cottage for a month or for two weeks, whatever. That was nice, too. There was also a place . . . called the Country Club. A big, big building. It was dominated primarily by all Jewish families. They'd come in and get a room or two rooms— it was two floors— and what a time we used to have! They had one big, big kitchen there, where all the women used to come in with their pots and everything else and cook their meals.

It was quite a place. You don't see those things anymore. . . . The rooms were bedrooms. And we had big porches all around it, went all around the building there. . . . It was on the main drag where the train was running, it was right by the Fresh Air Home. . . . At that time also Fort Screven was very much alive. We used their medical facilities in the event of an emergency or anything like that. **Samuel Radetsky, 45**

Tybrisa Pavilion, 1920
This bathing beauty is Gussie (Schine) Bono in front of the old pier at Tybee.
JVM 003 Savannah Jewish Archives General Photograph Collection, Item 2233

As a matter of fact, my family was living at Tybee when I was born. . . . My mother came on a train. There was no road then. . . . They lived in Savannah Beach all my life in the summertime. . . . My parents had a *minyan* at their house, every *Shabbes*. And we were saying *Kaddish*, my mother and father had a *minyan* every day there, in the mornings. **Martin "Maier" Rabhan, 75**

We used to go to Tybee every summer; never owned a house down there, always rented. We rented the first house on what they call Smith Row. This is where all the Jewish people lived around. . . . We lived right on the front. At that time there was no boardwalk to go in front; it was only dunes in front of it. You can't imagine how big the dunes were in those days. To get to the beach you had to go over two sets of them. I know that in those days those dunes must have been two to three stories high.

When you got to the beach you had a wide beach. You had a beach even at high tide [that] was as wide as a football field or more. . . . It would hold a lot of people. It was never crowded as we know it today. . . . All the Jewish boys of our age would go down there, and the Jewish girls they were down there also. It was just, it was just a great fun time the whole time that we were there, the whole summer long. Just good clean fun. . . . And the families used to be on the beach also, and . . . the fathers used to play with the sons. **Arthur "Bubba" Horovitz, 77**

My family had a summer place that they would rent at Tybee from the time I was about a year old. As a young adult, I used to stay down there with friends of mine. We would rent a room, one room for four boys, for the season, for seventy-five dollars, with two double beds in it, and that was for the whole season.

And we would go to the Pavilion every night. Usually in the afternoons, when the big name bands were down there and they were practicing, we would go there and listen to them practice and get to know some of the musicians. And the rest of the day we spent on the beach. It was no problem about being in the sun from about seven in the morning 'til about six in the afternoon. Nobody knew . . . about the ozone.

The dancing [at the Pavilion] was very good. There was no air conditioning in those days, and I can remember we all danced a lot. They'd have ten dances. You'd fill out your card during the week, and when you'd get there you knew who you were going to dance with. You could sit on the back of the Pavilion in a big rocking chair that they had there. Sometime it was so hot, I can remember that you would dance and dance. You had to wear a coat and tie, and you would begin perspiring, and most of the dancers were pretty close to each other and stuck together from the sweat.

They had a crystal ball. Sometimes they had a battle of the bands. They'd have two bands. . . . On Wednesday nights when everybody went up there, you'd pay fifty cents to get on the Pavilion. But on other nights . . . we used to wait outside until some of the couples went home around nine-thirty, and they weren't going back on the Pavilion, and they would give us their pass-out checks.

One of the football players from Benedictine was taking up the tickets, so I never had a problem. He'd give me a ticket and we'd go there every night. On Sunday night it was against the law to dance, so they used to put about five hundred Brumby rockers out on the dance floor— it was a tremendous floor— and have a concert. I think it was fifty cents to go up there on that night.

We went by train, and my dad . . . would go into town every day and he would buy chickens and pack it in dry ice and bring a watermelon, and he would send them out on the . . . train. And when I was a kid, my job was to take a little wagon and go down and meet the train and bring the chicken back home, and also take the watermelon over to Mr. [Lazar] May's icehouse. I can still remember going in there. It was freezing in there. And then on Sunday they would send me back there to get the watermelon. When all our company would come down for the weekend, we would slice the watermelon.

All the Jewish kids used to hang out on the steps right next to the old Pavilion, and that's where all the trading was done about who was going to dance with whom when you went up on the Pavilion. We were out on the beach all day, playing ball or riding waves. In those days, you didn't have surfboards. We just rode the waves with our bodies. **Sidney Raskin, 23**

We used to go to dances on the Pavilion in high school. We used to go to dances at the Tybrisa. Monday night we used to call Jewish night; it was two for one, and I don't remember going too many other nights there. . . . Only in the summer. And we used to congregate on the beach right there by the steps. All the Jewish kids would sit on the steps going out to the Tybrisa or around there, and that was where you just knew everybody. Nobody was introduced. **Ethyl (Richman) Rosenzweig, 25**

The train to Tybee, the train had no window screens and plush seats. West of Pavilion was a bath house. You had to pay twenty-five cents to undress and get towels. Picnic tables at Pavilion for families. Then go on beach. At evening, take train back to downtown to Randolph and President, then walked home or took trolley.

Cab Calloway, all-women's band, and other big bands played at Tybrisa. "Girl of My Dreams" was written by Sonny Clapp at Tybee and Blue Steele's band. As teens we would go as a crowd; if no money, we'd sit on steps outside and listen to music. Big crystal ball hung from center of Pavilion for dances. **Benjamin Silverman, 29**

The social group migrated from Tybee to Savannah and back and forth. Tybee was a big factor - social, teenage social life. A lot of people went to Tybee for the summer, and lot of people just went down every weekend on Sundays. . . .

It was the era of the big bands. I don't know whether people know what big bands are today—they might think it's a marching band—but it's a big orchestra that played the popular music of the day. Savannah, happily, was almost mid-way from Miami to New York, and these bands would play in Miami and migrate up North to New York, and Tybee was a stopping off point. They would spend a week at Tybee taking a, sort of a working vacation at the beach, and they'd practice every day on the old Tybrisa Pavilion. Saturday night before they left, they would give a dance and probably make expenses by charging admission for it. . . .

At that time I was a little too young to go to the Saturday night dances, but they were there every afternoon practicing on the Pavilion, and a lot of kids used to go up there and listen to them, and catch the breeze on the Pavilion, and listen to the orchestra play. **Herman Cranman, 36**

Sunday night they had a concert and we had some of the finest orchestras. Cab Calloway came through here one time. Bob Crosby came down, that was Bing Crosby's brother, came here. Louis Armstrong came through one night and gave a concert and a dance up there. There were a lot of them that came. Tommy Dorsey, Jimmy Dorsey's band came through here. **Sanford Wexler, 48**

Oh yes, we did have lifeguards. And we had a wonderful Pavilion. Saturday nights [were] wonderful for all of us. . . . Well, they had bands then, all the bands. That was the first date I ever had with Meyer [my husband]. He came down with a cousin of mine and we went to Tybrisa for the evening dancing on Saturday. . . . We just listened to the band rehearse. It was wonderful. . . . Well, we socialized, and then they had little waffles that they would cook on the Pavilion, on the boardwalk just as you went up. For a nickel we had a treat. . . . We used to wear little rubber shoes, bathing slippers. **Adele (Meddin) Schneider, 61**

They had the nice bands there, I think Bob Crosby and Blue Steele. Of course, Blue Steele was the one had a very popular song way back, "Girl of My Dreams" and all kinds of songs. Of course, that's when they had "Yes, We Have No Bananas" and all of those songs. That's going way back. **Beryl Bernstein, 67**

The most memorable thing about the Pavilion was, everybody will tell you, is the ball that was there. The lights, we'd cut the lights off and shine different colored lights on that ball, and it would roll around and the things would flash all over the place, and it was, it was something you hadn't seen before. **Arthur "Bubba" Horovitz, 77**

Some of the boys used to get together, me, Jake Fine, Harry Eichholz, and other different. But us three, we could rent a room at the [DeSoto Beach Hotel] at that time—now listen carefully—for two hundred dollars a year, for the whole season! Fifty dollars a man and we had, that was our room. We could come on any night. We had free linens, free anything, and towels. Fifty dollars a season. Two hundred dollars for the room. . . . We used to come down Friday afternoon and Saturday and Sunday, and go back Sunday night. **Sanford Wexler, 48**

One day [at our beach house], there was a little boy sitting [on] . . . a bench as you walk in the door. After he was there a while, I went up there and said, "Are you waiting on Leon?" "No, ma'am." "You waiting on Harry?" "No, ma'am."

Well, he looked a little young for Bernie, but I said, "Are you waiting to see my brother Bernie?" "No, ma'am. A car just hit me out front and I came in here to catch my breath." But you can imagine, he came in and no one paid attention! **Ida (Slotin) Wilensky, 34**

Tybee Island, c.1934
Nancy (Levington) Slotin and Ross Stemer are seen enjoying the beach. JVM 003 Savannah Jewish Archives General Photograph Collection, Item 2167

MISCELLANEOUS ENTERTAINMENT

For recreation at night, especially in the summertime, [my brothers] used to go sit in front of Nat Daubs' store and shoot the bull. . . . That was on York and West Broad. That was, I mean, just about every night except when it rained. He used to play pinochle with them once in a while, too, when they played in his house, 'cause Eva used to stay downstairs and watch the place and he would play pinochle with them. **Celia (Scheer) Hirsch, 1**

Sunday was a very big deal with us. We would get together, come to the Alliance and practice ball, and then, after, we would go to Coney Island Restaurant on Whitaker and Broughton Street. Wonderful hot dogs, five cents. And then we'd go to somebody's house and play. We'd shoot dice or we would play cards. The most you could lose was, what? Fifty cents or seventy-five cents! **Harry Eichholz, 57**

As we got older, in our teenage years, we went horseback riding on Bee Road, which was a country path at that time, and to Johnny Harris on dates to dine and dance. The whole floor was a dance floor, no tables as now, only the booths around the dance floor for eating. We also went to the Tybrisa Pavilion at Tybee for wonderful dances where many of the big bands got their start, the Dorseys, Bob Crosby, and many others.

As kids and teenagers, we also went swimming at the old . . . DeSoto Hotel swimming pool, and also at the Y.W.C.A. The DeSoto was a lovely old hotel with wide verandas all around, great for sitting and watching the St. Patrick's Day parade.

As we got older, [we had] dates at the Tavern and later the Sapphire Room, both in the hotel. It was a crime that the hotel was torn down because it was really unique, a grand old lady. . . . Later, when we married and had children, by then we would all go to the wonderful J.E.A. swimming pool with all our kids. **Elizabeth "Libby" (Levy) Price, 69**

We used to have a night of humor. . . . I had a couple of favorites that I . . . really liked. . . . Hymie and Moshie [are] on their way to Hawaii and they're having an argument on the plane, and [Hymie] says, "I wish you would stop saying Hawaii - it's Havaii." And Moshie says, "It is Hawaii." [Hymie] says, "No, it's Havaii. Wait, wait, wait, we'll settle it when we get there. We'll ask a native." So as soon as they got to Hawaii and went down to Waikiki Beach, they went up to the first native they could find and said, "Would you please settle something for us? Is it Hawaii or Havaii?" And the native says, "It's Havaii." And Moshie said, "Thank you." And the native said, "You're velcome." **Stephen Traub, 32**

We went on hay rides. Oh, we had a good time. We really did. It wasn't too much like a date, per se. We would go in groups, you know. And they had the crystal ball at the Tybee Tybrisa [beach pier]. My mama always said, "I wish you'd look at her shoes. They look like the morning after the night before." I was wearing out my shoes. We had dance cards and we used to fill in.

It was good times . . . but we took them for granted. That's the way it was supposed to be. It was really good times. We had a lot of fun. We went on hay rides. We went to dances. The Alliance had big goings-on up on Barnard Street. It was nice. **Sadye (Steinberg) Rabhan, 22**

I would like to just talk a little about my parents' social life because they had a very active social life here in Savannah. They had a number of very close friends; . . . they went out probably every weekend and they traveled a lot. They went to New York and their friends—we'll mention their names because I think that's important—they were very close with Ben and Cecil Friedman, Mae and Joe Lesser,

Mary and Morris Levy, Rose and Harry Zarem. . . . My father, because he represented a lot of different people, they had a lot of close relationships with . . . Sam and Kate Robinson and the Ehrenreiches and Levingtons.

My father and mother participated in not only the Jewish social activities, but they also participated through the years with a number of the gentile social activities. Not that they were invited to their homes, but if there were major functions in the city they participated. Their close friend B. I. Friedman was a city alderman [from] about 1936, '38 through the Second World War. My father was a city alderman in 1949-1954, and through this exposure to the entire city they were able to participate in many of the social functions of the city. **Martin Karp, 42**

CHAPTER 8: CHANGES IN SAVANNAH

EXPANSION

The most important changes that I saw was in the Old Fort area in that district. First of all, we saw the streets that were sandy become paved. The street-car track, all that was dug up and taken away. Changes were being made constantly, and we in business began realizing there was a vast change of everything on Broughton Street. The trend was going south. **Louis Silverman, 29**

Savannah, in my growing up years, was a small town. When my family moved to Victory Drive, some of our relatives told us good-bye, we were going so far out. Of course, now, my goodness, what used to be the southern part of Savannah is now midtown, and the south is way, way out. Well, for example, the other two synagogues, the Conservative and Orthodox, were also in the downtown area. As people moved their homes out south, and they don't ride on the Sabbath, they had to build new buildings. . . .

The growth of Savannah is phenomenal. Of course, it's just huge now, and the historic part of town, well, it's only been in the last maybe twenty years that it's been as apparent to Savannahians as it is now, because when I was growing up we had no tours, or I mean it was just there and we knew it was there. . . .

Also there was no crime in those days. Well, not the way it is now. We left our doors open, our windows open at night when we went to bed. Of course, now crime in Savannah, I hate to say, is really terrible. Traffic also is terrible. . . . Of course, that's because of all the people that live here now. But traffic was absolutely nothing. My father taught me to drive by going out Victory Drive because there was no traffic there. . . .

My grandmother came to live with her children. That's what was done in those days. There weren't . . . any retirement homes as we have them now. But actually I think this way is better [at Savannah Square]. I've been offered by both my children to come live with them, but I don't think I will ever do that. I think the retirement home idea is a very, very good one. Here I don't have a house to worry about any more but I'm with lots of people all the time and it's really very nice. . . .

All the banks are getting larger. The corporations are getting larger. Everything costs more, so let's just hope that we don't outgrow our boundary. I'd hate to see Savannah end up in either the Savannah River or the Atlantic Ocean. **Elizabeth "Libby" (Levy) Price, 69**

The city at the time of World War II ended about 52nd Street. During the period of the war, the city really did not grow in area and size until the war was over. That's when the city began to move south once more. **Doris (Goldin) Lukin, 88**

Occasionally we'd go riding up to Victory Drive, which was the end of the city at that time, and ride Victory Drive. . . . In the early '30s, because we got married, we wanted to buy a house, and 60th, 54th, 60th, actually on the other side it was woods. 54th was pretty new then. **Benjamin Portman, 20**

A Growing City, c.1950
These gentlemen are planning Talmadge Bridge to span the Savannah River between Georgia and South Carolina. Left to right are Spence Grayson, John Bouhan, Raymond "Bus" Kuhr, and Harold Friedman.
JVM 003 Savannah Jewish Archives General Photograph Collection, Item 1409

There have been a lot of changes in Savannah, along with all the shopping centers and the malls and things like that. At one time Paulsen and 59th Street was the end of the street. Beyond that was nothing but woods and trees and that was it. But now, Medical Arts has moved out there and all the businesses and things, it's just tremendous. DeRenne Avenue opened up and Waters Avenue going way out. I remember when the Mall first opened up, Adele Schneider was so excited about the Mall she came over and we went over there. We went there twice to look at it and it was just, you know, a treat because the city was growing. **Bess (Eisenman) Center, 3**

When we first got married, my father-in-law owned the duplex apartment on Bolton, off of Habersham, and they lived downstairs and we lived upstairs. We lived there for a few years and then we moved to 51st Street, two blocks east of Waters Avenue. . . .

When we bought the house on 52nd Street, Raymond Rosen says to me, "I'll come to see you one day on my way to Florida." Listen, there were no streets, there was no pavement, and I thought, "We're going to have a lot of ants or something." **Sadye (Steinberg) Rabhan, 22**

[My parents] built a house out on 45th Street, and it was woods out there at the time, about 1916, 1917. . . . Ardsley Park it was called, but the streets were not paved. We used to play out in the dirt. There was a lot of clay in the street in those days, and mud and stuff. My family had an electric car, and eventually, I think, they got a little model A or T Ford or something and worked on up from that. We used to ride the electric [streetcar] around town. **Stephen Traub, 32**

My grandparents, my parents, and then my mother's brother . . . all lived at 32 East 31st Street, which has all been torn down now. It's a parking lot for . . . the church that's on the corner of Bull and Anderson. . . . When I was one year old, my dad decided that he was going to check out and buy his own home, which he did for $7,500, on the corner of 49th and Paulsen, 545 East 49th Street. That's where I grew up at, and I can remember as a . . . young kid, this was like the end of Savannah. . . .

Behind me was 50th Street and 51st Street, and then there was nothing but woods. And the only thing built in those woods was a Gould Home which was located on . . . 54th and Atlantic. But it was in the woods, I mean dead, dead, dead in the middle of the woods. We used to go back and play in the woods. . . . I remember Paulsen was a dirt street. **Julius Edel, 35**

The more affluent at that time had already moved to the south section of Savannah. When I say south, you were south of Victory Drive. I didn't know anybody who lived south of Victory Drive. **Walter Lowe, 54**

CULTURE AND TECHNOLOGY

As far as the trains were concerned, Savannah was one of the two places on the East Coast in which the trains had to back in. They didn't come in to

Savannah and just come in and go out. The trains were backed into the station and then they took them out. That was probably a thirty-minute delay.

Once they built the station out on Telfair Road and tore down the old train station to put the highway in, you probably cut thirty to forty-five minutes out of the trip to New York. So that was also a consideration. I remember many, many trips going to the train station. The train station was also in the '20s a place of social activity because there was a restaurant there and a lot of the dandies would go there on Saturday night. **Martin Karp, 42**

Lena [Shoob] was cute. One time, she said, "You know, I've got problems my mother never had. The telephone rings and I don't know where it is." . . .

When I was the president of Hadassah and lived half of my life on the telephone, I didn't complain. . . . I said, "If I could just have a telephone in the car . . . I would be in clover, because then I could do what I had to do and still talk." Well, honey, today I would have been a wonderful president! **Sadye (Steinberg) Rabhan, 22**

I think Savannah has changed a lot but it's for the better. The old parts of town have been improved and the south side gets bigger and we have colleges, more than just Armstrong. I went to Armstrong when I first came back to Savannah in the '60s and had to take some courses. Now Armstrong is a much bigger school, four-year school. We have the Savannah College of Art & Design, and we have Savannah State College which has been here for a very long time.

So I think we have many things that we have to be thankful for. Lots of concerts by the orchestra in the squares, on the river, at different churches. We are blessed with lots of cultural and very modern schools of art and design. Savannah has lots to offer everybody! **Suzanne (Ginsberg) Kantziper, 84**

TRANSPORTATION

GENERAL TRANSPORTATION

I remember when fire equipment was pulled by horses, and we used to go to the fire stations and look at the horses, as they were kept in the fire stations with the hay and food and everything else. . . . And on West Broad Street there was a stable, a stable for horses with a blacksmith, and in those days horses were used quite extensively. The police department had a mounted patrol; it had policemen who were on horseback just like they later had on motorcycles and on bicycles. **Benjamin Silverman, 29**

They all had bicycles. Savannah wasn't as big as it is today. The more affluent had cars and some rode . . . horses, and even the police were usually on horseback, but they did have a few automobiles. The kids went on roller skates, bikes, mainly. But we had trolleys. The electric trolleys in those days—this was just before World War II—when World War II came, they had pretty well been discontinued, and they were beginning to pull up the tracks to get the steel to help the war effort. **Stephen Traub, 32**

STREETCARS

When I was growing up, there was the streetcar and the streetcar was very big. . . . My mother and daddy said that when they got married in 1930, that if you caught the streetcar on 40th Street you could then ride from 40th Street to Isle of Hope on one token, but if you got on [on] Anderson Street you had to pay two tokens, and since at that point in time they were young and had more energy than they had money, they would walk to 40th street to catch the trolley. **Anchel Samuels, 86**

Early Transportation, 1916
Gussie (Schine) Bono on her bicycle in Savannah.
JVM 003 Savannah Jewish Archives General Photograph Collection, Item 2234

The streetcars were wonderful. We had an A. & B. belt car that went [down] Barnard and made a big circle, Barnard and Abercorn Street. It was the Abercorn and Barnard Street Belt, they called it. They'd go downtown and come by as far south as, I guess it went all the way to 40th Street. And then we had E. & W., then West Broad Street, and made a circle that way.

And then we had streetcar lines going to Port Wentworth and the sugar refinery [and] toward Isle of Hope, Thunderbolt, Montgomery. You'd get transfers to some of those cars. And a lot of those cars in the summertime, particularly, going to Thunderbolt, Isle of Hope, and Montgomery, were open-air cars. It was nice. **Samuel Hirsch, 52**

Well, to me, being a country boy, it was a joy to be able to come to the big city of Savannah and get on the streetcar for a nickel and ride even as far out as Victory Drive. . . . What a wonderful feeling! . . .

There was a Bona Bella route which left Broughton Street and it must have taken hours, and it meandered its way down Habersham Street, around where Leopold Brothers [was]. . . . The streetcar meandered down Gwinnett Street at some point and then took off towards Waters Avenue, and it wound up all the way out to Isle of Hope. When you got there, you had had a journey! **Albert Ullman, 33**

I remember those old trolleys. They ran with, the electrical circuit was, the cable overhead and then the wheels on the ground below, that completed the circuit. We would run behind the trolley and pull the rope down and disengage the pulley from the overhead cable, 'cause that'd stop everything, and the conductor would come back fuming and we'd be run off somewhere. Just kids. **Stephen Traub, 32**

Where the streetcar used to come down West Broad Street, we'd run behind the streetcar. And there used to be a trolley rod that the electricity rubber used to run on the wire up top. So we would take it, the rope, and loop it around so that it wouldn't go up and down, and as soon as the trolley hit a low spot, it would come off the electricity. At that time it seemed like it was a lot of fun. We didn't hurt anybody. The guy just cussed us out. **Arthur "Bubba" Horovitz, 77**

So gradually the city was moving out, and the streetcar ran on Abercorn Street and Barnard Street, and was called the A. & B. Line and made a circle. Of course, that was the days when the automobile was coming in. Paved streets were beginning to come in. The car track ran on Abercorn Street. The children put bottle caps on the rail so that it would disrail [derail] the streetcar, which the conductor always anticipated. I guess it was a life of simpler times. **Mildred (Wolf) Weichselbaum, 51**

I had two brothers. . . . One was younger and one was older. The one that was two years younger than me was playing with a little boy with a red wagon. And on the corner of Broughton and Montgomery, there was a streetcar that came that way. And the streetcar turned into the left and went around to the City Market so that people who lived on Bolton Street and Gwinnett Street, that's how they got to City Market, on this trolley. The trolley turned one corner to Montgomery and Broughton. My brother was in the wagon and the little friend of his took him across the thing while the streetcar was coming, and at the age of four he was killed. **Lena (Feinberg) Rosenzweig, 26**

Down the middle of East Broad Street and down the middle of West Broad Street was a car line. For a nickel you could go around the belt, all the way around. You could catch a trolley on East Broad Street and ride East Broad to Bay and Bay to West Broad, and West Broad right out to one of the streets that escapes my memory, and back to East Broad. . . . There was a double track and one car would go one way and one the other, and that's the way most of the people traveled.

They didn't have automobiles. They would travel by trolley. And there were overhead trolleys; there were these long rods that hooked up to the trolley on top by a pulley. And as kids, I remember some of the kids would run behind the trolley and yank on the cord and pull it off the line, and the trolley would stop, and then the conductor had to get out and put the line back up on the overhead line in order to start back up again. **Benjamin Silverman, 29**

JITNEYS

I think the jitney was five cents. They were . . . Model T's or Model A's, Fords, and they ran all over the city and that's what they were called, jitneys. **Philip Solomons, Sr., 30**

We lived [in] the second house from Whitaker on the north side of the street [36th Street] when there were jitneys. And the jitneys were cars, five passenger cars. I think it was a nickel to ride downtown and back. **Ida (Slotin) Wilensky, 34**

BUSES

The city really did not grow in area and size until the war, World War II, was over. That's when the city began to move south once more. The streetcars were changed, one by one, to buses, and eventually disappeared altogether. **Doris (Goldin) Lukin, 88**

Broughton Street was the center of the city when I grew up. . . . I would go on the bus 'cause we didn't have a car when I was small. Buses everyone rode, and to tell you the truth . . . it was [a] kind of friendly place, that if you stood at the corner of Washington Avenue, which was a stop, the chances were very good that someone in a car would stop and say, "Are you going downtown?". . .

In those days . . . you were not afraid of people you didn't know. . . . You never made an overt action . . . to ask a person for a ride. Quite the opposite. You would just be standing at a bus stop and people who had a car empty would stop and say, "I'm going downtown, do you need a ride?" And no, you didn't stop and look them over or consider, 'cause I think it was probably the furthest thing from anyone's mind that people would do you harm. **Jack Golden, 74**

We did not have car pools; we rode buses. It was safe and you got on the bus and went downtown. They had little tickets that you used, that took you. I think they were . . . ten dollars a book and you got twenty rides. **Harriet (Kanter) Konter, 43**

AUTOMOBILES

The Age of the Automobile, n.d.
Parked in front of Forsyth Park (left to right): Mildred Byck, Carlyn (Byck) Heitler, and Joseph Byck.
JVM 005 Congregation Mickve Israel Photograph Collection, Item 0075

They tell the whole story that my grandfather [after using a horse and buggy in his business] finally went to J. C. Lewis and bought a truck. . . . The first day he got the truck, and he was riding down the street and he got to the corner, and he reared back on the steering wheel and said, "Whoa, Tom. Whoa, Tom." And of course, Tom was the horse and the truck kept rolling. **Isser Gottlieb, 92**

[When my parents went on buying trips] they'd have to take a train. There wasn't an automobile. . . . The first one belonged to the doctor, and we used to pay his chauffeur a quarter to drive us around the block. . . . A car was really something different. Everything was horses. When you'd go any place, you'd rent a team of horses, . . . but a car was, oh, something wonderful! **Helen (Blumenthal) Hirshberg, 13**

I think my older brother was about eighteen months older than I was and I was about seventeen. So we were now fighting over the cars and having dates. . . . When it came my weekend for the car, one time my brother Freddy, he just got out there early and took it. When I was ready to heat the car, the car was gone. So next week I pulled the distributor out of the car so he couldn't go. I had the distributor in my pocket. . . . I could just slip it back in there and take off. **Arthur "Bubba" Horovitz, 77**

I remember my dad taught me to drive when I was fifteen. That was 1945. He took me out like on 52nd Street which was dirt. It was a dirt street. The whole city ended at DeRenne Avenue. **Lewis Kooden, 91**

I tell you a funny thing that happened one time. When they opened up Route 17, I was already a teenager, a big shot. We'd ride. When they opened up 17, it was a big mud-hole all the way. . . . They told you not to go, but people went. Everybody went and they got their cars muddy, slipping and sliding everywhere. So I told him, I said, "Pop, go a little faster." I said, "Because you know if you go faster you hold on the road better.". . . Pop said, "Listen, you can get out and walk if this is too slow." So I jumped out and walked through the mud for about a mile. Finally I was so exhausted. . . . He said, "Get back in the car." So I got in then. Boy, I didn't say nothing no more that day. **Benjamin Portman, 20**

PEOPLE

Tremendous changes, not all in the Jewish community. I don't know if you'd call it homogeneous, but we were very clingy, very, very cliquish, clingy kind of group. Now the kids belong to the golf clubs, the tennis clubs, and they mingle a lot more with the non-Jewish community, which is good. **Ethyl (Richman) Rosenzweig, 25**

One of the main differences I have to believe is the affluence, and as people became wealthier, moved to the suburbs. We lived in a fairly close knit community. . . . Now with the suburban Landings and developments around the edges of golf communities and tennis communities, the community is really fractured in that sense. [The J.E.A.] is still the center of the Jewish community actually, but I don't think it has the kind of allegiance or the attraction that it had for us. To us it was all entertainment. Playing checkers was a big deal in the afternoon, but now the kids play golf. **David Rosenzweig, 25**

My grandfather had been an alderman, . . . Abe S. Guckenheimer. . . . He was well known. He was . . . second generation in Savannah. He worked downtown. . . . I can remember walking Broughton Street with him. Back in those days, men wore hats; men tipped their hats. Incidentally, women downtown wore hats and gloves. I can recall being on West Broughton Street, . . . it had to have been near Montgomery, he dropped by to introduce me to some contemporaries of my mother's parents, the Gittelsohns, I. M. and Lena Gittelsohn. . . .

Anyway, we continued across Broughton Street to Whitaker where he was taking me to lunch at Morrison's Cafeteria. Great days of my childhood, having lunch, mid-day dinner with Grandfather all by myself. Anyway, seventy-five percent of the people on the street would call him by name and he'd call them by name. Savannah in those days had a population of 60,000-65,000 people and the downtown folks knew each other. That was something that stuck in my memory. Because you can walk downtown today and see hardly anybody you've ever seen before in your life. **Alan Gaynor, 62**

BUSINESSES AND DOWNTOWN

You know, a lot of buildings have been destroyed although we have been able to keep a lot. The old Adler's Department Store had a terrible fire, which was unfortunate, and that burnt down. There used to be, at one time, thirteen banks in Savannah, commercial banks, prior to the Depression, and now we have five or six.

The corner of Bull and Broughton had a wonderful old building where the Liberty Bank & Trust was. Where the restaurant Il Pasticcio is now, prior to that was Lerner's Shop and prior to that there was a hotel, an old building. I think Historic Savannah [Foundation] had lots of the buildings, or the Georgia Historic[al] Society, has pictures of some of the old buildings on Broughton Street.

I can tell you that the Lucas Theatre had the first great air conditioner. Everybody used to flock there in the summertime to cool off. Where the Weis Theatre building [was] in which is now the Trustees [Theatre], SCAD [Savannah College of Art & Design] owns it, that was a bowling alley that we used to go to during the Second World War.

There used to be a lot of soda fountains on Broughton Street. There were a lot of small merchants and as they expanded to take in two or three of the stores and you had a lot of wonderful men's stores, ladies' stores. I guess the great ambition for most Jewish merchants was to move from West Broad to Broughton Street.

A lot of people came in from, moved in from the country. Mr. Jake Fine had his first store in Metter, Georgia. **Martin Karp , 42**

Historic Buildings Lost, n.d.
This building, adjacent to City Hall for many years, was torn down to make room for parking.
JVM 005 Congregation Mickve Israel Photograph Collection, Item 0090

All business changes. You know, Fine's was our most important ladies' shop and Chaskin's was another one, and Lady Jane was another one. And then . . . Glendale Hat Shop . . . and Levy's Department Store and Adler's Department Store. It's just, Broughton Street is just completely gone. And so is West Broad. . . . The only ones that are left on West Broad now is B. & B. [Paint Company] and National Tailors. **Lena (Feldman) Solomon, 82**

I moved here in 1953. At that time Morrison's was about the only restaurant where you could get a decent meal. The J.E.A. was very, very small, not the size as it is now. Going out on Saturday nights was going to a movie. The changes now! Why, there's more eating places, of course, and there's more activities in any field you want to. You want culture, you want the arts, you want athletics, you have so much more. Economic conditions are so much better. There's very little unemployment here. **Charles Becker, 64**

TOURISM AND PRESERVATION

I wouldn't live anywhere else but the downtown area from the time I got here because I was fascinated by all the historic architectural buildings and the richness of the buildings. Even though they weren't all, you know, fully restored as they are now, there were a lot of still tenement buildings, a lot of empties, and so forth. But I was here at the beginning of the restoration period. I remember walking streets with Lee Adler on Sundays and looking at buildings and the possibilities of each. **Eric Meyerhoff, 18**

River Street was completely remodeled with a seven million dollar grant from the Federal government. Before this was done, I used to rent a warehouse in this area for ten dollars per month. So, you can easily understand what the River Street remodeling did for the tax base in Savannah. **Leo Center, 4**

Savannah's City Market, c. March-April 1954
The tearing down of the old City Market on Ellis Square was the end of an era.
JVM 003 Savannah Jewish Archives General Photograph Collection, Item 1822

River Street was a place to avoid. It was . . . more dangerous down there. We'd stay up on Bay Street, but we were very careful. It was not really the most savory neighborhood. . . . Savannah was getting pretty run down looking. Historic Savannah [Foundation] had not begun; the reclamation of these derelict buildings was not in progress. We had not begun that. Things were just beginning.

We were a sleepy southern town. . . . There was very little progress, but [while] you could look at it negatively, it was also a time of great stability for me. In the '50s and the '40s, things just stayed the same for a long time. That's hard for today's child to understand, when changes are coming faster than the click of their mouse. **Barbara (Smith) Levy, 19**

Savannah has just grown so. Now you feel when you go to a grocery store anywhere, you don't hear a Southern accent, you hear a Northern accent. You don't see anybody much that you know. You go into a Publix and all those places, it's so large and it's entirely different. But that's growth and I guess you have to expect that. Now Savannah's grown, particularly since that book, *Midnight in the Garden of Good and Evil,* came out. Savannah has been swarmed with tourists. I've never seen anything like it. **Bess (Eisenman) Center, 3**

CHAPTER 9:
FAMILY MEMORIES AND ANECDOTES

I can't recall what name the Savannah baseball team had in those days, . . . Crackers, maybe. . . . [My grandfather, Abe S. Guckenheimer] was occupying a pretty large house at 811 Whitaker Street. The guys on the Savannah baseball team boarded or roomed with him. I'm sure they didn't eat, well, they could have eaten there. He cooked German pancakes and lentil soup and salt mackerel, . . . and oyster stew, those were his great things. His trademark was he constantly smoked cigars so you'd get some cigar ash in your oyster stew, but it flavored it!

In any event, his house was always full in the summer of third-rate baseball players. The only one I can recall is Pretzels Pazula. . . . I don't know if he ever got to the big leagues. **Alan Gaynor, 62**

[My grandfather, Arthur Solomon, Sr.] was in the first graduating class from Georgia Tech with a degree in mechanical engineering, and the story that I heard was that he got the . . . wood [for his house at Grimball's Point on Isle of Hope], the cypress wood particularly, from a lumber company that was going bankrupt. He was able to buy the whole lot of cypress and the house literally was designed around what he had. It's very Arts and Crafts. It was built in 1913. He acquired the land in the early 1900s in pieces. **Jan (Solomon) Friedman VandenBulck, 94**

I have the wedding gift that Juliette [Gordon] Low [founder of the Girl Scouts] gave to my Grandmother Mildred [Kuhr]. It was a little cloisonne mirror that one would hang on a chain perhaps. It's a lovely little piece. **Joan (Levy) Levy, 95**

My grandmother raised geese and if the expression *"shtup a ganz"* means anything. My grandmother used to take . . . a goose at a time, put in her lap, wrap it in . . . her apron, and you . . . open the mouth and you dropped corn into the mouth, and then you pushed it down into the gullet. That was to fatten the geese so that by the time you got ready to eat them, they were very fat. **Selma (Greenberg) Dunn, 7**

They had parties out at Grimball's Point. They . . . went swimming out there and they had a girls' dressing and sleeping area and a boys' dressing and sleeping area. They had been going and using the river and the place forever. **Sue (Solomon) Herman, 94**

Among [my grandfather's] attitudes and philosophies was agnosticism, never atheism, but agnosticism. He could not bring himself to believe and to act upon the rituals of traditional Judaism. He was a man who, I'm sure, had a traditional upbringing, I'm positive. I've seen pictures of my great-grandmother, his mother, who lived here for a while. She wore a *sheytel.* I mean, it was a very traditional family. My grandfather was absolutely not traditional. He refused to walk into a synagogue. Yet he was very, very best friends with the rabbi of the Orthodox synagogue. . . .

On holidays he closed his shop, and I remember we used to have to put a quarter in the hot water meter in the house, and he would dress as though he were going to synagogue, . . . and he would wait for the break on the holidays. He would greet everyone, wish them luck, *yom tov*, a good fast if it were Yom Kippur. And he would then turn around, proceed to go right around the corner and get in his car and drive away. He was just a wonderful, wonderful human being and a humanist, certainly respectful, but respectful of traditional Judaism, but not prepared to practice it. **Robert Friedman, 38**

A Savannah Family, n.d.
Martin and Louise Beck with their dogs.
JVM 005 Congregation Mickve Israel
Photograph Collection, Item 0029

My grandfather [Arthur Solomon, Sr.] and his wife, our grandmother, lived [at Grimball's Point] from 1932 until his death in '62, when Mother and Daddy moved in the house. And now my husband Charlie and I live in the house. It's a large piece of property with lots of azaleas and camellias 'cause our grandfather was very involved. . . .

[The house] was built by my grandfather and it never had a drop of paint on the inside. He had some sort of process done to the cypress. It's never needed paint. I think he had lots of friends who were in the business 'cause it's like recycled doors and recycled glass and he designed the whole thing around, I think, the building material he got. He was very creative and very mechanical and was quite proficient in doing things like that. **Jan (Solomon) Friedman VandenBulck, 94**

My mother's maiden name was Kayton . . . [and] my father's name was Rosenheim. . . . [My parents decided to change our] . . . name from my father['s] to my mother['s] for the purpose of perpetuating the Kayton name which was better known in Savannah. . . . They thought it was better if the three of us [my older brothers and myself], in the one family make the change. . . .

There is an amusing story that comes to mind. My dad was in a business that occasionally he would bring someone home to meet the family, and one day he came home with a gentleman and introduced him to his wife . . . and then he introduced him to the three boys, Allan Kayton, Robert Kayton, and John Kayton. The guest looked perturbed, to say the least, and couldn't understand it. My dad said, "They're my wife's children by her first husband." And he said, "Oh, I understand." Dad waited like Jack Benny would have waited, and then he said, "I'm the first husband." **John Kayton, 65**

[Arthur Solomon, Sr.] was a county commissioner for forty-six years. His interest in gardening actually started from his mother. Her name was Sarah Alexander Solomon. . . . She came from England and had a garden in England, and then encouraged him in that respect. **Sue (Solomon) Herman, 94**

My mother [Ruth Byck] became very interested in Senior Citizens because my grandmother, Ida Boley Byck, . . . lived with us, and was a part of our family as long as I could remember. Besides going to market and helping my mother cook, she really didn't have any functions except to play cards and stay up in her room and read. Seniors at that time, which is going back into the 1940s and early '50s, were really just put aside. There were no programs for them and mother became very interested because of my grandmother and her situation to do something to make seniors feel needed and worthwhile.

So, together with Mr. Harley Morrison, whose nickname was "Nippy" Morrison, and Mr. Hunter Leaf, they formed a committee to engage seniors in various opportunities and to see that they were engaged somehow to make sort of a contribution to their lives. She was instrumental, they were instrumental in starting what was called Golden Age Clubs where they got together and talked about various cultural affairs, music. They engaged Marge Mazo who was a local Jewish musician of note to give talks. . . .

They were able to get certain contracts for seniors to work on, as far as building pallets. . . . They encouraged older senior citizens to make certain quilts and dolls and other woven goods, and jellies, and these were sold in a gift shop that was run by senior citizens. Through that they were able to get a little home, so to speak, in Forsyth Park. It was attached to the old fort down there.

Mother made a lot of studies about other senior citizens' groups throughout the country, and was asked to attend a White House Conference on Aging, invited by the president at that time. . . . I believe that was Truman, if I'm not mistaken. She did not attend, but had a lot to do with the founding of what was to be called Senior Citizens Incorporated, which is now located . . . on Bull Street at the foot of Washington Avenue.

This was one of her ideas, after the building was up, was to get . . . some sort of movement going for the blind. A building was built, named in her honor, . . . which was called the Ruth Byck Auditorium and was dedicated to her in the early 1970s. Blind occupied it for a number of years and then they got quarters of their own, and Mother became interested in dementia of senior citizens, and the auditorium was then turned over to what was now called the Alzheimer's Program for dementia problems in older citizens.

She was given numerous awards - the Exchange Club, the Gold Deeds Award, and from the Jewish War Veterans, and from the Sertoma Club, and various other organizations, as well as the City of Savannah awarded her a key to the city. She was very proud of these awards and very proud of the movement that she started. **David A. Byck, III, 72**

[Grandfather Arthur Solomon, Sr.] was one of the founders of the American Camellia Society in 1946, '45, '46. It was, as they say, conceived in Savannah, but actually incorporated in Macon, Georgia. **Jan (Solomon) Friedman VandenBulck, 94**

[My father, Alexander Meddin,] was the City Champion Handball player in 1921, and they gave him a little silver medal. . . . They used to call him "Gator Meddin" 'cause Daddy was quite a swimmer. **Adele (Meddin) Schneider, 61**

I wouldn't be exactly certain of the exact locations they came from, but I know Daddy came from Poland and I want to say that Mama did, too. Mama and Aunt Ida Berman came to this country as orphans and were actually managed, I'm going to say managed, by two bachelor uncles, the Subotnicks,

Morris and Joe Subotnick, up in Augusta, Georgia. That was early in 1900 somewhere.

An interesting story is, I remember as a child, we'd go over to the Little Sisters of the Poor on 37th Street, where it was located. And I'd say, "We're Jewish. What are we going over to the Little Sisters of the Poor for?" "To visit." Then it came out, Mama would tell us stories. The bachelor uncles, they didn't know what to do with two young women who came to this country, so they put them . . . in the convent day school. They knew they'd be well taken care of, well educated, etc., taught the right values. So Mama used to, after she married Dad, she liked to pay homage, . . . visit once or twice a year with her sister. **Leon Slotin, 47**

Savannah Gentlemen, n.d.
Pictured left to right: Joseph Byck, an unidentified individual, and Sigmund Sonnenberg.
JVM 005 Congregation Mickve Israel Photograph Collection, Item 0036

I could do an hour standup on my Aunt Eva Sadler and my Aunt Hilda Broome. Just those two. My Aunt Bloomie was the driver; my Aunt Eva had very, very poor eyesight, but she was the co-pilot. And my aunts, how they managed to drive around this city for the many years that they did without getting in an accident, is beyond me.

Now, my Aunt Bloomie drove, but she couldn't park. . . . She would drive down to Broughton Street and stop the car and get out and ask a passerby whether he could park the car for her. It's a good thing that car-jacking was no art in those days, because he would have driven off with my Aunt Eva in the car. **Walter Lowe, 54**

Lena Fox was my grandfather's youngest sister. . . . *Driving Miss Daisy* was written by Aunt Lena's son [grandson], Alfred Uhry, about the antics of his grandmother having to have a chauffeur. The story is based on Aunt Lena's visits to Savannah. . . . When Aunt Lena would visit my grandfather at 27 East 50th Street, Will [the chauffeur] would sit in the kitchen with the cook or . . . he would stay out with the famous car, and I would sit on the grass at my grandfather's house and we would talk to Will. The story involving Miss Daisy is essentially true. **Jane (Guthman) Kahn, 93**

The sisters were a very, very tight-knit group. From what I can remember, I don't think that there were very many times when they all spoke to one another. And my wife, who was a sweet, sensitive, beautiful girl, used to take my mother to her card game. They were card fanatics, all the women except my Aunt Hilda Broome. I don't think she played cards. To the others, it was a mission. It wasn't a joy to them. So, one time my wife took my mother to play cards, and my Aunt Bloomie, who I said was the sweetest of them, was there, and I guess my mother spoke to all of the sisters more than the others did.

But this one occasion, what happened was, and I do remember it, she and my mother got in a terrible argument over whether the afghan, the patches, were crocheted or knitted. They stopped speaking over that. So when my wife, who was not used to that in her family, picked my mother up to take her home, she says, "You don't know how happy I am that you and Aunt Bloomie are speaking to one another again," because they were playing cards at Bloomie's house. My mother says, "What do you mean, we're speaking?" She said, "Well, you played cards." She says, "We don't have to speak to play cards." **Walter Lowe, 54**

In 1951, my life took another direction, a significant other direction which, in great part, was due to . . . the J.E.A. I was nominated and went to Tel Yehudah Camp in New Hampshire. . . . It was a Young Judaea camp, and it was, of course, *Zionist*. I went, and the only way I can describe it is, it was an amazing experience. I was like hungry for this kind of experience. Not the, the social part, yes, but the ideas and meeting people from everywhere, notions of Israel. So camp was over and we came back. . . .

We were sitting in a movie one night. I don't remember what the movie was, but we started talking and Israel came up, and I said, "I am going to Israel next year." They looked at me like I was crazy and laughed. . . . No one had gone to

Israel, and certainly no one from Savannah. . . . My father rejected it, just out of hand. My mother encouraged me. . . . We couldn't afford it. My grandfather, who was anti-*Zionist*, was the only person who was fully supportive. He was anti-*Zionist* because he was anti-state. He was very upset that Israel had become a state in a world which needed no new states. . . .

Savannah Jewish Federation and J.E.A. came up with the money to send me to Israel. And I went. I went in 1952. I had just graduated high school early. I was . . . sixteen years old. I had like two months of the experience of Israel as a new country. . . . We traveled and worked and learned throughout the country. You know, you have to understand Israel was very, very new. . . . Well, you know, it changed my life, those two experiences, Tel Yehudah and Israel. **Robert Friedman, 38**

Mr. Phillip Kaplan had the grocery store on Jefferson and 35th streets, on the corner. . . . Mama would send Maria, who was like a maid that lived with us, and we'd go around there to cash checks. . . . So one day I was worrying Mama for some money and she said, "Here's a check.". . . We go around to Mr. Kaplan's store . . . and Mr. Kaplan is so used to seeing us that he gave us money. I think it was a check for five dollars.

The next thing you know Mr. Kaplan calls Mama and said, "I've got a check here the bank sent back." "You didn't cash that check for Leon, did you?" "Yeah, it was made out and signed by Mrs. Chaim Yankel [colloquial, a nobody]." He didn't even look at the check. **Leon Slotin, 47**

When I went to get a passport to go to Israel the first time, I needed a birth certificate. When I got the birth certificate, it showed my birth date as October 20th, 1921, and I had always known, or thought I knew, that my birthday was in November. . . .

My Aunt Annie Melaver . . . was . . . on her deathbed. I walked into the room. . . . I said, "You know, I got my birth certificate the other day and I noticed the birth date was not the day I'm used to . . . November 20th." So she managed to smile and actually laugh and she said, "You know, when you moved to New York . . . I arranged to get a birth certificate for you.". . . . The cutoff date to go to school was the last of October, and she said, "We certainly didn't want to keep you out a whole year, so I told your mother we're going to get you a birth certificate with the October birth date.". . .

When I went to go for my Social Security I had the birth certificate, but I knew I had to tell the truth . . . [to] the person that was interviewing me. . . . I says, "I've just got to tell you the truth. My birthday's November the 20th." I'll never forget what she said. She said, sounded like an old Jewish lady. She said, "Don't make trouble. . . . If we start messing with this it will take years before you get your first check." So we left it alone. **Walter Lowe, 54**

**Sports and Fun in Savannah,
c.1922**
Abro Robinson up to bat in front
of the old downtown J.E.A.
JVM 003 Savannah Jewish Archives
General Photograph Collection, Item
2166

CHAPTER 10: LOVE IN SAVANNAH

FALLING IN LOVE

I met my husband through the J.E.A. . . . On Rosh Hashanah they always tried to have the soldier boys in to have dinner with the families . . . so they wouldn't feel so lonely. . . . They asked my mother to take some soldiers. She says, "I have, I can squeeze one in." And he happened to be my [future] husband. I didn't think much of him at the time. . . .

After that . . . he brought my mother this, these vases and a little snowman. . . . He took his whole salary and bought that in appreciation for having him over for dinner. He'd come always when mother was cooking supper, and I would get off from work and walk home and he would be sitting in the kitchen with my mother talking. I'd say, "What you doing here?" He said, "I'm visiting your mother.". . . Mama used to laugh, "He's sitting waiting for you." He started courting me. . . . I guess . . . the war had some good effect. It got rid of a lot of old maids. **Gertrude (Scheer) Barr, 1**

My husband came here with the first contingent to Hunter [Air] Field in 1940, and he helped pitch the first tent. . . . For Yom Kippur they let them off, and he came into town with a friend of his, and they came to the B. B. Jacob and I was there. . . . This was during recess in the middle of the day and we met in the basement, downstairs of the J.E.A. . . . There were a whole lot of us and we decided . . . to go out that night after Yom Kippur. We rode around, . . . and the rest is history. We were married two years later. **Beatrice (Heyman) Goodman, 39**

I met him [Abe] on the dance floor at the Alliance. . . . After the dance, we went to the Union Station for pie and coffee. . . . And then he says to me, "Can I take you home?" I said, "Well, why not." He had this little jitney [vehicle] that was the same age as me. . . . And then I started going with him and that was it. That was it! **Sadye (Steinberg) Rabhan, 22**

Now we were at Ellie Rossbach's house for dinner and Sammy Adler was there. I said to Eleanor at the table, I said, "You know, I was going with a nice

Jewish girl from Brooklyn but I introduced her to somebody she got engaged to.". . .
So Sammy got out his book, he had a book from going up to some club . . . and he
gave me a list of about six girls. The first two, Pat Somebody didn't have a Jewish
name; the second one was Gloria "Kelly" Stephins.

And so the next trip to New York, I picked up the phone and I called for Pat.
Well, her roommate was Kelly and Pat wasn't there. And so I started talking to
Kelly. I said, "Well, why don't you have dinner with me." And so that's how I met
her, over the telephone. . . . So I took her out to dinner. She says I took her to the
Rexall Drug Store but that's a lie. I took her to hear a band to find out whether she
could dance or not, cause that was my big love. . . . I didn't particularly care for
her, but it was something about her that I liked. **A. J. Cohen, Jr., 6**

He came to visit my cousins. That's who he stayed with, and I remember
distinctly the first time I set eyes on him. I believe in fate. I believe that everything
is what we call in Jewish "*besheret.*" Everything that happens, I believe, is meant to
be. **Lena (Feinberg) Rosenzweig, 26**

Socials for Servicemen, March 1951
The J.E.A. sponsored several programs for servicemen when many future
husbands met their wives. Left to right: four unidentified people, Irvin
"Yitsie" Rosenthal, Joan (Galin) Wolson, unidentified, Ida (Radetsky) Cooper,
unidentified, Naomi Brown, and Doris (Waldman) Gellins.
JVM 003 Savannah Jewish Archives General Photograph Collection, Item 0590

[My wife's] cousin was complaining to my sister-in-law that they'd been having trouble with me trying to find somebody for me to marry 'cause it was time for
me to get married. I was already thirty-three, thirty-four years old. Nothing seemed

to satisfy me. She said, "I've got the girl for him . . . cause she's the same way, . . . she can't find anybody she likes.". . . So she says, "If I give you a girl's name and address will you write her a letter?" I said, "Sure, what have I got to lose?"

I wrote her. She gets a letter from me and she says, "Who's this? I don't write anybody I don't know anything about. I'm not going to answer that letter." Her dad says, "I know the family and they're very lovely, they're nice people. What have you got to lose, a stamp? Write the letter. That don't mean you've got to marry the guy. Write him a letter.". . .

She wrote the letter and that was the beginning of writing to somebody I didn't know. And it got to the point that where we wrote, I wrote every day, a special delivery letter every day, day in and day out. . . . I really had her hooked, sanded, everything. She really, she went hook and barrel. **Sam Steinberg, 31**

In Savannah I paid absolutely no attention to Matt, because Matt was a real ragamuffin and wild. He always had holes in his knees because he used to play so hard and I thought I was a grown-up lady. . . . When he enlisted in the army . . . he stopped in New York and stayed at my house, . . . and he began to pay tremendous amount of attention to me. . . . This started it. . . .

He went to Harvard and he wrote me practically every day. I had two boxes of letters, . . . it had to be close to two-thousand letters. . . . I responded daily. I never missed a day, . . . every single day for three years, without stop. **Pearl (Spivak) Levy, 44**

There was also a lady that was a German immigrant, she was coming to *shul* also and she lived a few blocks from *shul*. . . . I became befriended with this lady. . . . She said, . . . "My daughter wants to have you tonight or the following Saturday for a birthday party.". . . So I went there. . . . What hit me was three chairs with three girls. Two had crossed their legs and one did not. Now in Italy, a lady does not cross her legs. . . .

The lady of the house comes to me and says, "What can I do for you?" "Well, I'd like to have some water." So I drink some water and while I was drinking water, I was looking at this lady. She said, "Max, you have something else on your mind. What is it?" I said, "Who is that lady? . . . Is she married? . . . Is she engaged? . . . If she's not engaged, I think that's my wife." Just like that. **Marcus "Max" Kreh, 59**

He [Larry] said, "I got so tired of being with people that weren't Jewish and wanted to meet some Jewish people." And he said, "I walked down Broughton Street looking for Jewish names on stores and I saw Levy Jewelers." And he said, . . . "I went in there and I said I'm Jewish." He didn't look Jewish. He said, "I'm Jewish. I want to date some Jewish people. Do you happen to know anybody that's presentable that I can go out with?" Miriam [Levy] was there and she said,

"Yes, I've got a cousin I think you'd like." So she told him to call me. **Annette (Berman) Gray, 87**

I actually had met Ronnie when I was nine years old. He came to my sister's thirteenth birthday party. . . . One of my . . . cousins, who was also there, said to me, "Bunny, which of these boys would you pick? You know, to marry." . . . I chose Ronnie for me, . . . for myself because he had gotten down on all fours and was playing with me. . . . I was nine and he was almost thirteen, I guess. I never saw him again until I was sixteen and I was a counselor at camp and we were out by the swimming pool. **Phillipa "Bunny" (Sherman) Cohen, 90**

B'nai B'rith Girls' Dance, 12 June 1946
Dances helped bring young couples together (left to right): Harry Robbins, Cherry (Hirsch) Kutler, Harry Yellin, Pauline (Dinerman) Fishel, Joseph "Jody" Zerman, and Jo Ann (Landy) Fogler.
JVM 003 Savannah Jewish Archives General Photograph Collection, Item 0168

Leah Adilman . . . called me one day and said she had her roommate from the University of Pennsylvania coming to Savannah, would I have a date with her? . . . I had a date with Marge and we started going together. I was just getting started and we finally drifted apart and Marge got married to a man named Julian Uhry from Atlanta. . . . Julian Uhry died on the golf course. He was playing golf and died. . . .

A couple of years after that, Leah Adilman called me again and said, "Albert, I have a visitor. Would you date her?" Of course, it was Marge and we started going together and we finally got married. **Albert Mazo, 50**

It was during 1958 that I met my future wife, Ellen. It turned out that her father, Edwin Rothschild, and my father, David A. Byck, Jr., were roommates in college. . . . Edwin . . . was best man at my father's wedding. **David A. Byck, III, 72**

We had not dated until I was fifteen when he [my future husband Leonard] asked to take me to a ball. . . . One of our friends who was sixteen at the time was having a big dance at the old General Oglethorpe Hotel. They were looking for all the Jewish boys who were eligible to take the girls and that was always a difficult situation in Savannah. There were never enough Jewish boys.

So Jane [Rosenblum, my sister] had found a date and so my dad said, "Well, I'll talk to Mr. [Jacob Isaac] Kantziper 'cause I know he's got a son." And that's how I got, that was my first date with Leonard. **Suzanne (Ginsberg) Kantziper, 84**

Mother and Dad were very concerned that I spent too much time with one or two [boys]. I think they were more concerned that I wasn't dating a lot of different people instead of just one. I think that was just a natural parental concern. . . . I almost couldn't go out on my first date with Merrill because my parents did not know who his parents were. And until he walked in and mother took a look at him and sort of figured out that she knew his sister, then she would allow me to go out. After all, she did not know his parents and they were not about to let their child leave the premises. **Barbara (Smith) Levy, 19**

When we [my twin and myself] started dating, we used to have the times of our lives. . . . We would switch dates. . . . Nobody knew. **Evelyn (Center) Goldberg, 10**

The other day I was looking through my memory book . . . from high school years, and all my dance cards are in there. And every single one of them were Jewish boys. **Ida (Slotin) Wilensky, 34**

When I got out of college, every Wednesday I would have a date with a certain person. And I would pick her up about one when she got off from her work, and we would go down to the Savannah Line, which consisted of four ships that carried passengers and cargo . . . to New York . . . and Boston. . . . We always found somebody . . . having bon voyage parties. So we would go aboard and go to one or two of the parties, and have snacks and drinks. . . . Then when they'd say, "All ashore, who's going ashore," we would get off the ship. . . .

We'd go to the Lucas Theatre where after six you'd have to wear a coat and tie, and it cost thirty-five cents apiece to go to the movie. . . . That would get out about nine-thirty, and from there we would go out to Johnny Harris, and we could buy barbecue sandwiches for twenty-five cents apiece and Coca-Cola was five cents. They had slot machines out there, so if you'd get lucky maybe you'd win a quarter or fifty cents for the evening. And that was a ritual. **Sidney Raskin, 23**

Savannah Wedding, c.1909
Held at 408 East Broughton Street, this wedding celebration included: Rae (Schwartz) Beasley, Fanny (Schlessenger) Schwartz, Hannah (Schwartz) Weil, Lena (Feinberg) Rosenzweig, and Helen (Schwartz) Perlman.
JVM 003 Savannah Jewish Archives General Photograph Collection, Item 2127

Lewis [Kooden]. . . said he wanted to marry Barbara [my daughter] and I said, . . . "Just a minute. I don't want any repercussions. Honey, come in here." So I took him into the bedroom . . . and showed him Barbara's closet and I said, "Now, I want you to look and see what's doing in here. I want you to see all the shoes and all the dresses and whatever is hanging. . . ." He always [says], "You warned me, but I didn't listen." [or] "Oh, she went to buy something. You warned me, why didn't I listen!" **Sadye (Steinberg) Rabhan, 22**

After I was liberated, I had been in prison camp for ten months. . . . I didn't know what was going on in Savannah or anywhere else. . . . On the way home there was a troop ship that I left France with and I ran into Bubba Horovitz on the boat. . . . During one of our many conversations he mentioned he wanted to congratulate me, that he heard I had become engaged. . . . I said, "Well, I don't know anything about being engaged." He got a little embarrassed and flustered. . . .

We landed in Boston, . . . I put in two telephone calls, one for my family and one to Helen. . . . I talked to my family and they didn't mention anything about

[it]. I asked how Helen was and whether they heard from her, whether they were keeping up with her, and so forth, and they said yes and that was it. . . .

She had actually become engaged by proxy while I was a P.O.W. . . . This was arranged by my father. . . . My father knew how I felt about Helen and he figured that Helen, if she felt the same way, she would accept his offer of engagement to me, and he asked Arthur [Cranman, my uncle] to take her out and ask her if she would marry me while I was indisposed. Arthur did that and she accepted. . . . The first time I found [out] I was engaged was when Helen's mother came on and said, "Congratulations, son, how does it feel to be engaged?" I almost dropped through the floor. . . .

I was very happy about it. . . . Being liberated, coming home and finding yourself engaged was kind of a difficult thing mentally to really keep up with. I was overcome with everything that had transpired. **Herman Cranman, 36**

My mother-in-law, let her rest in peace, she moved to Tybee that Sunday morning and she came late. She came an hour late to our wedding. We waited for her. So I said to her, "Mama, how come you're so late?" She said, "Well, you don't get married twelve o'clock Sunday. You get married one o'clock." I said, "Well you should of told me when we sent out the invitations." **Sadye (Steinberg) Rabhan, 22**

I spent my honeymoon at the DeSoto Beach Club. . . . We only had three days, so we decided to go to the DeSoto Beach Club. And at that time, it was during the war, and you couldn't crack a shade, even . . . at night. If they saw a glimmer of light . . . **Beatrice (Heyman) Goodman, 39**

There were one or two that married out of the faith. . . . When they did marry out of the faith, the family would sit *shivah*, . . . seven days of mourning if they married a non-Jew. . . . They didn't know the child after that. They sat *shivah* as if she was dead. There was no contact at all. **Lena (Feinberg) Rosenzweig, 26**

I never went out with any young man who was not Jewish. I had a friend from school who used to come by in the afternoons, but I really think he didn't come to see me. He came to use the, play my piano because he enjoyed playing the piano and he didn't have one of his own to play on. **Marion (Abrahams) Levy Mendel, 17**

I never went out with non-Jewish boys. . . . When I was in grammar school, they used to have dances called the Panther Dances. . . . My mother would let me go with kids from my class. But then it was just sort of an unwritten thing, I think, when I got into high school other boys would ask me out, Jewish boys, and so I just never dated non-Jewish boys. **Phillipa "Bunny" (Sherman) Cohen, 90**

We had one marriage where a Reform guy married an Orthodox Jew and you would have thought that it was an inter-marriage, . . . there was such scandal in the community. **Ida (Slotin) Wilensky, 34**

My brother married out of the faith. . . . My mother was remarkable. She said, "I don't want to lose my son," and she invited Margaret . . . to have dinner at two o'clock, two o'clock every day and that was my mother's doing. **Anne (Lewis) Buchsbaum, 2**

Newlyweds, 8 June 1923
Pictured are groom Jacob Ulman and his bride Ida (Weitz) Ulman.
JVM 003 Savannah Jewish Archives General Photograph Collection, Item 2268

LOVE FOR THE CITY OF SAVANNAH

I would not trade Savannah for any city in the world, its people and its community. I really wouldn't. I've been all over the world, and I've been all over the United States, and I've seen people and things, and nothing, nothing would I compare to Savannah. And that's the truth. **Reuben Schneider, 28**

I always thought there was a certain amount of greatness in this city. . . . We've produced a number of very remarkably talented people in this city. A lot of them have left the city, but they've made a name for themselves and they've made a name for Savannah. Anywhere you go in the world, especially today, when you say you're from Savannah, they always want to know about it. . . . I think Savannah has always had a very cosmopolitan people growing up and living here. **Martin Karp, 42**

I'd like to say that I think [Savannah is] still the most beautiful city in the world, and it's as friendly as it can be. I don't mind living here for the rest of my life. **Ida (Bronitsky) Stein, 56**

The people are just so very, very friendly. . . . We just enjoy living here! **Charles Becker, 64**

When I came to Savannah, I've been very, very happy here. I love the people and I love the city, and if I was a writer or poet, I'd like to write about Savannah. **Helen (Blumenthal) Hirshberg, 13**

Savannah happens to be a very nice place to live. Everything is close enough here that even when I was in business I was able to see my children. . . . I was in business. It took me five minutes to go from my house on 55th Street to downtown, so it was always very close. The people here in Savannah were very, very friendly. I always made a lot of good friends and have been very happy here. **Julius Rudikoff, 46**

Savannah is my home. I've never lived anywhere else. As a matter of fact . . . you're lucky if you've come to Savannah to live. I think it's a nice, friendly community. It really is. . . . I think it's wonderful! I have no way of knowing because I've really never lived anywhere else. I'm happy right here! **Sadye (Steinberg) Rabhan, 22**

I think the squares, the streets, the homes, the trees, the vegetation, makes [downtown] a very interesting, historic, compact place to live. I think a lot of people like urban living. . . . You can walk out on the streets early in the morning or even in the late evening and there is always activity. **Martin Karp, 42**

I must tell you that if you can make a decent living, the living is so easy in Savannah. It is much less of a strain, the weather is relatively good, and it's just much easier living here than elsewhere, as far as I'm concerned. **Walter Lowe, 54**

Well, [Savannah's] just wonderful! It gives you a peace of mind to know that you're in a, to know that you're living in a city that you see people that you have seen since you were a child. I like also the fact that Savannah has so many newcomers and I get a chance to meet new people, and these people are wonderful. They're from all over the world and everybody has a story to tell and it's just fascinating to me. **Phillipa "Bunny" (Sherman) Cohen, 90**

Growing up in Savannah, 1935
Left to right are these friends: (front row) Sandra (Cohen) Glass and Shirley (Robbins) Ghingold; (back row) Harry Robbins, Frances (Samuels) Rokoff, and Mary (Weitz) Friedman.
JVM 003 Savannah Jewish Archives General Photograph Collection, Item 2306

LOVE OF THE JEWISH COMMUNITY

In New York, I just always remembered it as so many people, and there wasn't a sense of unity. As soon as I came to Savannah, I felt the family aspect of the Jewish people in Savannah, and I mean that very strongly. **Norton Melaver, 15**

I think that there is a closeness of Jewish people. They're always there to help you out. I have found out in my life that if you give, you receive. I feel very, very lucky that I have so many wonderful friends that have been so caring. . . . They always are there for you. We're cliquish, I know there's a lot of cliques going in Savannah, but nevertheless, it's just, there's a closeness. There is a closeness! **Evelyn (Ward) Karsman, 53**

The Jewish community in Savannah, from the very earliest days, . . . has always opened their arms. . . . Even though I lived in a small country town, there was always that wonderful treat of coming to Savannah on Sunday, going to the old J.E.A. building, and associating with Jewish children. . . . There were many other young Jewish people from other various small towns around Savannah, and this is where we all got together and met the Savannah kids, and went into the A.Z.A., and joined the organizations, and got sort of assimilated into the Savannah Jewish community. **Albert Ullman, 33**

A Day at the Beach, Summer 1957
At Tybee Island, enjoying the beach, are friends and family: (front row) Gerald Gottlieb; (center row) Riette (Rabhan) Pollack, Lucy (Amato) Gottlieb, and Lee (Movsovitz) Rosenzweig Dor-Shav; (back row) Ann (Portman) Strother, Mary (Weitz) Friedman, and Marilyn (Klein) Cranman.
JVM 003 Savannah Jewish Archives General Photograph Collection, Item 2309

I can tell you one thing, we had a happy home. We had a kosher home, we weren't *shomer Shabbes*, 'cause our business had to be opened on Saturday. But we were all so close, and there was always singing and dancing in our house. During the war [World War II] all the soldiers used to come to our house. Papa used to leave the door open. You know, in those days you didn't have to lock up. And we'd wake up in the morning and find them on the couch in the livingroom, on our front porch where we had a glider, chairs. I mean, everybody was friends.

And they'd come into Papa's store when they'd get off at Union Station on West Broad Street. And he'd talk to 'em and say, "Come to our house and eat." And my poor mother, I don't know how she had enough for everybody. But there was always company. We always had family in the house and friends, and there was just always people. And we all loved to sing the Hebrew songs and dance. It was just a lot of fun, we had a very happy upbringing. We didn't have a lot of money but we had love and joy in whatever we did! **Bertha (Plotkin) Freedman, 8**

APPENDIX A:
GLOSSARY

alav ha-sholom	of blessed memory
aliyah	honor of being called up to recite a blessing over the Torah
Ashkenazic	term to describe Jews from central and eastern Europe
Bar Mitzvah	ceremony for thirteen year old boys, upon reaching age of religious responsibility
Bat Mitzvah	ceremony for thirteen year old girls, upon reaching age of religious responsibility
bema	dais in the synagogue
besheret	fate, destiny
Bnos Hesed Shel Emeth	female burial society
bubbe	grandmother
bubbe mayses	grandmother's tales, fairy tales or lies
cantor	clergy who leads congregation in chanting of prayers
challah	bread for Sabbath
Chanukah	holiday—Festival of Lights
chazan	Hebrew for cantor
cheder	Hebrew school
Chevra Kedisha	male burial society
Conservative Judaism	adherence to tradition with some departures in keeping with times and circumstances
daven	to pray
gefilte fish	fish cakes or fish loaf
gelt	money
goyem	gentiles/other nations
Haftarah	chapter from the Prophets read after the Torah portion on Sabbath mornings and holidays
hametz	leavened food, not kosher for Passover

Holocaust	World War II attempt by Nazis to destroy the Jewish people
Kaddish	mourner's prayer
kapores	atonement for sin
kasher	to make kosher (suitable for consumption according to biblical dietary laws)
kichel	small, plain cookie
kike	derogatory term for a Jew
Kristallnacht	9-10 November 1938, "The Night of Broken Glass" when Jewish businesses were victimized
kuchen	coffee cake made from sweet yeast dough
latke	potato pancake, traditionally eaten on Chanukah
l'chaved	in honor of
mandel bread	similar to biscotti
mechitzah	partition in synagogue to separate men and women
melamed	teacher
mensh	a person with a good heart
meshugge	crazy
meshullah	collector of funds
mezuzah	container for the Shema prayer on doorpost of a Jewish home
mikveh	ritual bath
milchik	dairy products
minyan	quorum of ten males for religious services
mitzvah	commandment; used in the vernacular as "good deed"
mohel	religiously trained man who performs circumcisions
momzer	bastard
musaf	additional service on the Sabbath and Jewish holidays
Orthodox Judaism	strict adherence to traditional, biblical, and rabbinic law
Pesach	holiday— Passover
Purim	holiday—Feast of Lots, read from the Book of Esther
pushke	container for charity
Reform Judaism	liberal approach, eliminating tradition regarded as irrelevant to the present
Rosh Hashanah	holiday—Jewish New Year
schnapps	strong liquor
Seder	Passover feast

Sephardic	term to describe Jews from Spain, Portugal, or North Africa
Shabbat (Hebrew)	Sabbath
Shabbes (Yiddish)	Sabbath
Shavous	holiday—giving of the Torah; harvest of the first fruits in Israel
sheytel	wig
shiddach	marital match
shivah	mourning period, generally seven days
shlogn kapores	ritual for atonement for sin
shmaltz	fat, drippings
shmatte	rag
shmiches	rabbinical ordination
shochet	ritual slaughterer according to Jewish dietary laws
shofar	ram's horn
shoklen	swaying during prayer
sholem aleichem	"peace unto you"
shomer Shabbes	observer of the Sabbath
shtetl	small village in Eastern Europe
shtup a ganz	stuff a goose
shul	synagogue
shule	school
shvartze	black person
Siddur	prayer book
succah	outdoor booth used during Succoth
Succoth	holiday—harvest festival, Feast of Tabernacles
tallis	prayer shawl
talmid chachem	expert on the Talmud
Talmud Torah	Hebrew School
tante	aunt
Torah	Five Books of Moses
trayf	not kosher
Tu B' Shevat	holiday—new year for trees
tuchus	buttocks
tzimmas	stew of fruits and vegetables
yahrtzeit	observance of the anniversary of a death
yarmulke	skullcap
Yiddish	language spoken by Jews chiefly in eastern Europe
Yiddishkeit	Yiddish lore, culture, and customs
Yom Kippur	holiday—Day of Atonement
yom tov	Jewish holiday
zeyde	grandfather
Zionism	movement for establishing and supporting Israel as a Jewish national homeland

APPENDIX B:
JEWISH ORGANIZATIONS

Note: For those organizations where no information was found, simply the name is listed.

Aleph Zadik Aleph (A.Z.A.)
National B'nai B'rith organization for high school age males; the first local chapter (No. 206) was organized in 1936.

American Joint Distribution Committee (J.D.C.)
Organized nationally in 1914 to help distressed Palestinian Jews and war refugees during World War I; since then continued on a global scale through the distribution of supplies and funds and the establishment of care, health, and educational facilities.

Arbeiter Ring *see* **Workmen's Circle**

B'nai B'rith (I.O.B.B.)
International Jewish service organization founded in United States in 1847; Savannah chapter chartered in 1860. Activities and sub-groups include Hillel Foundation, Anti-Defamation League, B'nai B'rith Women, B'nai B'rith Men, B'nai B'rith Youth Organization, A.Z.A. and B.B.G.

B'nai B'rith Girls (B.B.G.)
B'nai B'rith organization for high school females; the first local chapter was organized in 1944.

B'nai B'rith Men
Local chapter organized in 1860 as B'nai B'rith Association of Savannah; in 1866 the group received national charter for first local chapter of Joseph Lodge I.O.B.B. No. 76.

B'nai B'rith Women
Local chapter No. 446 was organized in 1944. B'nai B'rith Women is now renamed Jewish Women International.

Boy Scout Troop #2

Organized in 1913 through the Jewish Educational Alliance with Joseph Litman as the first scoutmaster.

Congregation Agudath Achim (A.A.)

Organized as an Orthodox synagogue in 1903, A. A. joined the Conservative movement in 1945 as the first Conservative congregation in the state; in 1919 A.A. purchased its first building on Montgomery and York streets.

Congregation B'nai B'rith Jacob (B.B.J.)

Organized in 1861 by a group of Ashkenazic Jewish immigrants who broke from Mickve Israel; B.B.J. is the oldest congregation in the United States continually affiliated with Orthodox Judaism; and built their first synagogue on Montgomery Street.

Congregation Mickve Israel

The third oldest synagogue in United States, Mickve Israel was founded in 1733 by original Portugese and German Jewish colonists of Savannah; originally an Orthodox congregation, the Reform congregation completed its Gothic Revival synagogue in 1878.

Congregation Yeshurun

Formed in 1930 by a Conservative group, however they dissolved in 1934 due to financial woes.

Flowers of Zion

Young Judaea club, for girls.

Georgia Hussars

Organized in 1736 by General James Edward Oglethorpe, the Hussars are still active as a unit of the Georgia Army National Guard.

Girl Scout Troop #4

Organized in 1922 through the Jewish Educational Alliance.

Grace Agula Club

Hadassah

An international Jewish women's organization, founded in 1909 by Henrietta Szold, which provides medical services and training in Israel. The Savannah chapter was chartered in 1918, and primarily fund-raised through Junior and Senior divisions.

263

Harmonie Club

Men's social club founded in 1865 for members of Mickve Israel to play cards, and hold family dinners and dances; for over fifty years the club was located at the corner of Jones and Bull streets.

Hebrah Gemiluth Hesed (H.G.H.)

Fraternal philanthropic society organized in 1887 for charity and benevolence.

Hebrew Immigration Aid Society (HIAS)

National organization headquartered in New York.

Hebrew Women's Aid Society

Forerunner founded in 1853 as the Ladies' German Benevolent Society; Hebrew Women's Aid Society was organized in 1930 for the relief of the suffering and needy.

Herman Myers Literary Society

Organized in early 1920s and named for Savannah's first Jewish mayor.

Herzl Club Literary Society

This youth literary and debate club for boys age thirteen to sixteen (associated with Young Judaea) was named for Theodor Herzl, founder of modern Zionism.

Jewish Educational Alliance (J.E.A.)

Chartered in 1912 to promote knowledge and education of English language and law to immigrant Jews, the J.E.A. has occupied three buildings: between 1914 and 1916 they leased a building on the northeast corner of Barnard and Harris streets; in 1916 they moved into a new building on Pulaski Square; and in 1955 they moved into their new facility on Abercorn Street.

J.E.A. Men's Club

Organized in the 1920s through Jewish Educational Alliance, the Men's Club sponsored social events, youth activities, and the local Golden Gloves tournament.

J.E.A. Women's Club

Organized around 1921 through the Jewish Educational Alliance.

Junior Hadassah

Savannah chapter founded in 1918 and evolved into the Business & Professional Group (B. & P.) in the 1950s. It split from Senior Hadassah in 1960s and became Shalom Hadassah.

Kadema Club

A Conservative youth group sponsored by A.A. for grades fifth through eighth.

Knights of Judah

Young Judaea club for boys.

Nathan Schultz Club

A debating society active during the 1920s and 1930s.

National Council of Jewish Women (N.C.J.W.)

Organized to teach immigrants, the N.C.J.W. began the Golden Age Program through the Jewish Educational Alliance.

National Jewish Welfare Board (J.W.B.)

National welfare organization serving Jewish military personnel in the Armed Forces and authorizing agency for rabbis entering the Armed Forces to serve as chaplains; during World War II was one of the civilian welfare agencies brought together by the United Service Organizations (U.S.O.).

Southeastern Federation of Temple Youth (SEFTY)

Regional organization of youth groups sponsored by local Reform congregations.

Torpian Society

Social club active in Savannah during the 1920s.

United Jewish Appeal (U.J.A.)

National group formed in 1934 to aid distressed European Jews by unifying United States' Jewish fundraising and relief efforts; in 1947, it shifted focus from war refugees to the support of the creation of a Jewish state.

United Service Organizations (U.S.O.)

National organization formed in 1941 by a request from Franklin D.
Roosevelt to provide recreation and a "home away from home" for
United States Armed Forces servicemen on leave; the U.S.O. took in six
civilian agencies including the National Jewish Welfare Board. The national
organization worked partially through local U.S.O. centers like Savannah's
Jewish Educational Alliance.

Workmen's Circle (Arbeiter Ring)

Cultural group organized by internationalists to foster Jewish identity through
Yiddish culture and education, and to reduce hardships of the working class;
local Branch 383 was organized in 1908, maintained a Yiddish shul and began
the Workman Circle Credit Union.

Xanadu Club

Young Judaea

Youth group of Hadassah organized nationally in 1909.

Zangwell Club

A debating society for boys age ten to thirteen active in the 1920s and named
for Israel Zangwell, British "New Humorist" novelist who penned the epic
novel of Jewish immigration, *Children of the Ghetto*, and coined the term
"melting pot theory" in a 1909 play. Zangwell was quoted saying,
"Yiddish incorporates the essence of a life which is distinctive and unlike
any other."

APPENDIX C:
SJA ORAL HISTORY COLLECTION FINDING AID

The Savannah Jewish Archives has in its care a large oral history collection, from which the content of this book was drawn, known as JOH 003 Savannah Jewish Archives Oral History Collection. The oral history collection, which is open and available to the public, includes cassette tapes of the original interviews, typed transcripts for all interviews, and photographs of all of the interviewees.

Each oral history is assigned an item number in the order it is received into the collection; this number is used to identify the tapes, transcripts and photographs corresponding to that interview. The following is an alphabetical list of oral histories by interviewee name used in this publication. Each listing includes the item number, the interviewee's name, date of the interview, and birth and death date and place if known.

We encourage everyone to visit the Archives and explore this rich source of information!

Subject	Interview date	Birth date & place	Death date & place
76 Arkin, Marvin	2001	1921, Savannah GA	
1 Barr, Gertrude (Scheer)	1998	1922, Savannah GA	
64 Becker, Charles	2001	1928, Brooklyn NY	
70 Becker, Meyer "Johnny"		1922, Tsientsin, China	1992, Savannah GA
67 Bernstein, Beryl	2001	1912, Savannah GA	
76 Blumenthal, Herbert	2001	1920, Savannah GA	
68 Bono, Murray	2001	1921, Savannah GA	
2 Buchsbaum, Anne (Lewis)	1996	1898, New York NY	2000, Savannah GA
72 Byck, David A., III	2001	1929, Savannah GA	
66 Cantor, Betty (Blumenthal)	2001	1917, Savannah GA	
3 Center, Bess (Eisenman)	1997	1912, Savannah GA	
4 Center, Leo	1997	1918, Savannah GA	
5 Clark, H. Sol	1997	1906, Savannah GA	2003, Savannah GA
6 Cohen, A. J., Jr.	1997	1920, Savannah GA	
90 Cohen, Phillipa "Bunny" (Sherman)	2003	1940, Savannah GA	
97 Cotler, Allan	2003	1918, Brooklyn NY	

36	Cranman, Herman	1998	1924, Savannah GA	
83	Danziger, Herta (Sanger)	2002	1911, Breslau, Germany	2004, Savannah GA
7	Dunn, Selma (Greenberg)	1998	1923, Savannah GA	
35	Edel, Danyse (Greenwald)	1999	1931, Macon GA	
35	Edel, Julius	1999	1929, Savannah GA	
57	Eichholz, Harry	1999	1914, Savannah GA	
8	Freedman, Bertha (Plotkin)	1997	1928, Savannah GA	
71	Friedman, Erwin "Ernie"	2001	1931, Savannah GA	
85	Friedman, Karl	2002	1928, Savannah GA	2004, Savannah GA
38	Friedman, Robert	1999	1935, New York NY	
9	Garfunkel, Benjamin	1983	1913, Savannah GA	1987, Savannah GA
37	Garfunkel, Charlotte (Shipper)	1999	1918, Trenton NJ	2003, Savannah GA
62	Gaynor, Alan	2001	1928, Savannah GA	
10	Goldberg, Evelyn (Center)	1997	1919, Savannah GA	2002, Savannah GA
74	Golden, Jack	2001	1934, Savannah GA	
39	Goodman, Beatrice (Heyman)	1999	1920, Savannah GA	
11	Gordon, Robert	1997	1920, Savannah GA	
40	Gottlieb, Alan	1999	1928, Savannah GA	2003, Savannah GA
92	Gottlieb, Isser	2003	1938, Savannah GA	
87	Gray, Annette (Berman)	2002	1920, Savannah GA	
12	Guthman, Aaron	1964	1867, Philadelphia PA	1967, Savannah GA
80	Heller, Rupert	2002	1927, Savannah GA	
94	Herman, Sue (Solomon)	2003	1938, Savannah GA	
1	Hirsch, Celia (Scheer)	1998	1918, Savannah GA	
52	Hirsch, Samuel	2000	1909, Atlanta GA	
13	Hirshberg, Helen (Blumenthal)	1997	1895, West Branch MI	1997, Savannah GA
77	Horovitz, Arthur "Bubba"	2001	1923, Savannah GA	
78	Javetz, Abe		1909, Austria	1989, Savannah GA
78	Javetz, Rachel (Chernoff)		1913, Savannah GA	1994, Savannah GA
93	Kahn, Jane (Guthman)	2003	1933, Savannah, GA	
84	Kantziper, Suzanne (Ginsberg)	2002	1936, Savannah GA	
41	Karnibad, Nathan	2000	1917, Brooklyn NY	
42	Karp, Martin	2000	1929, Savannah GA	
53	Karsman, Evelyn (Ward)	2000	1913, Savannah GA	2001, Savannah GA
65	Kayton, John	2001	1906, Savannah GA	2001, Savannah GA
43	Konter, Harriet (Kanter)	1999	1924, Savannah GA	
91	Kooden, Lewis	2003	1930, Chicago IL	
10	Kramer, Fannie (Center)	1997	1913, Savannah GA	2003, Savannah GA
59	Kreh, Marcus "Max"	1993	1900, Genoa, Italy	1993, Savannah GA
14	Leffler, Martin	1997	1917, Savannah GA	2003, Savannah GA
14	Leffler, Matiel (Roos)	1997	1926, Savannah GA	
89	Levin, Audrey (Galkin)	2003	1926, Jacksonville FL	
19	Levy, Barbara (Smith)	2000	1935, Savannah GA	
95	Levy, Joan (Levy)	2003	1942, Savannah GA	
44	Levy, Pearl (Spivak)	1988	1898, Brest Litovsk, Poland	2000, New York NY
54	Lowe, Walter	2001	1921, Savannah GA	

88	Lukin, Doris (Goldin)	2003	1924, Savannah GA	
50	Mazo, Albert	1999	1915, Savannah GA	2002, Savannah GA
15	Melaver, Norton	1997	1926, Brooklyn NY	
16	Mendel, Calmon	1998	1910, Savannah GA	2002, Savannah GA
17	Mendel, Marion			
	(Abrahams) Levy	1998	1917, Savannah GA	
95	Mendel, Marion			
	(Abrahams) Levy	2003	1917, Savannah GA	
18	Meyerhoff, Eric	1997	1929, Arolsen, Germany	
96	Meyerhoff, Harriet (Cranman)	2003	1946, Savannah GA	
60	Newman, Sol	2001	1923, Birmingham AL	
8	Plotkin, Samuel	1997	1915, Savannah GA	
20	Portman, Benjamin	1998	1915, Savannah GA	1998, Savannah GA
69	Price, Elizabeth "Libby" (Levy)	2001	1917, Savannah GA	
21	Rabhan, Frances (Ehrlich)	1997	1905, Swainsboro GA	2003, Savannah GA
75	Rabhan, Martin "Maier"	2001	1920, Savannah GA	
22	Rabhan, Sadye (Steinberg)	1998	1907, Savannah GA	2002, Savannah GA
45	Radetsky, Samuel	1999	1921, Grudno, Poland	
23	Raskin, Sidney	1997	1916, Savannah GA	
24	Robbins, Minnie (Bronitsky)			
	Feinberg	1998	1906, Zetl, Poland	2001, Savannah GA
25	Rosenzweig, David	1997	1917, Savannah GA	
63	Rosenzweig, David	2001	1917, Savannah GA	
25	Rosenzweig, Ethyl (Richman)	1997	1918, Savannah GA	
26	Rosenzweig, Lena (Feinberg)	1996	1906, Savannah GA	1997, Savannah GA
27	Rotkow, Fred	1996	1901, Lithuania	2001, Savannah GA
49	Rubnitz, Irvin "Sonny"	2001	1930, Savannah GA	
46	Rudikoff, Julius	1999	1916, New York NY	
86	Samuels, Anchel	2002	1936, Savannah GA	
81	Schildkraut, Maxine "Midge"			
	(Lasky)	2002	1940, Savannah GA	
61	Schneider, Adele (Meddin)	2001	1920, Savannah GA	
28	Schneider, Reuben	1998	1914, Providence RI	2001, Savannah GA
29	Silverman, Benjamin	1997	1911, Savannah GA	2000, Savannah GA
29	Silverman, Louis	1997	1897, Kobryn, Russia	2000, Savannah GA
55	Slotin, Harris	2001	1929, Savannah GA	
47	Slotin, Leon	1999	1924, Savannah GA	
82	Solomon, Lena (Feldman)	2002	1915, Poughkeepsie NY	
30	Solomons, Philip, Sr.			
	[restricted]	1998	1919, Savannah GA	
73	Spiers, Helen (Levington)	2001	1922, Savannah GA	
56	Stein, Ida (Bronitsky)	1999	1909, Zetl, Poland	
31	Steinberg, Sam	1997	1901, Savannah GA	1997, Savannah GA
58	Tenenbaum, Ralph	1998	1910, Kolonia, Poland	1998, Savannah GA
79	Traub, Herbert, Jr.	2002	1917, Savannah GA	

Jewish Community Picnic, c.1915
Identified in this photograph are Mendel Rosen, Hannah Molly (Klugman)
Rosen, Rae Levy, Edith (Lipsitz) Sader, Naomi Mazo, Sara (Levy) Kaplan,
Dena (Levin) Ehrenreich, Fred Ehrenreich, Etta (Levin) Slifkin, Lena (Slotin)
Ehrenreich, Mina (Mazo) Levington, Isaac Levington, and Malke Mazo.
JVM 003 Savannah Jewish Archives General Photograph Collection, Item 1837

INDEX